CHANGING LABOUR MARKETS, WELFARE POLICIES AND CITIZENSHIP

Edited by Jørgen Goul Andersen and Per H. Jensen

First published in Great Britain in January 2002 by

The Policy Press
University of Bristol
Fourth Floor, Beacon House
Queen's Road
Bristol BS8 1QU
UK

Tel +44 (0)117 331 4054
Fax +44 (0)117 331 4093
e-mail tpp-info@bristol.ac.uk
www.policypress.org.uk

© The Policy Press 2002

Reprinted 2004

British Library Cataloguing in Publication Data
A catalogue record for this book is available from the British Library.

Library of Congress Cataloging-in-Publication Data
A catalog record for this book has been requested.

ISBN 1 86134 272 1 paperback

Jørgen Goul Andersen is Professor of Political Sociology, and **Per H. Jensen** is Associate Professor, both in the Centre for Comparative Welfare State Studies, Department of Economics, Politics and Public Administration, Ålborg University, Denmark.

Cover design by Qube Design Associates, Bristol.

Front cover: Image supplied by DigitalVision.

Printed and bound in Great Britain by MPG Books, Bodmin.

Contents

Notes on contributors

Asmund Born is Associate Professor at the Copenhagen Business School, Denmark. He has published extensively on risk and power in organisations, and the connection between language and power.

Denis Bouget is Professor in Economics at the University of Nantes, France. He specialises in social policies for social exclusion, long-term care for older people, public local assistance, and the comparison of social welfare systems. He is Director of the Maison des Sciences de l'Homme (MSH) Ange Guepin, Nantes and Chairman of COST A15: 'Reforming Social Protection Systems in Europe'.

Gary Craig is Professor of Social Justice at the University of Hull, UK. His research interests include community development, local governance, poverty and inequality, and 'race' and ethnicity. Before returning to academic life in 1988, he worked for many years in large scale community development projects.

Bert de Vroom is Associate Professor of Public Policy at the University of Twente, the Netherlands. He has published widely on regulation and governance in the field of Aids policy, labour market and welfare policy. He is currently Coordinator of the COST A13 working group 'Ageing and Work'. His recent projects include an international comparative study into the development of transitional labour markets.

Jørgen Goul Andersen is Professor of Political Sociology, Centre for Comparative Welfare State Studies, Ålborg University, Denmark. He is working group coordinator of COST A13: 'Changing Labour Markets, Welfare Policies and Citizenship', coordinator of the Danish Election Programme and the ISSP Programme, and a member of the Board of the Danish Democracy and Power Programme. His research fields include comparative welfare state research, election research and political power and democracy.

Anne Marie Guillemard is Professor of Sociology, with a Chair at the University of Paris-Sorbonne, Department of Social Sciences. She holds a PhD in Sociology from the University of Paris-Sorbonne. She is a member of the European Academy of Sciences and the Institut

Universitaire de France, is on the editorial boards of *Revue Française de Sociologie* and *European Review* and is Vice Chair of COST A13. She is the author of numerous articles on sociology of social policies and the welfare state, and on the sociology of ageing and the life course.

Knut Halvorsen is Professor in Social Policy in the Department of Economics, Local Public Administration and Social Work, Oslo University College, Norway. He is currently also the Research Director of the Centre of Social Research at Oslo University College.

Torild Hammer is Senior Research Fellow at NOVA, Norwegian Social Research. She is currently coordinating a research project on youth unemployment in Europe, funded by the European Commission.

Per H. Jensen is a sociologist and is currently Associate Professor in Comparative Welfare State Studies at Åalborg University, Denmark. Since 1981, he has conducted several comparative research projects on labour markets and welfare states. He is currently Chair of the COST A13 network.

Ruth Lister is Professor of Social Policy at Loughborough University and is a former Director of the Child Poverty Action Group. She has published widely around poverty, income maintenance and women's citizenship, including *Citizenship: Feminist perspectives* (Macmillan, 1997).

Birgit Pfau-Effinger is Professor of Sociology at the University of Jena, Germany. She has published widely in comparative sociology and social policy, the sociology of inequality and labour markets, family sociology and gender studies. She is a member of the COST A13 network.

Peter Plougmann is founder and CEO of Oxford Insight A/S. He specialises in labour markets, industrial development issues and scenario building. He has worked with these issues within political administration, research and consultancy for more than 20 years. He has international experience of the EU, Nordic countries, Hungary, the Baltic nations, Australia, Hong Kong, Taiwan and the US. He has been involved in research and evaluation activities for the OECD, the European Commission, the Nordic Council of Ministers and the UN/ILO.

Willem Trommel is Associate Professor of Public Policy at the University of Twente, the Netherlands. He has published on welfare state reform, information technology and labour market change, and public governance. He is a member of the COST A13 'Ageing and Work' working group and is currently preparing empirical research in the field of transitional labour markets.

List of acronyms

ACA   Allocation Chômeurs Âgés

AC   *Agir ensemble contre le chômage* (an association of unemployed workers, France)

ALMP   active labour market policy

ANPE   *Agence nationale pour l'emploi*

APEIS   *Association pour l'emploi, l'information et la solidarité des chômeurs et des travailleurs précaires* (an association of unemployed workers, France)

ARPE   Allocation de Remplacement pour l'Emploi

ASA   Allocation Spécifique d'Attente

ASFNE   Allocation Speciale du Fonds National de l'Emploi

ASS   *allocation de solidarité spécifique*

ASSEDIC   *Associations interprofessionnelles pour l'emploi dans l'industrie et le commerce*

CAF   *Caisses d'allocations familiales*

CCAS   *Centres communaux d'action sociale*

CEPA   Center for Economic Policy Analysis

CFDT   *Confédération française démocratique des travailleurs* (a trades union, France)

CFTC   *Confédération française des travailleurs catholiques* (a trades union, France)

CGT   *Confédération générale du travail* (a trades union, France)

CRE   Commission for Racial Equality, UK

CSG   *contribution sociale généralisée*

DDASS   *Direction départementale d'action sanitaire et sociale*

DKr   Danish kroner

DM   German mark

EAPN   European Anti-Poverty Network

ECRI   European Commission against Racism and Intolerance

ERA   Early Retirement Allowance

EU   European Union

FDI	foreign direct investment
FNE	*Fonds National de l'Emploi*
FO	*Force ouvrière* (a trades union, France)
FF	French francs
FUS	*Fonds d'urgence sociale*
GDP	gross domestic product
HRM	human resources management
ICT	information and communication technologies
ILO	International Labour Office
IT	information technology
LISV	National Institute for Social Insurance
MNCP	*Mouvement national des chômeurs et des précaires* (an association of unemployed workers, France)
MUS	*Mission d'urgence sociale*
NAIRU	Non Accelerating Inflation Rate of Unemployment
NAWRU	Non Accelerating Wage Rate of Unemployment
NGO	non-governmental organisation
OECD	Organisation for Economic Co-operation and Development
RMI	*Revenu Minimun d'Insertion*
SEU	Social Exclusion Unit
SVR	Social Insurance Council
TEC	Training and Enterprise Council
TUC	Trades Union Congress
UN	United Nations
UNEDIC	*Union interprofessionnelle pour l'emploi dans l'industrie et le commerce*
US	United States
VUT	voluntary early retirement scheme
WAO	Disability Benefit Act
ZW	Sickness Benefit Act

Glossary

ACA   early exit programme, France

Activation   job training in a subsidised temporary job, most
                        frequently in the public sector or (in Denmark,
                        most typically) education

ANPE   the agency in France in charge of the state's
                        public employment services, including careers
                        guidance and registering the unemployed

ARPE   early exit programme, France

ASA   early exit programme, France

ASFNE   a programme providing incentives for companies
                        not to dismiss older workers, France

ASS   public social assistance scheme, France

ASSEDIC   local branches that manage unemployment
                        benefit, France

Aussiedler   ethnic German migrants

male   the model of a household unit with a male
breadwinner   breadwinner and a female housewife/home
model   carer, on which most welfare policies are
                        historically based

CAF   local branches for distributing family benefits,
                        France

CCAS   local social centres responsible for coordinating
                        social policies at a local level, including
                        community care, France

CSG	'generalised welfare contribution' – a tax earmarked for social policies, France
DDASS	local government offices responsible for implementing health and social policies, France
départments	the French administrative regions
flexicurity	welfare policies that combine a relatively generous social protection with demands for more market-oriented flexibility, for example, the Danish combination of weak employment protection, relatively generous unemployment benefits (for a long duration), and ALMP
FUS	a temporary social relief fund, France
Gasterbeiter	'guest workers' – immigrants employed in Germany, particularly from southern and eastern Europe
Jobseekers' Allowance	general unemployment benefit, UK
MUS	a group of voluntary representatives responsible for distributing FUS benefits in France
passive welfare policies	used by adherents of ALMP to characterise transfers without an offer or requirement of work, education or 'rehabilitation'
Préfet	local representatives of central government, France
recommodification	used to describe the development of 'politics against markets' to 'politics for markets' in social and labour market policies, for example, policies providing better incentives or more market-oriented benefits
RMI	minimum income support scheme, France

social assistance	means-tested financial help provided to those whose other sources of income is not adequate for subsistence
third way	efforts to formulate a new, more centrist and more market-oriented social democratic political formula, inspired by Tony Blair's New Labour but appearing in a variety of forms
UNEDIC	a non-profit organisation in France that provides a contributory social insurance scheme
VUT	voluntary early retirement scheme, the Netherlands
welfare regime	Esping-Andersen's concept of a welfare model encompassing particular mutually reinforcing configurations of the welfare state, the labour market and the family

Preface

This book ms the first major outcome of COST Action A13, 'Changing Labour Markets, Welfare Policies and Citizenship'. The purpose of COST Action A13 is to examine the effects of social security systems and welfare institutions on the processes of social and political marginalisation. COST is an intergovernmental organisation for coordination of scientific and technical research, aiming at coordination and formation of networks on a European level between nationally-funded research projects. Some 80 experts, appointed by 17 countries, participate in the COST A13 network which will remain in force for five years (spring 1998-2003). For further information about the COST Action A13, see

We are grateful to the Department of Economics, Politics and Public Administration, Åalborg University, Denmark, for its generous support to the publication of this volume.

Jørgen Goul Andersen and Per H. Jensen
Åalborg, November 2001

ONE

Citizenship, changing labour markets and welfare policies: an introduction

Jørgen Goul Andersen and Per H. Jensen

Changes in the labour market are seen as one of the most serious threats to the economic sustainability of European welfare states, and to the fulfilment of the ideal of 'full citizenship' among their citizens. Globalisation and technological change (sometimes described as the transition to a 'knowledge-intensive society') generate a marked decline in labour market fortunes among lower-skilled and other vulnerable segments of the labour force. This not only leads to social marginalisation, so the argument runs, but also becomes a barrier to economic growth: inflexible labour markets with high minimum wages mean that unemployment becomes structural so that an economic upturn leads to increased competition for skilled labour and thus to inflation rather than significantly reduced unemployment. This in turn undermines the financial foundation of generous social protection.

Because social protection of the unemployed contributes to high minimum wages and provides 'poverty traps', it unintentionally serves to reinforce labour market and social marginalisation. Thus, in the new global economy, European welfare states allegedly have to adapt by accepting larger wage differentials, imposing stronger work incentives, and/or providing activation of unemployed people to enhance their productivity (OECD, 1994, 1997; to some extent, this is even echoed in Esping-Andersen, 1999). Significant political differences prevail as to the proper combination of such measures, but in broad terms, the above-outlined diagnosis of unemployment and marginalisation has been dominant in the 1990s and around the millennium. Not least, comparison with the job-generating capacity of the American economy has been seen as an indication that European welfare states are caught by some 'Euro-sclerosis' which can only be cured by deregulation, increased wage differentials, improved incentives and more targeted social security. At the same time, such measures have been presented as the only ones that are able to solve the social problems of marginalisation and citizenship, which is the core dependent variable of this book. By citizenship, we do not only refer to social rights, but also to *practices* – to being effectively a 'full member of society' (see below).

This diagnosis could well be right. However, on closer inspection, solid knowledge about labour market change, its interrelationship with welfare policies and, in particular, its joint impact on citizenship appears quite rudimentary and fragmented (Gallie and Paugam, 2000, p 1). Also, the highly different fortunes of European welfare states around the millennium, both in terms of unemployment, and in terms of marginalisation and citizenship, cast doubt on previous interpretations and suggest that less deterministic perspectives are needed. We need to know much more about different paths to lower unemployment and ways to avoid labour market marginalisation. We need to know to what extent early retirement should be considered an aspect of labour market marginalisation. In particular, we need to know much more about social marginalisation and loss of citizenship: how should this be defined and measured? What is its incidence? Under what conditions can it be avoided?

This book presents some contributions to building more detailed comparative knowledge based on new and more complex approaches which:

- focus on *citizenship* as a key variable; in particular, on the possibilities of maintaining 'full citizenship', that is, full integration in social and political life, for all citizens, regardless of labour market position and market fortune
- focus on *welfare arrangements* as a core factor that may block (or unintentionally aggravate) labour market marginalisation, or alleviate its further consequences in terms of citizenship
- recognise marginalisation as a *multidimensional* phenomenon, which demands more clear distinctions between, for example, labour market marginalisation, economic marginalisation, and social and political marginalisation, and recognition of the complex links between these dimensions: one form of marginalisation does not *automatically* lead to another
- recognise the need to *differentiate*, along such dimensions as gender, age, ethnicity or values, when analysing marginalisation and citizenship; the marginalised are composed of heterogeneous groups with quite different problems, and processes of marginalisation must be analysed,

for example, in relation to pathways in and pathways out of the labour market, family structure and gender roles, ethnic divisions, and changing work orientations.

Figure 1 delineates an analytical framework that points out the need for more careful examination of the relationship between changing labour markets, welfare policies and citizenship, a framework that facilitates meaningful communication between different disciplines and theoretical

Figure 1: The relationship between changing labour markets, welfare policies and citizenship

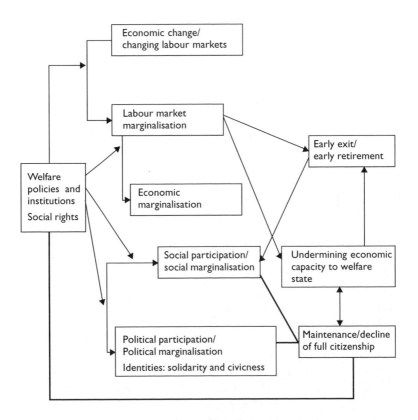

perspectives. This calls both for conceptual development and clarification, and for providing comprehensive empirical knowledge about the problem at hand. This book has three key aims:

- to contribute to a theoretical clarification of the key concepts of changing labour markets, welfare policies, citizenship and marginalisation, and the linkages between these key concepts
- to take some first steps towards applying such a framework empirically to illuminate how European welfare states have handled similar problems (unemployment, early retirement and immigration) via policies that give different emphasis to social rights, are based on different conceptions of the relationship between social rights and citizenship and have different effects
- to discuss conditions and new directions of change by contributing to an understanding of the complex interplay between external challenges, institutions, and agency in this policy field.

We will now expand on these points, clarify the concepts, and briefly introduce the contributions to this book.

Changing labour markets and welfare policies

Globalisation and technological change are at the heart of the notion of changing labour markets in the late 20th and early 21st centuries. Both processes – globalisation being to a large extent the result of political decisions rather than just exogenous factors[1] – tend to improve the life chances and the quality of working life for large segments of the population. However, at the same time they may also have social and economic effects that worsen the situation for more vulnerable segments of the population. Other things being equal, globalisation and technological change both tend to produce increasing economic and social inequalities. They may also threaten to produce a 'surplus population' of low-skilled workers. Those who possess a low level of skills, a low capacity to cooperate and a low adaptability to change are exposed to an increasing risk of ending up unemployed or in 'precarious jobs' – jobs with irregular working hours, with poor rates of pay, without regular contract and so on. When combined with labour market structures that protect people with a fixed employment contract, this can create strong insider/outsider divisions. Still, globalisation and technological change may take on different forms in different societies, depending on the particular labour market that exists and the social regulations in place. A broad summary of the changing labour markets and social processes facing European welfare states is provided by Peter Plougmann in Chapter Two.

Welfare policies and citizenship

There have also been strong external and internal pressures to change welfare policies that have been accused of being costly, inefficient and counterproductive. This holds not only for traditional strategies, such as Keynesian strategies of deficit budgeting designed to stimulate aggregate demand, but also for social protection measures, such as generous unemployment benefits. These social protection measures have been dubbed 'passive' policies, in contrast to 'active' measures that enable the unemployed to find a new job, or strategies of providing incentives that motivate or force people to find work.

However, the core issue in this contest over strategies reaches beyond questions of budget constraints and efficiency to combat unemployment. It is also about different conceptions of citizenship and its relationship to welfare policies. Adherents of universal, generous measures of social protection claim that economic security and avoidance of stigmatisation help to empower unemployed people, enabling them to remain 'part of society' and participate in social and political life, and also improve their chances to find an appropriate job. Adherents of activation tend to believe that employment is a precondition of being 'part of society'. Some scholars have discussed how activation programmes may be prepared in more 'empowering' ways; other scholars tend to equate activation with 'workfare', which is aimed at controlling and maintaining work ethics. At the political level, preoccupation with the rights of unemployed people has declined in favour of increasing stress on duties to be actively job seeking, to be willing to take any job, and to participate in activation programmes (Hatland, 1998; Clasen et al, 2001). Finally, adherents of incentives, targeting and de-universalisation of social security have not only been preoccupied with the economic aspects but also with dangers of 'poverty traps', and with the cultural and moral aspects such as the possible development of a 'dependency culture' (Murray, 1984; Dean and Taylor-Gooby, 1992; Halvorsen, 1998) that may even pass on from one generation to another and generate exactly the opposite effects of what was intended by social protection.

The focus of discussions about social stratification has increasingly changed from class and class inequality to a concern with social integration and exclusion. The focus of policy discussions about unemployment has to a large extent changed from a preoccupation with equality and poverty, to a concern for social exclusion and citizenship. Consequently, the concept of citizenship has increasingly become a core issue in debates about the effects of the welfare state. Below, we elaborate on the concept of citizenship and its relation to marginalisation, another keyword in this book.

Concepts of citizenship and marginalisation

Defining citizenship

In his seminal essay, Marshall (1965 [1949], p 172) defined citizenship as a comprehensive set of rights, "from the right of a modicum of economic welfare and security to the right to share to the full in the social heritage and to live the life of a civilized being according to the standards prevailing in society". As pointed out by Lister (1998), the concept of citizenship is analytically composed of two or three dimensions: rights and duties; participation; and identities or orientations. Participation and identities may also be summarised under the common umbrella of 'practices'. The three dimensions are as follows:

- *Rights (and duties)*: Marshall distinguished between civil, political and social rights and pointed out their inherent connection. This means that citizenship is a multidimensional concept, both as far as rights and participation are concerned.
- *Participation*: Marshall emphasised rights as a precondition of full citizenship (as a type of 'empowerment'). However, the acid test of full citizenship is the actual fulfilment of these rights, that is, social and political participation. It is debated whether the right and obligation to work should be considered part of citizenship, but at any rate, these concepts provide the opportunity to distinguish between participation in the labour market, in social life (which has several aspects), and in politics.
- *Identities or orientations*: this is sometimes spelled out as a separate dimension, and it occupies an important role not least in normative discussions about 'civicness', that is, about what constitutes a 'good citizen'. Discussions about dependency culture(s), stigmatisation, social trust, solidarity and social responsibility and so on all belong to this category. Also, there is an important normative discussion here, for example, between liberal, social democratic, republican and communitarian ideals of citizenship. For instance, workfare is strongly linked to a communitarian notion of citizenship.

These three dimensions of citizenship have been emphasised differently in European countries; in some countries, they have hardly been recognised at all since these countries are not familiar with the concept of citizenship as anything other than formal (state) citizenship. However, there is also a difference between a French tradition, which has emphasised the 'rights' dimension, and the predominance of the dimensions of participation and identity in Britain and Scandinavia, not least due to the efforts of feminist scholars. In Britain and Scandinavia, both normative discussions about the proper role of citizens (vis-à-vis public authorities and each other), and empirically orientated discussions about the nature and quality of political participation and democracy are often phrased in the language of citizenship. The concept of citizenship and current challenges to citizenship are elaborated on in more detail in Ruth Lister's contribution in Chapter Three.

Defining marginalisation

Tentatively, we may define marginalisation as participation that, involuntarily, is less than complete (Svedberg, 1995; Johannessen, 1998)[2]. As with citizenship, we may distinguish between marginalisation in different arenas. Marginalisation has frequently been equated with labour market marginalisation and has been operationalised simply as a certain unemployment rate over a certain period. However, this is misleading if any broader meaning is attached to the term, as is normally the case. In the first place, labour market marginalisation does not by definition imply social marginalisation. Next, such operational concepts do not necessarily measure an involuntary situation of destitution, powerlessness and limited control that is actually experienced. For instance, unemployed people during a recession cannot be considered marginalised if they have maintained their *ability* to find a job as soon as the business cycle turns upwards. By the same token, people are not politically marginalised in a substantive sense if low participation represents a deliberate choice, and if they have maintained their *ability* to act in defence of any preferences they have if they choose to do so, that is, if they remain efficacious (Andersen et al, 1998).

Like citizenship, marginalisation is a multidimensional phenomenon that relates to different arenas in society so that we have to distinguish, at least, between labour market marginalisation, social marginalisation, and political marginalisation. To these dimensions, it is tempting to also add economic marginalisation (financial hardship), even though this is more difficult to conceptualise in terms of participation. However this may be, one form of marginalisation does not automatically lead to another. Several authors have pointed out that in all probability there exists a complex interaction between political, social and economic marginalisation (Berghman, 1995; Andersen, 1996). An individual can be economically marginalised while remaining culturally integrated (Strobel, 1995). For example, people living in a ghetto, and under difficult economic conditions, can be active in the organisation of social and cultural activities (Jordan et al, 1994).

Labour market integration is often considered to be the most important integrative mechanism in the individual–society relation (Pixley, 1993; Seiersted, 1996). Others have questioned whether the labour market is *that* important for social integration (Andersen, 1996). Modern societies are highly differentiated, with a large number of alternative, integrative arenas, such as family, friends and civil society, and a large variety of organisations (Johannessen 1998; Lorentzen 1997). In principle, it is perfectly possible to be integrated (have full participation) in such arenas without being employed. Labour market participation may even be the dependent variable in relation to participation in other arenas: people often acquire a job via their social network. None the less, "the extreme form of marginalisation occurs when prolonged unemployment is reinforced by the disintegration of social networks that bind the individual to the community" (Gallie, 1999, p 140). From this point of view, integration may be dependent on provisions of sufficient resources to secure the autonomy of the individual.

Much confusion as to the causes and effects of marginalisation may originate from the fact that marginalised people are often lumped together as one single and unified group. Instead, it is important that different marginalised segments are differentiated in terms of social background factors, such as gender, age, class and ethnicity, as well as in terms of different orientations or lifestyles. Similarly, it is necessary to differentiate the effects that the welfare state institutions have along the lines of the 'citizen-identity' dimension, for example, by gender, age, class, ethnicity. It is also necessary to take as a point of departure the various problem areas that the welfare state addresses. We shall differentiate on the basis of labour market status (unemployment), age (early exit/early retirement) and ethnicity, as we consider these problem areas of the welfare state to be potentially quite differently structured, while at the same time being of major importance and a major challenge for most European welfare states. We would have liked to include more areas, in particular, disability, but have had to limit it to the few areas just defined.

Chapter themes

In Chapter Two, Peter Plougmann summarises the changing labour markets and social processes facing European welfare states. He then identifies and discusses some of the core tendencies and challenges.

The next three chapters focus on the changing interactions between welfare policies and citizenship. In Chapter Three, Ruth Lister presents the concept and provides a brief overview of the tradition of citizenship, including the significant contributions of feminist research to its renaissance and further development. Next, she elaborates on the concept and on the relationship between citizenship and the welfare state. She then clarifies how the concept of citizenship serves to point out the important qualitative changes in welfare policies, and how the notion of citizenship and its transformation may be applied to identify and to address the core contemporary challenges to welfare states.

In Chapter Four, Jørgen Goul Andersen elucidates the changing welfare policies in Denmark and discusses their relationship to changing conceptions of citizenship. The Danish experience is interesting from a comparative perspective as Denmark was among the first countries to recover significantly from persistent mass unemployment (1975-95) without sacrificing an unusually high-income equality. However, since the economic upswing, Denmark has moved from a state of 'ultimate universalism', coming close to a basic income system, to a quite strongly activation-orientated welfare regime with ever more emphasis on the right and duty to work. The chapter discusses the advantages and pitfalls of this development from social protection to activation, all from a citizenship perspective.

The Dutch welfare state has changed along partly similar lines but also made significant moves from a social rights oriented policy model towards an incentive-orientated policy regime. Chapter Five by Willem Trommel and Bert de Vroom highlights how such institutional change in the Dutch welfare state has come about, and how it has affected citizens' rights. Contrary to the arguments about welfare states' resistance to change, it is argued that the development is an outcome of agency, and of institutional learning in governance networks. The welfare state changes are seen as a deliberate, premeditated and conscious break from the historical welfare state traditions previously held in the Netherlands.

The next three chapters address the question of how, and/or with what effects on citizenship, various European countries handle similar social problems of unemployment, youth unemployment, and integration of immigrants. In Chapter Six, Jørgen Goul Andersen and Knut Halvorsen present an account of the 'standard interpretation' of unemployment and labour market marginalisation in Europe that has guided policy recommendations across Europe. This is compared with available evidence about the underlying assumptions, and with recent developments in unemployment and policies across Europe. In Chapter Seven, Torild Hammer addresses the relationship between welfare regimes and political citizenship among unemployed youth to test whether more generous financial support constitutes a resource for participation, or whether welfare dependency – regardless of the level of support – is associated with political passivity and alienation. This analysis is conducted on the basis of a six-nation comparative study of unemployed youth and compares, across two welfare regimes, the Scandinavian and the more residual British systems. Not least from a citizenship perspective, and from the ideal of 'full citizenship', ethnic minorities constitute a 'critical' group that runs the risk of becoming excluded from full citizenship both in terms of the formal and sociological meaning of civic, political and social rights, and in terms of participation in different arenas of social action. Labour market marginalisation is a particularly important issue here. This issue is addressed by Gary Craig in Chapter Eight, which surveys the labour market situation for people from ethnic minority groups across a number of European countries.

The next two chapters look at how citizenship can affect welfare policies. Another group that has been increasingly marginalised within the labour market, at least in a formal sense, is older workers. However, facing the prospect of rapidly ageing populations and increasing dependency ratios in the future, most governments have engaged in strong efforts to reverse the trend towards early retirement. In Chapter Nine, Anne Marie Guillemard and Bert de Vroom discuss how governments may be able to accomplish this task, based on a comparative analysis of policies in France and the Netherlands.

Do people who are marginalised in the labour market become subject to fatalism or do they manage to react against it? It is a classical sociological observation that marginalisation is infrequently met by social mobilisation (Lazarsfeld et al, 1933; Schlozman and Verba, 1979; Bagguley, 1992). However, France is an exception because unemployed people there have been subject to mobilisation and protest actions. In Chapter Ten, Denis Bouget elaborates on French exceptionalism and discusses the particular preconditions in the French social protection system for creating a protest movement by the unemployed in France.

From a different angle, Birgit Pfau-Effinger argues in Chapter Eleven that the integration of women within the labour market is not a simple reaction to state policies. Rather, welfare state institutions are embedded in society and, as a result, properties of welfare policies may be explained by central cultural values and ideals in society and the way these change, just as individuals refer to cultural values and ideals. As such, the behaviour of individuals is influenced by gender arrangements, which refer to complex mutual interrelationships between cultural values, policies and institutions. Different gender arrangements are associated with different ideals of gender equality, of integration and of action.

Throughout this book the concept of marginalisation is loosely used to describe a state of involuntary lack of participation and a state of insufficient resources. However, the concepts of marginalisation and exclusion are polysemic and are subjected to critical reflection in Chapter Twelve by Asmund Born and Per H. Jensen. They argue that integration within the labour market typically comes to be seen as the only possible action in relation to the phenomenon of marginalisation. The concepts of integration and exclusion often entail a strategy of 'normalisation' to a particular, dominant, lifestyle, as evident in policies inspired by communitarianism.

The concluding remarks by Jorgen Goul Andersen and Per H. Jensen in Chapter Thirteen summarise some of the main findings of the preceding chapters and discuss how an approach based on an elaboration of the concepts of marginalisation and citizenship as analytical concepts covering the three dimensions of rights (civil, political and social), participation (in society's different arenas), and identities may improve understanding in the field.

Notes

[1] Not surprisingly, there is much disagreement about whether globalisation is really that new, the extent to which it is an autonomous, exogenous force that simply demands adaptation, and the restrictions it imposes. Compare, for example, Giddens (2000), Krugman (1996), Hirst and Thompson (1999).

[2] Operationally, it is not so difficult as it may seem to determine what is 'involuntary' absence of participation. Not being excluded, and having the full capacity to participate but deliberately choosing not to participate does not designate marginalisation. The measurement of such a condition has a long-standing tradition in political science where this is usually referred to as a question of political efficacy; it seems that analogous concepts may be applied in other fields.

References

Andersen, J.G. (1996) 'Marginalisation, citizenship and the economy: the capacities of the universalist welfare state in Denmark', in E.O. Eriksen and J. Loftager (eds), *The rationality of the welfare state*, Oslo: Scandinavian University Press, pp 155-202.

Anderson, J.G., Halvorsen, K., Jensen, P.H., Johannessen, A., Kangas, O., Olufsson, G. and Øverbye, E. (1998) *Unemployment, early retirement and citizenship: Marginalisation and integration in the Nordic countries*, CCWS Working Papers No 4, Åalborg: Department of Economics, Politics and Public Administration, Åalborg University.

Bagguley, P. (1992) 'Protest, acquiescence and the unemployed: a comparative analysis of the 1930s and 1980s', *British Journal of Sociology*, vol 43, no 3, pp 443-61.

Berghman, J. (1995) 'Social exclusion in Europe: policy context and analytical framework', in G. Room, *Beyond the threshold: The measurement and analysis of social exclusion*, Bristol: The Policy Press, pp 10-28.

Clasen, J., Kvist, J. and van Oorschot, W. (2001) 'On condition of work: increasing work requirements in unemployment compensation schemes', in M. Kautto, J. Fritzel, B. Hvinde, J. Kvist and H. Uusitalo (eds) *Nordic welafre states in the European context*, London: Routledge, pp 198-231.

Dean, H. and Taylor-Gooby, P. (1992) *Dependency culture: The explosion of a myth*, London: Harvester Wheatsheaf.

Esping-Andersen, G. (1999) *Social foundations of postindustrial economies*, Oxford: Oxford University Press.

Gallie, D. (1999) 'Unemployment and social exclusion in the European Union', *European Societies*, vol 2, pp 139-67.

Gallie, D. and Paugam, S. (2000) 'The experience of unemployment in Europe: the debate', in D. Gallie and S. Paugam (eds), *Welfare regimes and the experience of unemployment in Europe*, Oxford: Oxford University Press, pp 1-22.

Giddens, A. (2000) *The third way and its critics*, London: Polity Press.

Halvorsen, K. (1998) 'Symbolic purpose and factual consequences of the concepts of 'self-reliance' and 'dependency' in contemporary discourses on welfare', *Scandinavian Journal of Social Welfare*, vol 7, pp 56-64.

Hatland, A. (1998) 'The changing balance between incentives and economic security in Scandinavian unemployment benefit schemes', working paper, SEFOS, Bergen, presented at ISSA conference, Jerusalem, 25-28 January.

Hirst, P. and Thompson, G. (1999) *Globalization in question: The international economy and the possibilities of governance* (2nd edn), London: Polity Press/Blackwell.

Johannessen, A. (1998) *Marginalisering og ekskludering – samme eller forskjellige fenomen?* HiO-notat No 6, Oslo: Oslo College.

Jordan, B., Redley, M. and Jones, S. (1994) *Putting the family first: Identity, decisions, citizenship*, London: UCL Press.

Krugman, P. (1996) *Pop internationalism*, Cambridge, Mass: MIT Press.

Lazarsfeld, P., Jahoda, M. and Zeisel, H. (1933) *Marienthal: The sociology of an unemployed community*, London: Tavistock.

Lister, R. (1998) 'Vocabularies of citizenship and gender: the UK', *Critical Social Policy*, vol 18, no 3, pp 309-31.

Lorentzen, H. (1997) 'Integrasjon og utstøtning i sivilsamfunnet', *Dansk Sociologi*, vol 8, no 1, pp 61-77.

Marshall, T.H. (1965 [1949]) *Class, citizenship and social development*, Cambridge: Cambridge University Press.

Murray, C. (1984) *Losing ground*, New York, NY: Basic Books.

OECD (Organisation for Economic Co-operation and Development) (1994) *The OECD jobs study: Evidence and explanations*, vols 1-2, Paris: OECD.

OECD (1997) *Implementing the OECD jobs strategy*, Paris: OECD.

Pixley, J. (1993) *Citizenship and employment: Investigating post-industrial options*, Cambridge: Cambridge University Press.

Seiersted, F. (1996) 'Teknologi og arbeidsledighet', *Nytt Norsk Tidsskrift*, vol 2, pp 149-60.

Strobel, P. (1995) 'From poverty to exclusion: a wage-earning society or a society of human rights?', *International Social Science Journal*, vol 48, no 2, pp 173-89.

Svedberg, L. (1995) *Marginalitet*, Lund: Studentlitteratur.

TWO

Internationalisation and the labour market of the European Union

Peter Plougmann

We are currently witnessing radical changes in the European labour market that are challenging the institutions of the European welfare states. A new international division of labour is creating new opportunities as well as new threats for the European labour force. More and more employees of the old manufacturing industries are displaced or substituted due to the new international division of labour and the implementation of new technologies. Knowledge workers and service workers are replacing traditional white-collar workers at increasing rates. Many young people do not even regard a regular job as something rewarding but instead take advantage of the new opportunities to become 'free agents' and self-employed and engage in the networking of the new economy. The transnational corporations have enormous influence on the location of production and the distribution of wealth and are the main actors behind the internationalisation and new global division of labour. New powerful social dynamics are entering the scene, created by the growing importance of locality and of the competence of the labour force, the potential impact of global migration trends, and an increasing political awareness of the role of social capital as a condition for industrial innovation and social inclusion.

This chapter will discuss the future of some significant features of the European Union (EU) labour market by looking at the process of internationalisation and discussing the fundamental social and political dynamics of change that are already having an effect on European firms and wage-earners as well as on the European welfare states.

State of the European labour market

Despite the increasing level of employment many EU countries are still characterised by a low employment rate. The EU average is currently

61%, a decline since the 1970s when the rate stood at 64% and it has not yet recovered to the 1990 level in spite of four years of job growth. By contrast, the employment rate in the United States (US) was similar to the European rate in 1970, but has now risen to 75%. The EU average masks major regional differences, particularly in the highly performing smaller European countries and the UK. The difference in employment rates between the US and the EU is almost entirely explained by the higher numbers employed in the service sector in the US, which accounts for 90% of the net job growth (Sarfati, 2000).

The EU has a high and persistent unemployment level, which for more than a decade has been more than double that of the US. Although European economies are almost all highly developed welfare states, they show a great diversity of labour market performance: job creation in the Netherlands has, relatively speaking, outstripped that in the US in the 1990s; in the 1970s, Denmark achieved an employment-population rate which was not achieved by the US until the mid-1990s; Austria's unemployment rate was until 1998 substantially below the US rate (Schettkat, 2001).

With the recovery from the mid-1990s, the gap between the EU and the US is narrowing, but the gap is still there and cannot be explained by different measurements (see Table 2.1).

The third feature of the EU labour market, which is important to notice, is the diversification of employment forms. Although standard employment is still the dominating form in the EU, atypical jobs have increased and constituted 27% of all employment forms in 1998 (22% in 1991). An overview of the three forms of atypical jobs in the EU shows that:

- part-time work has increased significantly – close to 80% of the net job creation in the EU since 1994 has been part time
- temporary employment, which increased from the beginning of the recession in the early 1990s, continued to grow in 1998, representing 40% of all job increases
- self-employment involves 15% of the current EU workforce.

The worldwide development of atypical jobs reflects the demand for greater labour market flexibility, which results in part of the cost of social protection being shifted to the individual worker or to the welfare system depending on specific policies in different countries. This is fast becoming one of the most challenging dynamics within the EU labour market.

Table 2.1: Unemployment rates, approximated US concept (%)

Years	France	Germany	Italy	Netherlands	Sweden	UK	EU mean*	Canada	USA	Japan	Australia
1961-70	1.8	0.6	3.2		1.7		1.8	4.7	4.7	1.3	2.0
1971-80	4.3	2.3	3.8	4.8	2.1	5.0	3.7	6.9	6.4	1.8	4.4
1981-90	9.5	6.1	6.6	9.2	2.5	10.1	7.3	9.4	7.1	2.5	7.7
1991-98	11.6	8.1	10.6	6.0	8.1	8.7	8.8	10.0	6.0	3.0	9.3
1999	11.1	9.0	11.5	3.5	7.1	6.1	8.1	7.6	4.2	4.7	7.2

Source: Computations based on BLS international comparative labour force database

EU mean = unweighted average of the unemployment rates of the listed countries (Schettkat, 2001)

Unemployment and social wellbeing

Conventional wisdom suggests an inverse relationship between unemployment and social wellbeing: when unemployment goes up, social wellbeing goes down, and vice versa. However, social wellbeing is not only determined by unemployment. Many other conditions affect social wellbeing, such as the level of annual earnings, job security, and access to other income provided by social policies of the welfare state. The correlation between unemployment and social wellbeing is not a uniform one. Countries with a strong social safety net are able to maintain a satisfactory level of social wellbeing for their respective unemployed population – even in periods of high unemployment. Countries with weaker social institutions may see a large segment of their population suffer, despite a lower aggregate jobless rate. This has been the case in the US during the last couple of decades. In contrast, a substantial number of EU states have succeeded in maintaining relatively strong social safety nets even in times of high unemployment. It is worth recognising the existence of different welfare state regimes within Europe.

Different welfare state regimes

Different welfare state regimes provide different settings for the wellbeing of wage-earners. Countries such as Denmark and Sweden represent a welfare state model that differs significantly from the models of the US, UK and some continental European countries by maintaining a universal social coverage in case of unemployment based on an assumption of the individual rights and needs of the labour force.

Gallie and Paugam (2000) have developed an interesting taxonomy of different welfare state models, using three criteria for "unemployment welfare regimes":

- proportion of unemployed covered by insurance benefits
- the level and duration of the benefits
- the scope of the active labour market policy (ALMP).

Based on these indicators it is possible to construct a taxonomy of four different welfare state regimes (see Table 2.2).

The European countries are not uniform in the way in which they have organised the political and social institutions put in place to assure the wellbeing of their wage-earners. The problems of combating unemployment during the 1990s have triggered a number of policy changes in Europe.

When describing the policy changes in the 1990s, Casey and Gold (2000) underline that the Netherlands, Sweden and Ireland all performed better in the recent period and add:

> Each of these countries displays neo-corporatist traits. However, each of them has been moving toward supply-side corporatism, which places a considerable premium upon decentralisation, ordered deregulation and a respect for the role of the market. The first two countries have also taken substantial steps to modify and adapt their systems of social protection. (p 99)

This could be seen as an attempt by these countries to mimic some of the notions of the US job-creation model. It does imply that the troubled process of European job creation has led to a strong political argument in favour of making EU countries adapt to the US labour market model, emphasising flexibility above all. However, it is far from all EU countries that regard the US job-creation model as the best model for Europe.

Table 2.2: Four different welfare state regimes as defined by the situation of the unemployed

Regime	Proportion of unemployed covered by unemployment benefit system	Level of compensation and duration of unemployment benefits	Active labour market policy	Country illustrations
Sub-protective	Very incomplete	Extremely limited	Generally non-existent	Greece, Italy, Portugal, Spain
Liberal (minimum protection)	Few	Limited	Weakly developed	UK, Ireland
Employment-centred	Variable (depends on the employability of the person in question)	Unequal	Extensive	France, Germany, Netherlands
Universalistic	Comprehensive coverage	High and generous	Very extensive	Denmark, Sweden

Relationship between unemployment and earning inequality

Before embracing the US model it is important to notice that there seems to be an inverse relationship between unemployment and earning inequality. The US currently has one of the lowest unemployment rates in the world, but also the highest degree of earning inequality. By the 1990s, the top decile of American families enjoyed an average income nearly 6.5 times greater than that earned by the bottom decile. In most European countries, unemployment rose, but the so-called P90/10 interdecile income ratio remained about 3 to 1 (Luxemburg Income Study, 1999).

In a study of earnings inequality in the period 1979-98, Howell and Hüebler (2001) provides evidence that earnings inequality growth was by far the highest in the US and the UK. Belgium and Italy experienced the largest declines in earnings inequality. While Japan and Denmark showed no change, four nations experienced moderate declines (Germany, France, Norway and Finland) and other OECD nations had moderate increases. The UK and the US stand out as the only countries where there has been a continuation of a pronounced rise in earnings inequality during the last two decades.

The European labour market has benefited from the growth period of the past 10 years. In contrast to the period at the beginning of the 1990s, the labour market at the beginning of 2001 is characterised by increasing employment and falling unemployment. However, the average European level of unemployment is still double that of the US.

The EU labour market is at the same time influenced by an increasing segmentation of those in employment and the under-employed on one side and those affected by long-term unemployment on the other. This has placed heavy demands on EU countries' national welfare systems. Even if many EU countries have taken notice of the US job-creation model, including the high level of flexibility it provides, only relatively few have taken steps to change radically the institutions and incentive structures of their respective national labour market. As a result, social wellbeing seems to be better and income inequality less radical in EU countries than in the US.

Important dynamics for the future of the European labour market

The question discussed in the rest of this chapter is whether the future European labour market can maintain its relatively favourable position for the next 10 years and at the same time cope with the challenges that stem from the new international division of labour within a process of reforming the existing welfare state regimes. To investigate this issue we will look at some of the more important effects of internationalisation and the emerging new economy.

There are some new central, structural and sociological issues, which we are inclined to overlook in the day-to-day debate that will be decisive for the future distribution of employment. The issues to be discussed in more detail are:

- new international distribution of work creates new world (dis)order
- the global distribution of paid work
- social and political changes: the role of the middle class
- the 'new economy'
- new social dynamics
- the emergence of industrial Hollywoods and the increasing importance of social capital
- the new regional competition about competence and employment in the EU
- the creation of increased social inequality in the growing mega metropolises
- an increasing risk of new migration waves (also in Europe).

The rest of this chapter will briefly outline a framework, based on these issues, for understanding the future employment trends in EU countries.

New international distribution of work creates new world (dis)order

Internationalisation is characterised by a number of significant economic and political features, including the extensive:

- global expansion of the goods and capital markets
- growth in the number of wage-earners on a global scale
- relocalisation of manufacturing production from western economies to the emerging economies, Eastern Europe and the Third World
- focus on the service economy, sustained by the information and communication technologies, particularly in the US and the EU, but also in the emerging economies.

Taken together these features create considerable changes in the international distribution of work and affect the creation and distribution of future power, employment, income and wealth on a global basis. There are many ways of understanding and describing this process. There is also no consensus on the dynamics and causes of what some call globalisation and what others just see as continued internationalisation. Similarly, there is no universal agreement on the positive or negative consequences of the new international distribution of work (Dunning, 1993; Barber, 1995; Korten, 1995; Beck, 1998; Cohen, 1998; Gray, 1998). However, no one questions the fact that major changes have occurred in the location of wealth creation and the distribution of value based on a new mode of production. The development of global virtual companies with no production facilities of their own, with no real national attachments and built on a flexible web of supply and demand relationships has created a fundamental new way of production.

There is no doubt that the transnational corporations have an almost universal influence on the distribution of work and production across national borders. This trend has made Ohmae (1994) underline the importance of the increasingly comprehensive and global world trade that is making regions adapt to the development strategies of large corporations. It has also made the former US Employment Secretary, Professor Robert Reich, emphasise that neither money, goods or services know any limits, and that the challenge for governments, business managers and trade unions in the 21st century is to develop policies that ensure an adequate, developed and competent labour force that reflects the requirements of the global economy (Reich, 1991).

A new world (dis)order has been created, which will change the conditions for the employment development of the EU countries. The global distribution of paid work is at stake. The impact on the EU labour market is still not clear, neither is the political response to the unacceptable social effects of internationalisation certain.

Global distribution of paid work

Growth in European employment has, as already indicated, occurred simultaneously with a massive restructuring of the industrial basis. A comprehensive relocalisation of the manufacturing production has taken place, as follows.

The emerging economies (such as, Korea, Thailand, Poland and China) have since the mid-1980s overtaken large parts of the traditional production lines (for example, steel, shipyards, cotton, textiles/clothing and quite a significant share of the automotive production) as well as, somewhat surprisingly, the new industrial production markets (computer hardware, and accessories, and consumer electronics).

The service sector, for example software and film production (India), computer entertainment and tourism (religious package holidays to Mecca from Indonesia and Malaysia), have experienced large growth rates. Europe is still leading in the tourism field, despite the high growth rates of both the US and Asia.

Europe still has the world's largest total production of cars (every tenth person within the European labour market works with cars in one way or another). In the field of energy production (power plants and so on), telecommunications (mobile telephones and global positioning systems) and all types of specialised industrialised markets, Europe holds a very good position. However, Europe has lost nearly the entire consumer electronics field to Asia and is clearly behind the US in the defence industries. This also applies to the production of computers and software. European manufacturers in the expansive media and entertainment industry lag behind their American competitors seen from a global view. It also seems that the European medical and biotechnology corporations are losing ground to their American competitors.

The EU continues to be one of the largest food producers in the world with an extensive export.

Social and political changes: the role of the middle class

These changes of the location of work have had a profound impact on the social and political framework of the European welfare states.

The age of Fordism created a well-organised and well-paid working class in the western economies. The traditional blue-collar working class is now disappearing as an effect of the restructuring of the manufacturing production of the western economies. In the wake of the decline of the working class the role and power base of political organisations, particularly the trade unions, are disappearing and/or changing. This is probably the most important sociological reason for the current changes in the political basis of the western welfare states.

At the same time the number of wage-earners in countries in Asia and South America is increasing. These wage-earners experience an almost paradoxical rise in earnings of unseen proportions while global exploitation and, in some areas, social, capitalistic oppression have never been more distinct than today.

However, there is a growing middle class that demands democratic influence and social security. The middle class of the emerging economies

---

is in a process of building a political identity, as seen in many of the former eastern European countries, in Mexico and Peru but also in Asian countries such as Korea, Thailand and some of the coastal regions of China. The economic crash in 1997/98 in Asia created a strong interest from the middle classes there in building sustainable financial and political institutions that can take care of, if not prevent, any radical social conflicts that might arise from potential future economic crises. Whether or not this process will lead to the creation of welfare states such as those in Europe remains to be seen, but it is still an interesting sociological and political development. This is especially true in a period or time where many are embracing the market without any major political reservations.

From an EU point of view, this tendency to question the fairness and effectiveness of the globalisation with regards to the wellbeing of the population is interesting. The fear of unfair international competition based on 'social dumping' has for some time preoccupied the political agenda in the EU. The process of EU enlargement has been slowed down considerably due to this problem. If the emerging economies succeed in building general labour market regulations and institutions that prevent 'social dumping', this will increase the wellbeing of employees in all involved countries. It is in the interest of Europeans that the middle classes of the emerging economies around the world are successful in organising themselves as a class and in building sustainable political institutions.

The global distribution of paid work is undergoing massive changes and the question is, 'What determines the future development of this factor seen from a European point of view?' One thing is obvious: the process of internationalisation has changed the employment landscape of Europe. Manufacturing is decreasing rapidly and new forms of services are taking root very fast. The demands for flexibility within the labour market have never been greater. The risks of increasing social displacement and increasing poverty in some European countries and regions are evident.

The need for fast adjustments and a proactive policy to cope with the structural changes in demand for labour is also obvious. The same is true when we look for initiatives to exploit the new opportunities provided by the so-called 'new economy'.

The new economy

The past 10 years have seen a new phenomenon emerge in the world economy, that of continued, high economic growth, increasing global employment rates, low inflation rates and low interest rates. This has made many economic and political analysts, from the Federal Reserve Chairman Allan Greenspan to the techno-cultural editor of *Wired* magazine, Kevin Kelly, argue in favour of the concept of the new economy.

It is claimed that the new economy is based on changes in the relationship between production factors, particularly technological development, the creation of a dynamic network economy and a decrease in union strength. The almost revolutionary development in computer technology, the Internet and, lately, biotechnology are highlighted as the most significant factors behind the market development of new products and an increasing productivity in the manufacturing sectors. This has reduced the overall costs and created the basis for the rising global employment rate. Whether that is the explanation for the fact that the Phillips curve no longer behaves according to theory (which states that wage pressure leads to inflation) still needs to be verified. New analyses indicate that it is the expansion in the number of working hours in the form of overtime work, extra jobs, and increased part-time employment in the US due to a fall in the real earnings of the majority of wage-earners that is the reason why we have not seen steep inflationary trends.

Observers also rarely agree on the positive presentation of the situation (Krugman, 1997). It is easy to argue that the global productivity capacity is not increasing with an unheard of historic speed. Global growth (including in the South-East Asian countries) reached close to an annual rate of 4% in the 1990s, which is better than in the 1970s and 1980s (both approximately 3% per annum), but still lower than in the 1950s and 1960s. Correspondingly, demand rates in the mature economies are able to keep pace with potential supply. Growth in the emerging economies contributes more to the global demand rate than to global supply rates. This is not least due to the fact that the earnings of the middle classes in many emerging economies (Asia, Eastern and Central Europe, South America) are growing in line with productivity development. In a few of the Asian Tiger countries wages are approaching the US level. Countries such as Taiwan and Singapore therefore import cheap labour from large areas of Asia to keep costs low. At the same time, the ethnic Chinese communities based overseas (totalling approximately 60 million people) are very active investors and are constantly establishing new production facilities to replace the too expensive ones, for example in Taiwan (Weidenbaum and Hughes, 1996).

Instead of supporting a theory about a new economy (Soros, 1998), some observers of the international economic developments find it to be financial speculation – not changes in the production factors – that affects current economic development trends. The international market

---

developments reached historic extremes at the end of the 1990s. Share prices on global stock exchanges fluctuated wildly and reflected the surplus supply of homeless capital. This has had a particularly bad effect on Asia, South America and Russia (Gough, 1998; Godement, 1999). The destruction of values, massive job cuts, hyperinflation and radical changes in the relative strengths of different social classes were the results. This development then strengthened the stock markets in the US and the EU. Rising share prices reflect the influence of the speculative capital, which is a danger signal warning about future instability in the US and the EU. The heavily fluctuating technology shares, primarily in dot-com companies in 2000, reflect that the risk of the effects of speculative capital is immediate. Rising share prices based on speculation will at some point in time need to be adapted to the real value of the companies (profits and equity), both in the American and the European economies. The consequence for the European labour market could easily be a new period of rising unemployment rates.

At the beginning of 2001 the situation is in many ways characterised by the dot-com bubble economy's rapid collapse. The open question is whether the old, traditional industries will gather the productivity improvements and new business concepts represented by the dot-coms and incorporate them in the future global production system. There are many indications that this will be the case and this new crisis will probably result in a strengthening of the transnational corporations. That would reduce the negative effects on employment rates globally and particularly in the US and the EU. To understand the impact of this process we have to look more closely at some important new social dynamics.

New social dynamics

Looking for quick, superficial explanations for the current favourable economic situation and positive trends in the EU employment rates will be misleading. Instead, we need a structural understanding of what dynamics are crucial for the competitive development and future of the European labour market.

The most important new social dynamics are:

- the consolidation of industrial Hollywoods – regions of global excellence within specialised areas of production, regarded by every one as the world leader; talent, capital and companies all want to be like this, or even better to be part of the cluster of competence that constitutes an industrial Hollywood

- the increasing importance of locality, that is, dependence on the scope and development of social capital
- the 'New Middle Ages', in which the new real form of competition in the EU takes place between urban regions and rather than between nations
- urbanisation development and migration
- flexibility demands on labour, which are distinctly rising as a consequence of the impact of internationalisation.

Industrial Hollywoods

Free movement of financial capital is not the same as free movement of physical capital. Fixed capital, investments in human capital and the importance of regional social capital will not be moved overnight (Storper, 1997). Consequently, regionalisation and social capital will play an increasingly important role in the future (Putnam, 2000). The consequences for the employment rate and competency development requirements are best illustrated by the concept of industrial Hollywoods:

- The international distribution of work is based on continuous specialisation. This does not only include the specialisation of job tasks, products and markets, but also a specialisation of the composition of competences and geographic clusters of cooperating companies.
- In all sectors and product fields centres of excellence have been established, which are market leaders globally. These are regions and geographic areas that are hyperinnovative, globally competitive and therefore attract capital and talented manpower from all over the world.
- This creates a positive development circle – the best regions become even better. Hollywood represents such an example for the film and TV industries, which is what led to the term industrial Hollywoods.

When considering the importance of internationalisation to the European labour market, it is clear that qualified labour – in spite of an increasing geographic mobility – almost more than any other production factor has a locality. It is crucial to understand what factors encourage the innovative ability of a region, thus ensuring employment on a long-term basis. The concept of social capital in this context emerges as one of the essential factors in the development of industrial Hollywoods in Europe.

Social capital

An increasing number of regional development studies show that cultural values, sociological relations and political conditions that either promote or hinder the development of human relations regionally, affect the innovative ability and the long-term economic growth of a region (Shuman, 1998).

According to Putnam (1993, 2000), social capital makes the difference. A central concept in social capital is trust, between citizens and companies and between citizens and institutions in a given region. There is still a great deal of debate about the unambiguousness of trust (Leadbeater, 2000). Putnam has been criticised for using wrong indicators for social capital in the US in his earlier work. The same applies to Fukuyama (1995) who has been heavily criticised for his handling of social virtues; but no one has dismissed the relevance of his thesis – that confidence-building relations also create employment and wealth. On the contrary, data from the European Value Systems Study Group shows clear indications of the existence of such a correlation in the EU. The latest studies show that regions such as Catalonia in Spain, Denmark and Ireland (which in a European perspective are regions rather than nations) and various constituent states in Germany, for example Bavaria, and other smaller regions in large EU countries display an interesting correlation between high scores on indicators for strong cultural identities and social trust while experiencing long periods of economic growth and a high level of adaptability. Social capital affects a region's ability to take advantage of the opportunities of the network economy and ensures that secondary innovation occurs in clusters of small and medium-sized enterprises, which is of crucial importance for the competitiveness of the regions. This trend leads to completely new forms of competition within the EU, which may be called the 'New Middle Ages'.

'New Middle Ages' or the existing form of competition in the EU

Competition is changing character, not least in Europe. There is no longer competition between nations or individual companies; instead there is competition between regions and cities. There are about 30 regions/cities in Europe, which in their mutual competition and various alliances create the basis for the localisation of new jobs and for the distribution of power and income (Delamaide, 1994; Bruton, 1996; Newhouse, 1997). It is a situation that is mostly reminiscent of Italy in the Middle Ages when lords and mercenaries were involved in conflicts and alliances with and against the papacy and each other. There was no national state and no democratic state power to mediate. Today, political power is becoming increasingly fragmented while a reorganisation of the economic productive use of existing social capital and innovative ability of the regions is taking place.

The future of job creation within the EU is becoming increasingly dependent on existing companies' ability to become a part of the production systems of the leading regions. Few companies and regions are in a position to do this. This forms the basis for a new distribution of jobs in the EU and potential social polarisation problems even today, a process that will intensify in step with the enlargement of the EU.

It will also make demands on the European welfare states to counter the negative consequences. Some liberal economists and political scientists do not find that the European welfare states are able to counter the problems. They claim that there are too many politically defined regulations of the European labour markets that are making the labour market too rigid. Instead, greater flexibility is needed. The central issue of flexibility will be dealt with later, but it must be mentioned at this point that other observers of European social and labour market development single out the institutional framework conditions placed on the labour market of the EU countries as beneficial to creating consensus. The existing institutional framework conditions prevent social conflicts. The framework ensures the existence of a well-qualified workforce and a relatively efficient allocation of labour.

A study by Auer (2000) of four small European economies (Ireland, Austria, the Netherlands and Denmark) shows that a high level of social security has to be combined with a high level of flexibility within the labour market – this forms the basis for an efficient allocation on the labour market that prevents mismatch problems and long-term unemployment.

The existing institutional framework for the European labour market also allows the different European regions to maintain and develop their great cultural and political diversity. Many economists and social scientists (Thurow, 1992; 1996) consider this diversity to be the European societies' greatest relative competitive advantage compared to the US and Asia.

Despite the positive assessment of the EU's existing social paradigm, it will require an enormous amount of political flexibility and production adaptability to accommodate the changes created by the new international distribution of work in the future. Not least, it will require an increase in the amount of confidence-building activities between companies, their managers/owners, employees, regional authorities and regional society if the potential social crises and uneven distribution of employment are to be avoided. At the same time, the social capital is being eroded, not least as a consequence of the spreading urbanisation process and new trends in migration throughout the world and within Europe. We need to now look at these social dynamics.

Mega metropolises and migration

A massive urbanisation process is still ongoing everywhere in the world. This causes massive sociological changes to take place, not least in the form of a proletarianisation of increasingly larger groups of wage-earners and migrating job-seekers. The cities will no doubt continue to grow and reshape in the 21st century. At the global level, mega metropolises with more than 25 million inhabitants will be dominated by slums and poverty along with many people available for work who can and will be subject to massive exploitation.

These mega metropolises will particularly be located in Asia, Latin America and Africa, but widespread social exclusion and economic polarisation will also be found in the large cities of the western countries. Many inhabitants of these giant cities will be forced to live in regions that are on the periphery of the labour market and will have opportunity to earn a decent wage or work under decent working conditions. Many poor people will – in a state of increasing desperation – live by and with violence, crime, prostitution and, in more extreme cases, selling organs and children to the industrialised countries.

It is necessary to ask what will happen when the approximately 100 million migrating former peasants from China realise that they cannot find decent employment in the cities and discover that they are excluded from the development in the distribution of wealth. One scenario, which is gaining strength, is that China will collapse and be divided into mutually competing regions, possibly followed by civil war. If that happens, China will not be able to maintain its current production for the world market. The large amounts of foreign direct investment (FDI) will then start to flow in other directions. This will have a massive effect on the international distribution of work.

Another scenario is civil wars in the Maghreb countries, where class struggle is couched in religion, leading to the beginning of terrorist activities and mass emigration to Europe. Pressure on Spain, France and Italy is already heavy (Weiner, 1995; Kornø Rasmussen, 1996; Coleman et al, 1999). This leads to a thesis about the proximity of new, great migrations. We can easily envision the following migrations in the next decade:

- **the great migration north:**
- from South America and Mexico towards the US (and Canada) combined with an increase in the cultural and political fragmentation of the US due to another demographic and ethnic distribution of the population – this is already happening
- from Africa towards the soft belly of the EU (Spain, France and Italy) with consequent political reactions (increase in the support for right-wing and populist parties)

- **the great migration east:**
- from the provinces of China to the coastal areas, possibly leading to an intensification of the social disparity and a political clash with the central government in Beijing; political instability will have a negative affect on FDI in China negatively, which will then flow elsewhere, for example the EU, thereby strengthening employment in Europe

- **the great migration west:**
- from Eastern Europe to Western Europe – this pressure will particularly be felt by Germany, Austria and perhaps then Scandinavia; as a consequence, as well as having a Third World labour market placed directly in the back garden, a massive migration wave will be reflected in a surplus supply of both unskilled labour and an increment in the supply of professional labour.

This might not all happen but is a definite risk that has to be taken into account when discussing the global distribution of work. There is sufficient reason to be aware that pressure from the proletarianised masses of labour will inevitably affect the future localisation and organisation of production. This will affect all known labour market conditions and it will probably not be possible to maintain the traditional industrial relations that currently exist within EU countries.

It is not just migration that is changing the framework conditions of the European labour market. New forms of management strategies put into action to exploit new opportunities and to increase the overall flexibility of the European production system are changing many known working conditions and terms of employment. These new management principles are another new social dynamic which creates a need for 'flexicurity'.

New forms of work organisation

New management and organisational principles, such as those labelled 'management by skills' and 'management of skills' and both based on the changing international forms of competition, give many European wage-earners new working conditions (Murphy, 1996).

'Management of skills' underlines the need for human capital investments at the company level, whereas 'management by skills' moves one step further by recognising the need of modern companies to rely on the tacit knowledge of groups of employees. The job of managers changes to focus on coaching and facilitating wage-earners, so that they have the necessary means to produce in an ever-changing competitive world. This development is considered to be a necessary adaptation to future demands made by many companies, trade organisations and policymakers. In the past few years, the Organisation for Economic Cooperation and Development (OECD) has – in line with the European Commission and many researchers – analysed changes in company structures, company strategies and the consequences of this to human resources management (HRM). A rough digest of the results of these analyses provides the conclusion that there is a clear trend towards an increased individualisation of wage-earners' attachment to the labour market. This trend is based on the companies' interest in:

• downsizing, to reduce the number of employees to an absolute minimum
• outsourcing, to focus on core skills and then purchase everything else from others
• increasing wage differentiation, to prevent the core labour force of a company leaving prematurely
• employment rate growth on non-standard terms, to ensure flexibility and profitability
• changes in management forms towards high skill and high trust organisational and management models, to generate efficiency effects and ensure costs are reduced
• increasing demands for prior education and competence and subsequent training, with the focus being on employees taking responsibility for their own learning.

The result of these interests is not just numerical and functional flexibility; it is the creation of an increasingly more globally-flexible production, distribution and service system.

The OECD estimates that approximately 25% of all companies

(particularly in the industrial sector) are driven by the development of an increasingly more comprehensive, flexible form of organisation. It is not the majority of companies or employees that are directly affected by the demands for increasing flexibility. A new trend is that companies in some service sectors are moving in the opposite direction towards old-fashioned Taylorisation and automation of work. However, it is evident that there is a clear trend towards an increase in flexibility within the European market.

There are great differences in the way the flexible organisation is realised. In countries such as the US and the UK the change is almost purely market driven. In Germany and Scandinavia and partly in Austria, the Benelux countries and France it is consensus driven, often with a strong strain of central initiatives. In Japan, and partly in Korea, the consensus initiatives are generally based at the company level. In the remaining OECD countries (Spain, Portugal, Greece, Turkey and Ireland) there are many different combinations of the approaches mentioned.

The effects on the structure of the labour market are an emphasis on non-standard and atypical employment, leading to:

- more short-term employees
- more potential for teleworking
- more room for self-employment (both for professional and unskilled workers).

The increasing interest by companies to maintain their core employees further adds to the tendency to polarisation of the European labour market.

'Flexicurity'

As flexibility becomes a reality, the concept of job security is becoming increasingly irrelevant for more and more employees. Employees can only create job security by using their current job to acquire the competences to change jobs and hence ensure continuous employment. The new concept is to create security via flexibility, termed 'flexicurity'.

This organisational development has positive and negative effects on the employees and the unemployed. There are many positive effects of increased flexibility and job rotation in the form of better career opportunities, the employee's work having increased influence and a better working environment due to less repetitive work.

The negative effects are often overlooked in the debate but the new organisational and management principles boost the trend towards the expulsion of labour that cannot adapt to the demands for more responsibility and continuing change. This is often older, low-skilled labour or highly specialised skilled people whose skills become obsolete due to structural and technological changes.

As a result, a polarisation of the labour market is taking place. Adapting to new forms of management and organisation is necessary for European firms to compete internationally, but the consequences for the wage-earners show the Janus head of this development trend. It is crucial to create a social pact between the ones (wage-earners and companies alike) gaining advantages and the ones that are affected negatively by this development.

The need for 'flexicurity' is probably the most significant challenge for the European labour market in the years to come. Demands for new flexible attitudes towards change among wage-earners will increase. This requires that wage-earners have access to certain welfare state benefits, such as a comprehensive unemployment benefit system, and opportunities for continuing adult vocational training. There is an increasing need for lifelong learning to be an integral part of working life. These are conditions that are far from present in all EU countries today. The European labour force needs to gain better access to continuous competence development if the current positive employment trend is to continue.

Demands for new competencies

Many types of European professional labour will lose their basis for demand in line with the new global distribution of work. The de-industrialisation of European industry will also limit the need for traditional, skilled labour and workers with a short-term education. The primary group that has lost employment opportunities has been those with short-term education. On the other hand, automation and the de-materialisation of the production process have already created new opportunities for workers with adult vocational training skills in these fields. The majority of flexible wage-earners are already utilising the new opportunities provided by the new economy.

The distribution of work in the global network of manufacturing systems determines a hierarchy of competences, with the highest competency demands continuing to be made by the highly developed countries, including Europe. However, the relative number of jobs in these fields will continue to fall in those countries.

Those hardest affected by this will be the traditional manufacturing industrial sectors and their employees. It is a gradual process in which the need for the traditional employee groups in industry and in trade will diminish. The speed with which this is happening will vary from one group of employees to another, but there will be no return to the 'good old days'.

Many of the traditional skilled groups of labour must – to a higher degree than today – adapt to the new flexicurity conditions. These changes have to take place on a broad scale and will take place in both the private and public sectors. The responsibility for acting in due time is shared by employers, wage-earners and their organisation along with government agencies.

It is the combined effect of new terms of employment and working conditions, the increased individualisation and the demand for more independent initiatives from individual employees combined with the ability to handle knowledge abstractly that will make further demands on both professional specialisation and personal qualifications in the future. Many young people will have to be prepared to accept a considerably more diffuse professional identity than before. This will be hard for some; as a result, governments must pay more attention to the drop-out problems among young people.

The breakdown of traditional demarcation lines between jobs is already a trend. Traditional notions that define a given labour market segment, such as maintaining a given profession or trade to secure professional identity, must in most cases be abandoned. Increasing internal competition between unions and still lower rates of unionisation are further weakening the unions nationally. This also makes transnational cooperation between unions difficult.

Not much that characterises these trends is revolutionary. Today, a large proportion of employees, who come from all types of education backgrounds, are not employed in the jobs or sectors that originally they aimed to work in. Already the labour force has proven to be very flexible.

Many new professions and job functions that did not exist previously are rapidly being developed. This applies particularly to the private service sector and to transnational companies.

New professions created in the information and communication technologies (ICT), life sciences and biotech sectors will create many new employment opportunities in Europe. This places heavy demands on the development of completely new competences. However, not all EU regions will benefit equally from this development. The successful regions will be those that understand the importance of developing knowledge-intensive production processes and services based on the development of new competence clusters and industrial Hollywoods.

One of the greatest challenges for the European welfare states will be to adapt to the new realities in the areas mentioned. Overall, the internationalisation process in its many different forms places considerable demands on reorganisation, new priorities (for example, on lifelong learning and flexicurity) and a complete renewal of our understanding of the welfare state system.

Perspectives

This chapter has highlighted some of the new dynamics imposed on the European labour market. The radical changes of the global division of labour leaves little room for errors when it comes to embracing the new opportunities of the new economy. To fit into the new global division of labour, European companies need to become even more flexible and employ an even more competent and effective workforce. The days of the traditional manufacturing industries are gone and the service and knowledge-driven economy arrived long ago. The competition between European regions has replaced the competition between nations. The importance of building regional social capital in order to compete successfully has become still more evident. To overcome the problems of creating enough jobs it is not sufficient just to embrace the US job-creation model; the efficient welfare state institutions must be developed further to create an institutional and political framework of 'flexicurity'. This will include creating a more universalistic form of welfare system than currently exists in many European countries.

References

Auer, P. (2000) *Employment revival in Europe*, Geneva: International Labour Office.

Barber, B.R. (1995) *Jihad vs. McWorld*, New York: Times Books.

Beck, U. (1998) *Politik der Globalisierung*, Frankfurt: Campus Verlag.

Bruton, A. (1996) *A revolution in progress*, London: Little Brown & Company.

Casey, B. and Gold, M. (2000) *Social partnership and economic performance, the case of Europe* .

Cohen, D. (1998) *Fehldiagnose Globalisierung*, Frankfurt: Campus Verlag.

Coleman, D., Esch, L. and Waden, S.Ö. (1999) *Indvandringen til Danmark*, Copenhagen: Spektrum.

Delamaide, D. (1994) *The new superregions of Europe*, New York: Dutton.

Dunning, J. (1993) *The globalization of business*, London: Routledge.

European Value Systems Study Group (EVSSG); various publications 1970-2000, Tilburg: Tilburg University.

Fukuyama, F. (1995) *Trust, the social virtues and the creation of prosperity*, London: Penguin Books.

Gallie, D. and Paugam, S. (2000) *Welfare regimes and the experience of unemployment in Europe*, Oxford: Oxford University Press.

Godement, F. (1999) *The downsizing of Asia*, London: Routledge.

Gough, L. (1998) *Asia meltdown*, Oxford: Capstone Publishing Limited.

Gray, J. (1998) *False dawn, the delusions of global capitalism*, London: Granta Books.

Howell, D.R. and Hüebler, F. (2001) *Trends in earnings inequality and unemployment across the OECD: Labor market institutions and simple supply and demand stories*, Center for Economic Policy Analysis (CEPA), New School University.

Korten, D.C. (1995) *When corporations rule the world*, West Hartford, CT: Kumarian Press.

Kornø Rasmussen, H. (1996) *Flygtninge og indvandrere i Europa*, Copenhagen: Handelshøjskolens Forlag.

Krugman, P. (1997) 'Is capitalism too productive?', *Foreign Affairs*, Sept/Oct.

Leadbeater, C. (2000) *The weightless world*, London: Demos.

Luxemburg Income Study (1999) Center for the Study of Population, Poverty and Public Policy (CEPS), INSTEAD, Differdang, Luxembourg.

Murphy, E. (1996) *Flexible work*, Hertfordshire: Director Books.

Newhouse, J. (1997) *Europe adrift*, New York, NY: Pantheon Books.

Ohmae, K. (1994) *The borderless world – power and strategy in the interlinked economy*, HarperCollins Trade Paperback.

Putnam, R.D. (1993) *Making democracy work*, Princeton, NJ: Princeton University Press.

Putnam, R.D. (2000) *Bowling alone – the collapse and revival of American community*, New York, NY: Simon & Schuster.

Reich, R.B. (1991) *The work of nations*, London: Simon & Schuster.

Sarfati, H. (2000) *The changing labour market in the OECD region – challenges to social policy and social protection reform*, AAHS Labour Market Shifts, Luxembourg: ILO.

Schettkat, R. (2001) *Regulation in the Dutch and German economies at the root of unemployment?*, Utrecht: Department of Economics, University of Utrecht.

Shuman, M. (1998) *Going local,* New York, NY: Free Press.

Soros, G. (1998) *The crisis of global capitalism: Open society endangered,* London: Little Brown & Company.

Storper, M. (1997) *The regional world: Territorial development in a global economy*, New York, NY and London: Guilford Press.

Thurow, L. (1992) *Head to head*, New York, NY: William Morrow and Company.

Thurow, L. (1996) *The future of capitalism*, London: Nicholas Brealey Publishing.

Weidenbaum, M. and Hughes, S. (1996) *The bamboo network*, New York, NY: Free Press.

Weiner, M. (1995) *The global migration crisis*, Addison-Wesley.

THREE

Citizenship and changing welfare states

Ruth Lister

Introduction

This chapter marries an overview of current developments in the theorisation of citizenship with a discussion of a number of trends in European welfare states, which have implications for gendered citizenship. These trends are reviewed in relation to four main issues:

- the pressures for residualisation of social rights
- the relationship between social rights and obligations and the 'recommodification' of labour through which the ability to uphold a socially acceptable standard of living is tied more closely, once again, to labour market participation.
- the implications of this recommodification for the recognition of care as an expression of citizenship responsibility
- supra-national citizenship, in particular with reference to the European Union (EU) and social rights and the treatment of 'outsiders'[1].

Although the chapter does not directly address labour market trends, current developments in citizenship need to be understood in the context of those trends, in particular the intensification of marginalisation, discussed elsewhere in this book. In turn, a clearer understanding of both the concept of citizenship and of the changing nature of social citizenship in different welfare states helps us to make sense of current responses to changing labour market conditions and to new patterns of marginalisation.

Meaning(s) of citizenship

Citizenship is one of those slippery terms that means different things to different people and is the subject of disparate understandings according to the national context. At one level it simply represents a legal status, symbolised in the possession of a passport. However, it also has a deeper, more substantive, sociological and political meaning, which describes the relationship between individuals and the state and the relationship between individuals within a national community.

As such, it is also a highly contested concept at every level, from its meaning to its political application. This is, in part, because of what it means for the type of society to which we aspire, but it also reflects citizenship's roots in two different, and at times antagonistic, political traditions: liberalism and civic republicanism. The former casts citizenship as a *status* involving primarily rights accorded to individuals; the latter casts it as a *practice* involving responsibilities to the wider society (Oldfield, 1990).

T.H. Marshall's famous essay on *Citizenship and social class* (1950), which provides the starting point for most subsequent discussions of citizenship, defined it primarily as a status. As is well known, he conceptualised citizenship rights as civil, political and social. Social rights, enshrined in the welfare states that emerged in the 20th century, promote the decommodification of labour by decoupling the living standards of individual citizens, to a greater or lesser extent, from their market value so that they are not totally dependent on selling their labour power in the market for their survival and wellbeing.

More recently, radical political theorists have suggested ways in which Marshall's triad needs to be extended to include, for example, reproductive rights and the right to participate in decision-making in social, economic, cultural and political life. The latter is echoed in attempts to develop a more active form of citizenship rights, through, for example, promoting user-involvement in public services. This idea of participation being a right of citizenship represents a bridge to the civic republican tradition that originated in ancient Greece and Rome. Here citizenship represents an obligation and the citizen is an active participant in governance and politics for the good of the wider community. There has been something of a resurgence in this tradition, especially in the US, in reaction against the individualism of the previously dominant liberal citizenship paradigm. Provided we adopt broad definitions of citizenship and the 'political', in line with feminist political theory, this more participatory understanding of citizenship is helpful in thinking about issues of democratisation and accountability in the welfare state.

However, the more prominent discourse on duties in today's welfare states centres on work obligations. The issue of work obligations is not a new one; Marshall discussed it in an often overlooked passage in his famous lecture. But, a voice from a different era, he suggested that "the essential duty is not to have a job and hold it, since that is relatively simple in conditions of full employment, but to put one's heart into one's job and work hard" (Marshall, 1950, pp 79-80). In conditions of considerably less than full employment in many European countries, exclusion from and marginalisation within fragmented and unequal labour markets serve to weaken the citizenship of those who do not possess the education and skills to compete.

Elsewhere, I have argued that it is not a question of whether citizenship is about rights or responsibilities, but "what is the appropriate balance and relationship between the two and how does that balance reflect gender and other power relations?" (Lister, 1997, p 21). I have also argued for a critical synthesis of the liberal and civic republican traditions: a rounded conceptualisation of citizenship that incorporates the dimensions of both status and practice. At the axis of the synthesis is the notion of human agency[2].

Citizenship as participation can be understood as representing an expression of human agency in the political arena: broadly defined, the rights that come with citizenship enable people to act as agents. Citizenship is thereby a dynamic concept in which process and outcome stand in a dialectical relationship to each other. Rights are not set in stone; they are always open to reinterpretation and renegotiation and need to be defended and extended through political and social action, not least in the welfare state arena. Such a conceptualisation of citizenship is particularly important in challenging the construction of women and other marginalised groups as passive victims, while keeping sight of the discriminatory and oppressive political, economic and social institutions that still deny them full citizenship.

However, there are dangers associated with this conceptualisation of citizenship. As a normative ideal, it risks creating a measuring rod against which many members of marginalised groups, most notably overburdened women but also, for instance, chronically sick or very severely disabled people, might once again fall short because of the demands they face in their private lives and other constraints. One way to avert this danger is to draw a distinction between two formulations: to *be* a citizen and to *act* as a citizen. To be a citizen, in the sociological sense, means to enjoy the rights necessary for agency and social and political participation. To act as a citizen involves fulfilling the full potential of the status. Those who do not fulfil that potential do not cease to be citizens in either the formal, legal or more substantive sociological and political sense.

Contemporary theorisation of citizenship

In the contemporary theorisation of citizenship, there are two aspects central to 'post-Marshallian' thinking. Both concern the tension created by citizenship's power to exclude as well as to include, often setting up a state of partial citizenship. The chapter will look at how thinking is evolving in relation to nation state 'insiders' and then to nation state 'outsiders'.

Insiders

One of the main criticisms of Marshall's theorisation of citizenship made today is that it reflected the perspectives of men and for the most part ignored those of women. Yet, citizenship, a supposedly universalistic ideal, was originally predicated on the exclusion of women and their inclusion has been on different terms to those enjoyed by men. There has thus developed a strong feminist critique of 'malestream' citizenship theory, which has contributed to the resurgence of an interest in citizenship as an academic and political tool. This has exposed the gendered processes of exclusion and inclusion and the ways in which these have been pivotal rather than accidental to traditional constructions of citizenship.

Moving on from simple critique, feminist scholarship is now attempting to 're-gender' citizenship from the perspective of women (Lister, 2000). Three broad approaches can be discerned, summed up under the three normative images of the 'gender-neutral' citizen, the 'gender-differentiated citizen' and the 'gender-pluralist citizen'. Crudely, for the gender-neutral citizen, the emphasis is on equal rights and obligations; gender should be irrelevant to their allocation. In the social sphere, the priority is to enable women to compete on equal terms with men in the labour market. The latter, in turn, opens up access to the social rights of citizenship linked to labour market status through social insurance schemes. In contrast, the 'gender-differentiated citizen', personified in the mother, appeals to difference not equality when promoting women's claims as social and political citizens.

However, such a maternalist construction of citizenship has attracted criticism for constructing "sexually segregated norms of citizenship" in which difference spells unequal and inferior (Jones, 1988, p 18). In response, a number of feminists, sympathetic to some of the values underlying the gender-differentiated model, are arguing for a non-maternalist conceptualisation of difference around the broader notion of care and an ethic of care, which is not confined to women. Drawing on theorising around care, they are making the case for the right to time to care and to receive care, as part of a more inclusive citizenship (Knijn and Kremer, 1997).

Some, though, such as Chantal Mouffe (1992), have criticised the gender-differentiated model, not from a standpoint of gender-neutrality but from a radical pluralist position in which gender is just one element of the individual's subject position and identity. Here we find the 'gender pluralist citizen'. Likewise, gender is only one of the motors driving partial citizenship. Both academics and activists have developed critiques of traditional constructions of citizenship, which have ignored the perspectives of black and minority ethnic groups, gays and lesbians and people with disabilities and which have served to exclude rather than to include these groups. The implications of age for citizenship are also beginning to be considered – from the perspectives of both children and young people at one end of the spectrum and frail, older people at the other. Increasingly, citizenship is being theorised from the perspective of 'multiple subject-positions' and identities and in relation to a 'politics of recognition' as well as 'redistribution' (Isin and Wood, 1999).

As the universalist conception of citizenship began to fragment before our eyes like some type of theoretical kaleidoscope, the question was posed by Stuart Hall and David Held (1989, p 17) as to whether there is "now an irreconcilable tension between [on the one hand] the thrust to equality and universality entailed in the very idea of the 'citizen'" and, on the other, this post-modern kaleidoscope of particular needs and perspectives. The contradiction between citizenship's universalistic claims and the exclusions in which it is has been implicated has led some to question its value for a progressive social policy and politics. Nevertheless, those very groups, which have been excluded from traditional constructions of citizenship, have used the language of citizenship to frame their demands, which suggests that it does still have a value. To take just one example, the fight for the realisation of full civil, political and social rights for people with disabilities has been represented as a "struggle for citizenship" (Barton, 1993, p 235).

Today, critical citizenship theorists are grappling with the tension identified by Hall and Held, as they attempt to rearticulate citizenship, so as to address its exclusionary dimensions and to reconcile its universalistic claims with the demands of difference, through what might be called a "differentiated universalism" (Lister, 1997).

Outsiders

At the same time, critical citizenship theorists are arguing for a more internationalist and multi-layered perspective. Citizenship theory, following Marshall, has tended to focus on the processes of inclusion and exclusion within the boundaries drawn and regulated by nation states. More critically, citizenship can be identified as "a conspiracy against outsiders" (Hindess, 1998, p 67) in a world divided into a series of states to which citizenship is attached. It is an issue that is taking on greater salience in the face of growing numbers of asylum-seekers and migrants, attempting to cross national boundaries in an increasingly economically polarised world.

The richer industrialised world has not been willing to countenance the free movement of labour alongside the free movement of capital (Massey, 2000). However, a combination of demographic trends and labour market shortages is causing some governments to encourage the immigration of workers with needed skills, such as in information technology (IT), to the possible detriment of the countries from which they have emigrated (*The Guardian*, 30 October 2000).

Other factors prompting a less nation-state bound perspective are: developments in the EU, including the construction of European citizenship; the impact of globalisation, in its various forms; the impact of environmentalism. Increasingly, citizenship is being theorised as multi-tiered, extending from the local through to the global, encouraging us to think about the transnational responsibilities of the more affluent nation states.

The global arena is also providing the stage for citizenship as a practice, with the emergence of what has been described as an embryonic global civil society through which social movements and non-governmental organisations are beginning to pursue their goals across national borders, often via electronic communications. In the EU, there are active networks of non-governmental organisations (NGOs), which play an important role in the development of policies at European level, including the European Women's Lobby, European Migrants Forum and European Anti-Poverty Network[3]. At a global level, an example is the 'global alliance of people's movements' that coordinated resistance to the unfettered free trade policies of the World Trade Organisation and the damaging effects of economic globalisation, culminating in demonstrations in Seattle (1999) and Prague (2000). Women have been particularly adept at developing global networks, to considerable effect in relation to the United Nations (UN) world conferences in the 1990s, particularly with regard to the development of a global women's human rights agenda.

Citizenship and changing welfare states

Economic globalisation is one of the most important contextual factors shaping current welfare state developments – either because of its direct impact in constraining the power of nation states (which tends to be exaggerated) or, perhaps more importantly, because of its perceived impact and the use that politicians make of that (see Sykes et al, 2001). There is a tendency, certainly in New Labour thinking in the UK, to treat economic globalisation as an inevitable and desirable process, outside of the power of politicians. The role of politicians is to reform labour market, education and training, and welfare policies so as to equip people to adapt to change. This position is reflected in the Anglo-German document, *Europe: The third way, Die Neue Mitte* (Blair and Schröder, 1999). This, for instance, repeatedly rejects the traditional 'tax and spend' approach, which has previously underpinned centre-left welfare state policies, as no longer sustainable or appropriate in the modern globalised world (Blair and Schröder, 1999).

Linked with this position is the belief in a trade-off between egalitarianism (as embodied in continental European models) and employment (as promoted through Anglo-American models) in the context of changing labour markets. Add to that demographic trends, in particular the combination of an ageing population and a fall in fertility rates, family trends, in particular the growing number of lone parent families, and ideological shifts, which are questioning the relationship between the state and the individual which stands at the heart of citizenship, and we have a situation of welfare states under pressure. In other words, the pressures are as much political as economic.

As welfare state analysts, such as Gøsta Esping-Andersen (1996) and Jane Lewis (1999), remind us that does not mean that all welfare states will react in the same way (see also Sykes et al, 2001). This needs to be borne in mind in the following discussion of trends in the ways in which national governments are responding to internal and external pressures placed on welfare states. This discussion is coloured by and draws on the particular experience of the UK.

Residualisation of social rights

One such trend, which can be discerned, in both Western and Eastern/ Central Europe, is that of residualisation. Robert Henry Cox concludes that in Europe:

> there is a movement away from the idea that the welfare state should provide an optimal level of assistance. Instead, there is increasing acceptance of the idea that the welfare state should do no more than guarantee a minimum level of support. (Cox, 1998, p 13)

He identifies the growing use of 'targeting' (not just by income) as a means of narrowing entitlement and encouraging personal responsibility through private welfare, particularly in the area of pensions reform. He refers to pension reforms in the Nordic countries, which involve a shift from a citizenship-based approach to one that is closer to the Bismarckian social insurance model. At the same time, in Western Europe traditional social insurance models of both the Bismarckian and Beveridge heritage are themselves being questioned and modified in different ways. In Eastern/ Central Europe there is pressure to adopt a residual safety net model of provision. As Jochen Clasen observes, in a study of developments in social insurance in both Western and Eastern/Central Europe, "in many European countries means testing has become more rather than less important, while the role of social insurance is being seriously questioned" (1997, p 2).

To varying degrees this reflects the inability of traditional social insurance models to provide adequate protection in the face of economic and social trends, including high levels of long-term unemployment and women's increased labour market participation (at least in Western Europe). However, in some countries, it also reflects a deliberate policy decision to downgrade insurance benefits in favour of means-tested benefits and private provision. Nowhere is this more so than in the UK. Under the Conservatives, there was a series of cutbacks in insurance benefits culminating in the reduction of insurance-based benefits for the unemployed from 12 to 6 months. As a result, between 1979 and 1997-98, spending on means-tested benefits as a proportion of total social security spending more than doubled from 16% to 34%. Whereas in 1979-80, 45% of the total benefit paid to unemployed people was contributory and 55% means tested, by 1999-2000, the proportions were 9% and 91% (Social Security Committee, 2000). New Labour is continuing the general process, in terms of greater reliance on both means-testing and private provision.

Social insurance stood at the heart of the Beveridge model of social citizenship. Conversely, means-testing has traditionally been seen as corrosive of social citizenship as, combined with greater reliance on private provision for those able to afford it, it divides off those in poverty from the rest of society and undermines the equal status which citizenship implies. It undermines the individual rights of women in particular, for, in the case of those in couples, they are less likely to have access to social security in their own right under means-tested rather than non-means-tested schemes. To the extent that this particular trend is typical of European welfare states, even if less pronounced than in the UK, (and there are counter trends such as the extension of social insurance in Germany) it raises questions about the future fabric of social citizenship and the individual social citizenship rights of women.

Relationship between social rights and obligations

The other key trend in European welfare states identified by Cox is that:

> social insurance and other benefit programmes are moving away from solidaristic principles and becoming more achievement-oriented. The notion of citizenship as the basis of an individual claim to support is changing. There is an increasing demand that citizens recognise obligations when they demand their rights. (1998, p 13)

'No rights without responsibilities' is proposed by Tony Giddens as a primary motto for the 'third way' (1998, p 65)[4].

Paramount among these obligations is work, or to be more accurate paid work. Whether it is the Blair government in the UK 'reforming welfare around the work ethic' or the Kok administration in the Netherlands issuing the rallying cry of 'work, work, and again work', paid work as the expression of citizenship obligation is the primary motor of welfare reform in many countries. We have the confluence of four rivers of thought:

- a North American New Right discourse, expounded by the likes of Lawrence Mead, which promotes work obligations as "as much a badge of citizenship" as rights (Mead, 1986, p 229)
- a reassertion of the Protestant work ethic[5]
- an emergent European discourse of social exclusion and inclusion, promoted by the European Commission, in which paid work is seen as the key to social inclusion

• a particular strand in feminist thinking, which prioritises paid work for women as the path to full and equal citizenship.

The European discourse is also a discourse of 'active' welfare states, the goal of which is to reconnect the workless with the labour market. This is contrasted with old-style passive 'dependency'-promoting welfare states that allegedly simply handed out benefits (although there have always been conditions attached to benefit receipt for certain groups). This is quintessential 'third way' thinking. Ilona Ostner (1999) has conceptualised it as the replacement of decommodification by the 'recommodification' of those capable of paid work but living on benefits. It is true that some welfare states, most notably Sweden, have for a long time pursued active welfare/labour market policies in recognition of the damage which unemployment does to citizenship. However, in Sweden's case it has been in the context of generous social security provision rather than the type of retrenchment we are seeing in many countries today.

Few would probably dispute the importance of tackling unemployment and worklessness, given its association with poverty and exclusion for many. However, the success of the work–welfare approach in promoting social citizenship and social inclusion is critically dependent on the availability of jobs. Even in the UK, where unemployment has fallen significantly from its previous high levels, there are parts of the country, most notably major cities, where there exists a 'jobs gap', which is unlikely to be filled by supply-side measures aimed at enhancing employability alone. In those continental European countries where unemployment remains high, the narrow equation of social citizenship and inclusion with paid work is even more questionable. For those who subscribe to the 'end-of-work' thesis (the idea that technological change means that there will no longer be sufficient paid work for all who want it), it might seem paradoxical that governments are just at this moment in history treating employment as *the* citizenship obligation.

Even where there are jobs, some, such as Ruth Levitas (1998), question whether inclusion on to the bottom rung of an unequal labour market, in which jobs are low paid, insecure and marginal, spells genuine inclusion and citizenship. It is not enough to posit employment as a badge of citizenship: the quality of that employment and the conditions under which it is performed must also be part of the paid work equals citizenship equation.

Care

This is not to say, though, that only paid work should be equated with citizenship. Levitas and others have also criticised the narrow definition of citizenship responsibility implicit in much current policy. Both unpaid community or voluntary activities and unpaid domestic care work are, in effect, devalued, when paid work is elevated to *the* citizenship obligation (even if politicians speak warm words about volunteering and caring).

Focusing just on care work, this approach ignores the arguments of those feminists who believe that care should be valued as an expression of citizenship responsibility. Selma Sevenhuijsen's *Citizenship and the ethics of care*, for instance, "documents a search for ways of placing care within conceptions of democratic citizenship" and aims to make care "visible as a cognitive, reflective and moral practice" (1998, p 32). More recently, she has argued that "the relationship between rights, obligation and responsibility cannot be theorized in an adequate manner without taking care into account in the fullest possible manner", by which she means care both as a "concrete activity" and a "moral orientation" or "an ethics or a set of values that can guide human agency in a variety of social fields" (2000, p 6).

At a time when feminists are placing increased emphasis on the value of care, policy towards lone parents is moving in the opposite direction in a number of countries. This is part of what appears to be a wider shift from a 'male breadwinner' to what Nancy Fraser (1997) has called a 'universal breadwinner' model in which the breadwinner role is universalised so that women can be citizen-workers alongside men. This exemplifies the gender-neutral model of citizenship referred to earlier.

This approach has been particularly controversial in countries where there has not traditionally been an expectation that lone parents should be available for paid work as a condition of benefit receipt, examples being the Netherlands and the UK. A decision to reverse that policy in the Netherlands provoked strong reactions. The original requirement that lone parents with children aged five and above should be available for full-time work has not been implemented successfully at local level, with many lone parents moving only into part-time jobs or remaining on assistance. After intensive public consultation and parliamentary debate, · the Government has announced increased childcare and educational support to help lone parents into work. Municipal authorities will administer a package of individualised help for those with children younger than five, without the introduction of a statutory obligation to seek paid work (which had been proposed at one stage) (Knijn and van Wel, 2001).

In the UK, there is still no obligation for lone parents to seek paid work, in the face of continued opposition to the idea. However, a new law is being phased in from April 2001, which will eventually require virtually all lone parents, along with other claimants fit for paid work, to attend interviews to discuss their work prospects with a personal adviser, as a condition of benefit receipt. Even though employment will not be obligatory, there will be a much stronger expectation that lone parents should see themselves as potential workers.

Research in both the UK and the Netherlands suggests that as the pendulum swings further towards constructing lone mothers primarily as workers rather than mothers, this does not accord with how some lone mothers themselves perceive their responsibilities:

> The qualitative evidence reveals the strength of the commitment of women in both countries to care and the complexities of the balancing act that they must perform in order to combine care with employment, and the sacrifices that they must make. (van Drenth et al, 1999, p 638; see also Duncan and Edwards, 1999)

If the pursuit of a 'universal breadwinner' model is to be successful, there has to be a decent infrastructure of social support – accessible and affordable quality childcare and measures that facilitate combining paid work and family responsibilities (including for those caring for older people, as well as those raising children). This has long been recognised in many European countries, although only belatedly in the UK, which is not to say that the infrastructure in place in each particular country is by any means always adequate.

Parallel with a movement towards the 'universal breadwinner' model can be found a separate set of policies more consistent with what Fraser calls "the caregiver-parity model". This model "aims to promote gender equity principally by supporting informal carework" (Fraser, 1997, p55). Prime examples are payments to those who stay at home to care for children or for older or disabled relatives (although gender equity is not necessarily the motivation for making these payments)[6]. This contrasts with Fraser's own vision for the 'post-industrial welfare state': the 'universal caregiver' model, in which men would combine paid work and care in the same way that women currently do. From a citizenship perspective, the model might be called that of the 'citizen-earner/carer' and 'carer/earner' as opposed to the 'citizen-worker' model that currently dominates.

As the European Commission has acknowledged, policy needs to create the conditions in which such a citizenship model can flourish. Back in

1986, a European Ministerial Conference (1986) issued a declaration on equality between women and men in political and public life, which endorsed the

> view that de facto equality between women and men in the world of work, in the family and other areas of life, will not come about without the full sharing between women and men of the duties and responsibilities that democratic citizenship implies. (European Ministerial Conference, 1986)

Since then the Council of Ministers has adopted a Recommendation on Child Care (1992) which includes as an objective the encouragement "with due respect for freedom of the individual [of] increased participation by men (in the care and upbringing of children) in order to achieve a more equal sharing of parental responsibilities between men and women".

As a strategy it has already been adopted by some Scandinavian countries, albeit with only partial success hitherto. Of particular significance has been the use in Sweden and Norway of paid parental leave to encourage paternal involvement in childcare through the adoption of the 'daddy quota', four weeks of leave reserved for the father. In Norway it has led to a dramatic increase in fathers' use of parental leave, from 1-2% to 70% (Millar, 2000). Writing from a Danish perspective, Birte Siim contends that, in some Scandinavian countries, the development of a dual breadwinner model, supported by a public social infrastructure, has meant that "family factors, like marriage and children, no longer represent a barrier to women's political participation" (1999, p 121). There has also been legislation (or discussion of legislation) in both Austria and Germany aimed at a more equitable division of domestic labour generally. What underlies such measures is a recognition that the ability of both women and men to be full and active citizens in the public sphere is shaped by their citizenship responsibilities, or lack of responsibilities, in the private domestic sphere. These are issues that are central to the contemporary citizenship agenda.

Beyond the nation state

Increasingly central is the question of the national limits to citizenship. As observed earlier, citizenship theory no longer takes for granted the boundaries of the nation state. This raises questions both about supra-national citizenship, most notably in this context the EU, and the treatment of nation-state outsiders.

The EU

The idea of European citizenship has been promoted by the European Commission since the mid-1980s as a means of capturing the loyalty of EU citizens to a developing political union. The status of 'Citizens of the Union' was formally enshrined in the Maastricht Treaty. Elizabeth Meehan has argued that:

> despite criticisms that European citizenship is cosmetic, the rights associated with citizenship are no longer regulated or guaranteed exclusively by the institutions of nation-states but have, in addition, an increasingly significant European dimension. (1997, p 69)

In some countries, such as the UK, women's social citizenship rights have been strengthened as a result.

There have been two official reports calling for the clear elaboration of social and other rights so as to strengthen the fabric of European citizenship. First, the Comité des Sages argued that if Europe wishes to become

> an original political entity, it must have a clear statement of the citizenship it is offering its members. Inclusion of civic and social rights in the Treaties would help to nurture that citizenship. (1996, p 13)

The Comité also underlined the indivisibility of civic and social rights. This same emphasis on the indivisibility of civil and social rights and on the need for such rights to be enshrined in the Treaties can be found in the more recent report of the Expert Group on Fundamental Rights and in the demands of civil society groups such as the European Anti-Poverty Network (EAPN). The Expert Group noted that the Amsterdam Treaty "marked a decisive step on the way to an ever clearer recognition of the principle of fundamental rights protection by the European Union", even if it did not lead to "an explicit recognition of particular fundamental rights" (Expert Group on Fundamental Rights, 1999, p 11). An EU Charter of Fundamental Rights has been formulated, although its scope is not as broad as that called for by groups such as the European Social Policy Forum.

Outsiders

The growing emphasis on the rights associated with EU citizenship throws into relief the position of non-citizens. In what has been dubbed the 'age of migration', the response of most western and northern nation states has been to raise the barriers, through tougher immigration controls, harsher interpretation of the rights of asylum-seekers and more exclusionary residence qualifications for welfare benefits and services – all summed up in the image of 'Fortress Europe'. However, as the Expert Group pointed out, such restrictions are "inconsistent with the universality of at least a substantial number of fundamental rights". Similarly, it argues, "asylum-seekers cannot be exempted from the EU's duty to respect fundamental rights" (Expert Group on Fundamental Rights, 1999, p 17).

Asylum-seeking is a gendered process, although this is often not recognised. According to a UN report, women refugees and asylum-seekers face "gender-based discrimination and gender-specific violence and exploitation" at all stages of their flight (UN, 1995, p 637; see also Bhabha, 1999). Women fleeing domestic sexual persecution, unprotected by their government, are rarely granted refugee status, although the UN High Commissioner for Refugees has urged countries to follow the US and Canada in acknowledging the right to refugee status of such women. This point was partially conceded in a landmark High Court case in the UK, which granted refugee status to two Pakistani women who had been subjected to domestic violence and thrown out of their homes by their husbands. The Court accepted that they had "a well-founded fear of persecution", and would be unprotected by the state, should they return to Pakistan (Islam v Secretary of State for the Home Department; R v Immigration Appeal Tribunal, ex parte Shah [1999] 2 AC 629, 2 All ER 545).

Conclusions

Citizenship has been used as a conceptual tool in this chapter to analyse a number of key trends in European welfare states, in the context of the labour market trends described elsewhere in this book, which represent a threat to citizenship in its sociological sense. While there are variations between individual countries, the general trend appears to be towards a narrower, more conditional and exclusive interpretation of social citizenship. How successful such models will be in combating marginalisation, in its various forms, is highly debatable.

More positively, the Amsterdam Treaty has broadened the competence of the EU with regard to some of the building blocks of citizenship: most notably combating social exclusion and discrimination in its various forms. Article 13 states that action may be taken at European level "to combat discrimination based on sex, racial or ethnic origin, religion or belief, disability, age or sexual orientation". Article 137 extends the EU's powers to combat social exclusion.

In conclusion, it is worth recalling the conditions of poverty, exclusion, marginalisation and discrimination, which the Amsterdam Treaty acknowledges. At the last official count in 1993, 17% of the total population of the EU and 20% of its children were living in poverty. Women on average continue to be disadvantaged relative to men. Racism and xenophobia are flourishing in a number of member states; homophobia and disabilism are still prevalent. In these ways, the citizenship of many members of the EU (and of the wider European continent) is undermined daily.

Notes

[1] The original paper on which this chapter is based also contained a section on agency and accountability, which included a discussion of user-involvement in welfare institutions and the implications of the 'marketisation' of care. This has been omitted for editorial reasons.

[2] See also Dagger (1997) for a rather different synthesis of the two traditions.

[3] It has been suggested, though, that some of these networks are dominated by professionals rather than by grassroots activists.

[4] For a discussion of welfare users' views about welfare obligations and responsibilities see Dwyer (2000).

[5] In a recent interview in the *Daily Mail* (a UK right-wing tabloid newspaper), Gordon Brown the British Chancellor of the Exchequer, explained that he "was brought up in a house where my father was a Church of Scotland minister and work was seen as a duty – part of the moral ethic" (9 March 2000).

[6] For an overview of policy developments see Daly and Lewis, 1998.

References

Barton, L. (1993) 'The struggle for citizenship: the case of disabled people', *Disability, Handicap & Society*, vol 8, no 3, pp 235-48.

Bhabha, J. (1999) 'Embodied rights: gender persecution, state sovereignty and refugees', in N. Yuval-Davis and P. Werbner (eds), *Women, citizenship and difference*, London/New York, NY: Zed Books.

Blair, T. and Schröder, G. (1999) 'Europe: the third way/Die Neue Mitte', reproduced in K. Coates (ed), *The third way to the servile state*, Nottingham: Russell Press.

Clasen, J. (ed) (1997) *Social insurance in Europe*, Bristol: The Policy Press.

Comité des Sages (1996) *For a Europe of civic and social rights*, Brussels: European Commission.

Cox, R.H. (1998) 'The consequences of welfare reform: how conceptions of social rights are changing', *Journal of Social Policy*, vol 21, no 1, pp 1-16.

Dagger, R. (1997) *Civic virtues*, New York, NY/Oxford: Oxford University Press.

Daly, M. and Lewis, J.A. (1998) 'Introduction: conceptualising social care in the context of welfare state restructuring', in J.A Lewis (ed), *Gender, social care and welfare state restructuring in Europe*, Aldershot: Ashgate.

Duncan, S. and Edwards, R. (1999) *Lone mothers, paid work and gendered moral rationalities*, Basingstoke: Macmillan.

Dwyer, P. (2000) *Welfare rights and responsibilities: Contesting social citizenship*, Bristol: The Policy Press.

Esping-Andersen, G. (ed) (1996) *Welfare states in transition*, London: Sage Publications.

European Ministerial Conference (1986) 'Declaration on equality between women and men in political and public life', 4 March, Strasbourg, MEG 86(8).

Expert Group on Fundamental Rights (1999) *Affirming fundamental rights in the European Union*, Luxemburg: Office for Official European Publications.

Fraser, N. (1997) *Justice interruptus*, New York, NY/London: Routledge.

Giddens, A. (1998) *The third way: The renewal of social democracy*, Cambridge: Polity Press.

Hall, S. and Held, D. (1989) 'Left and rights', *Marxism Today*, June, pp 16-23.

Hindess, B. (1998) 'Divide and rule: the international character of modern citizenship', *European Journal of Social Theory*, vol 1, no 1, pp 57-70.

Isin, E.F. and Wood, P.K. (1999) *Citizenship and identity*, London: Sage Publications.

Jones, K.B. (1988) 'Towards the revision of politics', in K.B. Jones and A.G. Jónasdóttir (eds), *The political interests of gender*, London: Sage Publications.

Knijn, T. and Kremer, M. (1997) 'Gender and the caring dimension of welfare states: towards inclusive citizenship', *Social Politics*, vol 4, no 3, pp 328-61.

Knijn, T. and van Wel, F. (2000) 'Does it work? Employment policies for lone parents in the Netherlands', in J. Millar and K. Rowlinson (eds) *Lone parents, employment and social policy: Cross-national comparisons*, Bristol: The Policy Press.

Levitas, R. (1998) *The inclusive society? Social exclusion and New Labour*, Basingstoke: Macmillan.

Lewis, J. (1999) 'Welfare states in transition – new topics and new challenges' paper given at Equality, Democracy and the Welfare State: Europe and the United States, European Forum conference, Stamford University, US, 10-11 May, 1999.

Lister, R. (1997) *Citizenship: Feminist perspectives*, Basingstoke: Macmillan.

Lister, R. (2000) 'Citizenship and gender', in K. Nash and A. Scott (eds), *The Blackwell companion to political sociology*, Oxford: Blackwell.

Marshall, T.H. (1950) *Citizenship and social class*, Cambridge: Cambridge University Press.

Massey, D. (2000) 'The geography of power', in B. Gunnell and D. Timms (eds) *After Seattle: Globalisation and its discontents*, London: Catalyst.

Mead, L. (1986) *Beyond entitlement: The social obligations of citizenship*, New York: The Free Press.

Meehan, E. (1997) 'Political pluralism and European citizenship', in P.B. Lehning and A. Weale (eds) *Citizenship, democracy and justice in the new Europe*, London: Routledge.

Millar, J. (2000) 'Expanding parental choice: some notes on policy options', paper given at Financial Support for Parents of Pre-School Children Seminar, One Parent Families/National Family and Parenting Institute, London, 17 February.

Mouffe, C. (1992) 'Feminism, citizenship and radical democratic politics', in J. Butler and J.W. Scott (eds) *Feminists theorize the political*, New York, NY/London: Routledge.

Oldfield, A. (1990) *Citizenship and community: Civic republicanism and the modern world*, London: Routledge.

Ostner, I. (1999) 'From equal pay to equal employability: four decades of European gender policies', paper given at Equality, Democracy and the Welfare State: Europe and the United States, European Forum conference, Stamford University, US, 10-11 May.

Sevenhuijsen, S. (1998) *Citizenship and the ethics of care*, London/New York, NY: Routledge.

Sevenhuijsen, S. (2000) 'Caring in the third way', *Critical Social Policy*, vol 20, no 1, pp 5-37.

Siim, B. (1999) 'Gender, citizenship and empowerment', in I. Gough and G. Olofsson (eds) *Capitalism and social cohesion*, Basingstoke: Macmillan.

Social Security Committee (2000) 'Memorandum submitted by the Department of Social Security', *The contributory principle*, vol II, London: The Stationery Office.

Sykes, R., Palier, B. and Prior, P. (eds) (2001) *Globalisation and European welfare states: Challenges and change*, Basingstoke: Palgrave.

UN (United Nations) (1995) *The world's women 1995*, New York, NY: UN.

van Drenth, A., Knijn, T. and Lewis, J. (1999) 'Sources of income for lone mother families: policy changes in Britain and the Netherlands', *Journal of Social Policy*, vol 28, no 4, pp 619-41.

FOUR

Work and citizenship: unemployment and unemployment policies in Denmark, 1980-2000

Jørgen Goul Andersen

The Danish welfare experience of the 1990s contains interesting lessons about the relationship between changing labour markets, welfare policies and citizenship in a globalised economy:

- The idea that European welfare states face a trade off between employment and equality is contradicted by the Danish 'job miracle' (from 1999), which brought unemployment down to one-half the European average, without sacrificing welfare or income equality. This is often attributed to the 'third way' policy of activation. However, 'sound' economic policy seems at least as important.
- It was possible, even during the recession, to overcome severe economic problems of the welfare state without serious retrenchments, let alone systemic change (Andersen, 1997a).
- Until the mid-1990s, Denmark pursued a remarkable policy – in retrospect dubbed 'passive' – that granted the unemployed access to full benefits for more than eight years. This policy even proved economically sustainable and may share responsibility for the quick reintegration of long-term unemployed on the labour market. At any rate, this policy embodied the ultimate 'social rights' conception of citizenship and was backed by the Social Democratic Party, which strongly resisted any change until it became the governing party from 1993.
- The significant changes in Danish welfare policies for the unemployed speak against the idea of welfare states' "resistance to change" (Pierson, 1998; van Kersbergen, 2000) but this is explainable in terms of the few 'veto points' in the Danish welfare system: only the last, and perhaps least significant, part of the reforms was made after consultations with

the social partners. The Danish reforms also speak against the idea of changes being made in response to crisis: on the contrary, the economic upswing was a driving force behind the reforms.

This chapter provides an overview of (un)employment policies in Denmark during the 1980s and 1990s, mainly from a citizenship perspective but acknowledging the importance of economic sustainability. From a citizenship perspective, work is not equal to social integration. The core concern from a citizenship perspective is to avoid exclusion from full participation in social and political life (Andersen et al, 1998). Nevertheless, this concern traditionally meant emphasis on full employment. Only from the late 1970s, priority was given to protecting the social and economic rights of the unemployed. However, during the 1990s, Social Democratic governments came to underline the duty to work, since work is considered the only source of full and true citizenship.

Employment and unemployment

The changing labour market policies should be seen against the background of the actual development in unemployment, which reveals very high figures in the early 1990s when mass unemployment seemed insurmountable, and a significant decline towards the end of the 1990s, which has gradually increased concern for shortage of labour power. An overview of Denmark's unemployment record in the 1990s is presented in Table 4.1. According to figures on registered unemployment, which on balance are the most reliable[1], unemployment has dropped from 12.2% of the labour force in 1994 to 5.4% in 2000, that is, from around 350,000 to 150,000. In the beginning, this improvement was described by many critics as 'window dressing'. Part of the initial decline is explained by growth in activation, leave and early retirement (see gross unemployment [B] in Table 4.1) – but especially from 1996 onwards, the decline is real.

Social protection for the unemployed in Denmark aims at securing full citizenship. Among the registered unemployed, about 80% receive unemployment benefits rather than social assistance[2]. Unemployment benefits are generous, with 90% replacement of past earnings. Because the ceiling is low (slightly less than DKr20,000 per year), unemployment benefit in practice is nearly a flat-rate transfer. In return for generous economic protection, employment protection is low: next to the UK, Denmark has the most liberal employment protection in the EU (Government, 1999, p 285). This combination is rather unique and is often believed to explain the high flexibility on the Danish labour market (Andersen and Christiansen, 1991; OECD, 1998; Madsen, 1999).

Changing problem definitions of unemployment

Although unemployment policies have often changed in response to urgent political-tactical needs, they have nevertheless been rooted in changing problem definitions of unemployment. Two of these changes coincided with a change of government whereas the third but perhaps most profound

Table 4.1 Net and gross unemployment in Denmark, 1993-2000

	1993	1994	1995	1996	1997	1998	1999	2000*
As % of labour force								
Standardised unemployment rate*	10.1	8.2	7.2	6.9	5.4	5.1	5.2	4.5
Official (registered) unemployment rate[†]	12.4	12.2	10.4	8.9	7.9	6.6	5.7	5.4
In 1,000s								
1 Registered unemploy-ment[†]	349	343	288	246	220	183	158	150
2 Activation, total	116	84	70	74	76	77	85	75
3 Leave from unemployment	–	25	45	37	24	22	13	6
1-3 Gross unemployment (A)	465	452	405	356	320	281	255	231
4 Transitional allowance[‡]	4	8	23	46	42	36	31	25
1-4 Gross unemployment (B)	469	460	428	402	362	317	286	256

* International Labour Office definition, survey-based figures

[†] National definition, calculated as full-time persons

[‡] Transitional allowance is a pre-early retirement programme for 50- to 59-year-olds who were long-term unemployed (closed for new entrance from January1996 and to be phased out by 2006)

Sources: OECD (2001); Statistics Denmark, *Statistikbank*.

change took place rather suddenly under the Conservative coalition government in 1988/89. Finally, there was a change in policy when the Social Democrats went back to office. But this was not associated with new problem definitions:

- Under the Social Democratic governments until 1982, economic thinking was dominated by the Keynesian conviction that government should *correct market imperfections*, in particular unemployment, by manipulating aggregate demand and other macroeconomic parameters. For a small, open economy, competitiveness and the balance of payment were also key concerns that should be balanced against short-term improvements of employment.
- This balance tipped radically in 1982. Although the Keynesian legacy was not given up entirely, the new bourgeois government brought in new economic philosophies stressing the negative side-effects of demand-stimulating policies, for example, the reaction of capital markets to expectations of inflation. The new government gave one-sided priority to *competitiveness*, arguing that this was the only sustainable way to fight unemployment. The Social Democrats reluctantly accepted this problem definition, in particular after the electoral defeat in 1984.
- Still, it was implicitly believed that sustainable economic growth would gradually eliminate unemployment. However, from 1988/89, attention was directed to structural problems within the labour market, in particular the mismatch between low skills and high minimum wages (Economic Council, 1988; Government, 1989). According to this philosophy, economic growth would not solve the unemployment problem: at a certain level, that of structural unemployment, increased demand for labour power would not bring lower unemployment but lead to bottlenecks and inflation, and thus to declining competitiveness and new recession. In the following years, this problem definition of *structural unemployment* was accepted by nearly all actors in the field: the major parties and interest groups. A precondition for the agreement on this problem definition was its compatibility with the interests of the actors. Employers, and Conservative/Liberal parties, could claim that minimum wages were too high[3]; trade unions, and Socialist parties could claim that qualifications were too low and should be raised through education and activation. However, social learning was also important: during the economic upswing of 1983-86, the philosophy of competitiveness seemed to be confirmed by actual events, since aggregate employment increased by some 200,000 full-time employed. However, in 1987 the wages of those paid on an hourly rate increased

by some 10%. What followed was a seven-year long recession. Even though there are strong arguments that the wage increases in 1987 were caused by political factors (collective agreements shortly before an election, see Ibsen, 1992; Andersen, 1993, pp 295-9) rather than economic ones (bottlenecks and wage drift), it became an 'institutional truth' that further improvements of unemployment were impossible unless structural unemployment was reduced. Without more 'flexible' labour markets, any attempt to fight unemployment would be in vain. Throughout the 1990s, this became the basic philosophy guiding economic policies altogether.

- As compared to this path-breaking change, there was less innovation in *ideas* (but certainly innovation in practices) associated with the Social Democrats' return to office in 1993. The Social Democrats reintroduced a few Keynesian ideas including the idea that the government could and should do something about unemployment. This became the short-term priority in economic policies, with emphasis on 'kick-starting' the economy by stimulating aggregate demand. But the long-term strategy was one of active labour market policy. In broad terms, the economic philosophies remained the same.

Changing employment and unemployment policies

As the changing philosophies of the bourgeois government in the late 1980s did not materialise in policies (apart from the policy of doing nothing) until the Social Democrats returned to office in 1993, the policies cluster in three 'policy regimes' that coincide with changing governments: what the bourgeois parties were politically unable to accomplish in 1989-92, was to some extent obtained in concessions from the Social Democratic minority governments in the following years. In Table 4.2, we describe the three clusters using a simple typology of policies. The table also represents a historical ordering – the failure of one type of strategy increased the attention given to possible alternatives.

Keynesian strategies 1975-82

Like other countries, Denmark was hit by the oil crisis in 1974, and when a Social Democratic government was elected in 1975, its main priority was to re-establish full employment. It resorted to the routine instrument of *stimulating aggregate demand*, most significantly a temporary halving of the value-added tax. Also, and continuously (but not always voluntarily), the government pursued a policy of large budget deficits. At the same time, *public employment* increased dramatically, partly due to a conscious 'switch policy' substituting private consumption with labour-intensive and domestically produced public consumption to avoid the constraints of a large balance of payment deficit. From 1975 to 1982, the number of full-time public employees increased from about 550,000 to 750,000 (Andersen, 1993, p 37).

As this did not have much visible effect on unemployment, new strategies of *lowering labour supply* were adopted in 1979. An *early retirement allowance* (ERA) was introduced, granting 60- to 66-year-olds membership of an unemployment insurance fund[4], the right to retire with maximum unemployment benefits for the first two years and a lower rate (gradually increased to 80%) afterwards. Also in 1979, *longer holidays* (from four to five weeks) were introduced as a means of reducing unemployment. However, active labour market policies (ALMP) had already started in the 1970s, especially for the young (see below).

Throughout this period, the government also pursued a strategy of improving *competitiveness* via a currency policy with successive small devaluations combined with a strong *income policy* with routine interventions in collective agreements. However, all efforts seemed in vain. By 1982, unemployment had increased to nearly 10%, inflation was 10%, long-term interest rates were above 20%, the balance of payment deficit was 4.1% of gross domestic product (GDP) (foreign debts reaching 34.5% of GDP), and state deficit had increased to 11.5% of GDP. For many years, this remained a traumatic experience also among voters (Andersen, 1991, p 68); it paved the way for new strategies – and for a new government as the centre parties withdrew their support for the Social Democrats.

Export strategy 1982-92

The new Conservative–Liberal government in 1982 announced a new strategy of 'economic reconstruction', which remained its political raison d'être throughout the next decade. Basically, it followed an anti-inflationary policy giving first priority to the balance of payment deficit and, more generally, to policies aimed at improving competitiveness and strengthening the market. From the very beginning, the most important elements were:

• liberalisation of capital markets, allowing free capital movements

Table 4.2: A typology of anti-unemployment policies in Denmark, 1975-2000

	Examples of strategies and sub-strategies
Demand/supply strategies	1 Demand strategy Stimulate aggregate demand Increase public sector employment
	2 Reduction in labour supply/job sharing Shorter working hours/longer holidays Early exit programmes Leave programmes (such as parental and education leave)
Competitiveness strategies	3 Competitiveness/export strategy Wage moderation (such as incomes policy) Currency policy: devaluations
Structural strategies	4 Activation/qualification strategy Education Job training Individual plans of action
	5 Market/incentive strategy Lower minimum wages (not adopted) Stronger incentives to work Lower unemployment benefits Shorter duration of benefits Tighter eligibility criteria Service strategy: subsidise household services
	6 Stronger controls/stronger requirements Stronger works test Stronger mobility requirements and more severe sanctions 'Workfare': duty to work in return for benefits

- a fixed currency policy linking the Danish Kroner (DKr) to the German Mark (DM)
- suspension (from 1987 abolition) of indexation of wages
- fixed budgets for the public sector and zero growth in public employment
- temporary freezing of maximum unemployment benefits (1982-85); but partly compensated by a 10% increase in 1988.

The first three elements were irreversible and soon became accepted (although reluctantly) by the Social Democrats as new cornerstones for the party's policies in the future.

However, unintentionally, lower interest rates due to lower inflation triggered a huge increase in private consumption financed by capital gains from homeowners. The long-run effects for the balance of payment were disastrous and contributed to a seven-year long recession from 1986-93. From the beginning, the government also had great plans of a 'bourgeois revolution', including a major restructuring of the welfare state and a significant reduction of taxes; but, in the end, public expenditures rose by 21% in real terms during the 'bourgeois decade'. None the less, this represented a tightening, and along with the recession, this solved Denmark's chronic balance of payment problem and, to a large extent, also its fiscal crisis (Andersen, 1997a). This happened without increasing economic inequality or poverty. On the contrary, Denmark obtained a slightly more *equal* distribution of disposable incomes in the 1980s, and (relative) poverty among the unemployed remained virtually non-existent (Andersen, 1997b).

Labour market policies were left nearly untouched. The generous unemployment benefit system (which had been significantly improved just before the oil crisis in the 1970s) was maintained and nearly approached a basic income system (see Table 4.3). *Access* was easy, since only one year of membership and six consecutive months of (normal) employment was required to achieve full entitlements. *Duration* was very long (some 8½ years) because entitlement to 2½ years of unemployment benefits could be prolonged twice for another 2½ years if the individual took part in a job programme. The *compensation level* of 90%, which is very favourable to low-income groups (and to citizenship), was maintained. Also, the *works test* appears to have been rather liberal. The unemployed could not refuse an appropriate job and were formally required to be actively job-seeking and able to take a job immediately. However, especially in recession periods, little was done to ensure an effective works test. To summarise, the policies of the 1980s did not constitute a basic income system; but it did move a long way in this direction[5].

Activation strategy 1993 onwards

Writing in retrospect, the government (Ministry of Finance, 1999) itself describes the changing labour market policy of the 1990s as a reform in three stages. The first stage was the 1993 Labour Market Reform, including

---

Table 4.3: The Danish unemployment benefit system, by 1992/93: close to a basic income

Unemployment benefits

1   Easy access: one year membership of Unemployment Assurance Fund, 26 weeks of employment within the last three years (2000: 52 weeks)

2   Long duration: 2½ years but right to participation in a job project twice, with entitlement to benefits for another 2½-year period. Including the job project period, this meant entitlement to more than eight years of full-scale support (2000: four years)

3   High level of compensation: 90% of former wage, with a relatively low ceiling. In practice nearly a flat-rate benefit. No differentiation according to family situation, seniority or duration of unemployment. (2000: not changed, except for 18- to 24-year-olds, who are required to take an education)

4   Moderate control with active job-seeking, depending on the business cycle (2000: tightened)

Early retirement

5   Early retirement allowance: 60- to 66-year-olds (who had been members of an unemployment insurance fund for at least 20 years) entitled to leave the labour market. Maximum unemployment benefits during the first 2½ years, 80% for the remaining period. (2000: significantly changed)

6   Transitional allowance: introduced by 1992, granting 55- to 59-year-olds (1993: 50- to 59-year-olds) long-term unemployed right to a transitional allowance (80% of maximum unemployment benefits) until early retirement allowance from the age of 60 (2000: abolished)

a 'check up' in the 1994 compromise over the 1995 state budget. The second stage was part of the compromise over the 1996 budget the following year. The third stage came in 1998 as part of the compromise over the 1999 budget. However, if we take a closer look, policies appear more ambivalent and contradictory, which also explains the different interpretations (Jensen, 1999; Torfing, 1999). Labour market and economic policies in the 1990s could be said to have followed two contradictory paths: a *basic income* path, and an *activation* path. Also, for quite a while an ambivalence remained in the activation path between strengthening the rights and the duties of the unemployed[6].

The basic income path

The basic income path was not immediately abandoned by 1993. On the contrary, because the government was keen to break the unemployment curve (preferably before the 1994 election!), the basic income path seemed to be expanded by new elements in the 1993 labour market reform: the transitional allowance was extended to include the 50- to 54-year-olds. New arrangements for parental and education leave, introduced in 1992, were significantly improved. In particular, parental leave was extended from 36 to 52 weeks of which the first 13 weeks became a *right* for parents with children up to the age of eight. The allowance was 80% of maximum unemployment benefits but in the mid-1990s, most municipalities provided additional support. Education leave was also improved. This required replacement by an unemployed person and acceptance by the employer but the allowance provided was 100% of maximum benefits. Both arrangements were open to the unemployed, who typically constituted about one half of the persons on leave until 1999. A third leave programme, a sabbatical leave, was introduced under the same economic conditions as parental leave but conditional on job rotation[7].

As these measures were popular, some ministers began to speak about the government's new philosophies of work and the changing relationship between family life and working life. However, leave policies had not yet become irreversible, and parental leave gave bottleneck problems from the very beginning; nurses and other groups who had never had any opportunity to take advantage of the liberal unemployment benefit system did not want to miss this single opportunity in a lifetime. Already in the 1994 'check up', it was decided that compensation for parental leave would be gradually lowered from 80% to 60%. In return, both parental and education leave were made permanent whereas it was decided that sabbatical leave be terminated. After an initial explosion, the number of persons on leave declined from 82,000 in 1996 to 34,000 in 1999 (*Statistisk Tiårsoversigt*, 2000), and the decline continued in 2000. Transitional allowance was closed for new applicants from January 1996. Education leave was closed from 2001. What remains of the new leave schemes, then, is a poor parental leave, mainly used as a prolonged maternity leave[8]. Together with a tightening of the unemployment benefit system, this means that the basic income path has been effectively closed.

New main path: the active line

The most significant change in the 1990s is the active line. This was firmly rooted in the philosophy of structural unemployment, in particular in the idea that structural unemployment derives to a large extent from a mismatch between wages and labour productivity. From this philosophy, five functionally equivalent policies can be derived:

- lower minimum wages
- stronger incentives to work, in particular less generous unemployment benefits
- stronger works test
- subsidies for low-productivity work
- activation: improved productivity through education and job training.

To avoid lower minimum wages and lower unemployment benefits, the labour movement accepted the other measures, in particular activation. It is the combination of activation, tighter controls and shorter duration of unemployment benefits – new rights and new duties – that characterise the Danish 'active line'. It is the changed balance between rights and duties that characterise its development since 1994.

Although the new policies have been described as a change from a 'passive line' to an 'active line', it is important to underline that ALMP as such is not an entirely new phenomenon. Although rooted in different philosophies, and far less goal-directed to bringing people back to employment, Denmark has a long tradition of active labour market policies. Already by 1977, municipalities and counties were required (in a law about youth unemployment) to establish employment projects, education and courses and so on for the young unemployed. In 1978, a job training programme was adopted, so that people in danger of dropping out of the unemployment benefit system were offered an 'appropriate' job, most typically in the public sector. In the mid-1980s, this was supplemented by subsidising education or establishing a private firm. In short, the old system was not characterised solely by 'passive support'. By 1992, DKr13.9 billion (about 1½% of GDP) was spent on active labour market policies (including rehabilitation), and calculated as 'full person years'; 116,200 persons participated in activation broadly defined (Commission on Structural Labour Market Problems, 1992). According to OECD definitions and calculations, spending on ALMP went up from 1.1% of GDP in 1986 and 1990 to 1.8% in 1994 and 1997 (Martin, 2000). By comparison, the unweighted EU average was 0.9% of GDP in 1985 and 1990, and 1.2% and 1.1% in 1994 and 1997, respectively (Martin, 2000, p 85). Denmark is not unique but only Swedish figures are *significantly* higher (2.1% in 1985 and 1997, and 3.0% when unemployment peaked in 1994).

An important difference is the changing balance between rights and duties. In fact, the first stage of the 1993 reform was ambivalent at this point. On the one hand, the maximum unemployment period was fixed to seven years of which the last three years should be on activation (education or job training) without the possibility of regaining entitlement to benefits. On the other hand, seven years (through leave occasionally extended to nine years) is a long time, and it only took 26 weeks of ordinary employment to become entitled to another seven-year period (see Appendix). The ALMP was decentralised to 14 regions, which should direct policy implementation according to specific regional needs, facilitating at the same time a higher level of responsiveness to the unemployed. Finally, but not least, the reform demanded that an 'individual plan of action' should be elaborated for all long-term unemployed. In a dialogue between the unemployed and the employment office, a plan of activation should describe how an activation could be designed in accordance with the wishes and the abilities of the unemployed as well as to meet the needs of regional labour markets so to maximise employment opportunity (Jensen, 1999). In principle, this constitutes a significant strengthening of rights, even though practices have not always followed the ideals (Olesen, 1999; Larsen and Stamhus, 2000).

This has been maintained, but successive reforms have given ever more emphasis to duties. The term 'job offer' was replaced by 'activation', and 'social rights' by the phrase 'right and duty'. The net effect is a fairly strong tightening of the social protection of the unemployed (Ministry of Finance, 1998; 1999, p 184). The trend towards a stress on duties was discernible before the 1993 reform. In 1990, a 'youth allowance' was introduced for 18- to 19-year-olds demanding early activation as a condition for receiving social assistance. By 1992, this had been extended to the entire age group below 25 years (in the 1998 'Law on active social policies' which replaced the law on social assistance, this was further extended to the 25- to 29-year-old age group).

From 1995, the three years of an 'active period' came to include the 'right and duty' to permanent activation without regaining entitlement to a new period of benefits. In the second phase of the reform (the compromise over the 1996 Budget), the duration of benefits was cut to five years, with 'right and duty' to activation after two years, and entitlements to benefits now requiring 52 weeks of prior ordinary employment. Various other requirements as to transport-to-work time and a duty to take jobs outside your trade were tightened. The third phase was negotiated with unions and employers' associations but included in the package agreement over the 1999 State Budget. Duration was now fixed to four years, with (what turned out to be a very costly) duty to activation after only one year, at least for 75% of the time (in education or job training). Those aged 50 to 54 who had until then maintained an infinite right to unemployment benefits, were now transferred to ordinary conditions, whereas the unlimited right to unemployment benefits was maintained for the 55- to 59-year-olds.

The third phase also included a reform of the popular early retirement allowance, which reduced the allowance to 91% of the full amount for those who retired before the age of 62, giving people a strong incentive to remain in the labour market until that age. Finally, as part of this reform, the pension age was lowered from 67 to 65 years. As most people retire earlier, this was also a means of retrenchment since pensions are considerably lower than unemployment benefits. Also, a quite expensive, earmarked early retirement contribution was introduced in addition to the ordinary fee to unemployment insurance, and early retirement was made contingent on 25 years' contribution. People who do not use their right to early retirement but continue to work until the age of 65 receive a cash payment (of some DKr14,000) as a premium.

Also in 1998, the Law on Social Assistance was replaced by a new set of laws including one on 'active social policy'. Both the title of the law and the wording of the paragraphs underline the duty to work and the loss of social assistance for those who refuse. As elsewhere, the effects will depend much on street-level implementation. However, there have been indications of unintended effects among some of the weakest groups who are not able for any type of activation. Finally, a reform of the Disability Pension, also emphasising the work line alongside some improvements in benefits, was adopted in 2000.

The effects of a formal tightening of the works test depend much on how it is implemented; little is known about actual practices but probably not all the possible requirements are exploited to the full by job officers if there are 'good reasons' not to do so. Also, there are probably channels of 'recirculating' people who drop out of the unemployment benefit system, for instance through temporary jobs in municipalities that have strong incentives to keep people in the state-financed unemployment benefit system rather than the locally financed social assistance and the co-financed disability pension system. On balance, the Danish unemployment benefit system has remained generous, both in terms of duration and the high level at which the minimum benefit is set. However, the main focus of these reforms is an ever-stronger emphasis on the duty to work, to some extent based on a communitarian notion of work as the core of citizenship and social integration.

However, this emphasis on duty to work is also strongly influenced by lower unemployment, which makes it easier to find a job, and more necessary from an economic point of view to avoid bottlenecks and inflation, which could reverse the economic recovery. At any rate, there

Table 4.4: An overview of labour market policy in Denmark in the 1990s: two paths

'Path of activation'		'Basic income path'	
1990-92	Tightening of policies available for young unemployed on social assistance	(1980s	easy access to unemployment benefits)
		1992	Transitional allowance for long-term unemployed aged 55 to 59 (compromise over 1992 Budget, December 1991)
		1992	Parental leave: 36 weeks. Conditional on job rotation and employers' acceptance
		1992	Education leave (from February 1993; access also for unemployed)
1993	Labour Market Reform I (mainly from 1994) Duration of unemployment benefits now seven years (plus leave) Right and duty to activation after four years, so last three years of period is spent on permanent activation without earning entitlements to continued benefits	1993	Labour Market Reform I: Parental leave (26 weeks) a right. Including unemployed. Up to 52 weeks conditional on employers' acceptance. 80% of maximum benefits plus frequently additional support from municipality Sabbatical leave (same compensation; conditional on job rotation and employer's acceptance). Education leave (also for unemployed). 100% of maximum benefits, regardless of previous income
	Individual plans of action for long-term unemployed		Transitional leave for all long-term unemployed people aged 50 to 59. 80% of maximum benefits
1995	Labour Market Reform II (from 1996) Compromise over 1996 Budget with Conservatives Duration of unemployment benefits now five years Right and duty to activation after two years	1994	Check up (compromise on 1995 Budget) Parental leave: allowance gradually reduced to 60% of maximum unemployment benefits Sabbatical leave phased out in 1999
1998	Labour Market Reform III (from 1999) Tripartite negotiations. Compromise over 1999 State Budget Duration of unemployment benefits now four years Activation after one year Reform of early retirement allowance	1995	(Compromise on 1996 Budget) Transitional allowance for 50- to 59-year-olds to be phased out; entrance closed from 31 January 1996
		2001	Education leave programme closed
1998	Law on social assistance replaced by new laws, including 'Law on active social policy', stressing duty to activation		Result: Citizen's wage path is closed

Note: For more details see Appendix.

has been a dramatic change within a few years from a system approaching a citizens' income system to a system that, according to the government's 'benchmarking' of duty to work, places the requirements of the Danish system nearly in line with those of Sweden where the duty to work has always been a core element in social and labour market policy (Andersen, 1996, p 161; Government, 1999, pp 290-1; Ministry of Finance, 1999, pp 183-7).

Finally, yet another functional alternative to generate jobs for the unskilled is the service strategy. This strategy, based on subsidising labour-intensive household services (in 2000 by 50%), was first proposed around 1990. It was strongly supported by the Ministry of Industry, and it became a 'pet project' of the Minister who was the leader of one of the small coalition parties (the Centre Democrats). A household service programme was implemented in 1993. Although it has enjoyed only half-hearted support by the government, by 2000 the sector employed more than 10,000 workers.

Why such changes?

Taken together, the labour market reforms of the 1990s represent a major change – including improvements but also a quite significant tightening of policy – which contradicts the conventional idea that welfare states are highly resistant to change (Pierson, 1998). This holds in particular for a welfare state like the Danish one, which is almost exclusively tax-financed and state-directed. This leaves few veto points for actors other than the political parties. Except for negotiations with the social partners over the 1998 reform (but not including the reform of the early retirement allowance which was the most controversial part), the changes were made without any formal consultations with the social partners who do not appear in the processes in any visible way. The tightening took place after the economic upswing, not in response to an economic crisis. Regarding the process as a whole, it looks much like a learning process where each new step reinforces the former, provided that it seems to work – and an institutionalisation or routinisation of the negotiations within government, and with the opposition (which is an integral part of Danish political life, since nearly all governments are minority coalition governments).

Apart from noting that a significant breaking of the path is possible, we may still speculate why the Social Democratic Party, which used to resist any attack on the rights of the unemployed, has changed its position so profoundly. Although a full explanation is beyond the scope of this chapter, relevant factors would seem to include that it was willing to, it was forced to, and it was not so afraid to do so:

- it was *willing to* because of the influence of ideas: a new orthodoxy of economic ideas, as well as communitarian ideas of social integration and citizenship; to some extent, activation also echoed traditional ideals of full employment; and perhaps even more importantly, a shortage of labour which gradually surfaced in some regions and sectors made it necessary and acceptable to push the unemployed somewhat harder
- it was *forced to* because of the political situation: the coalition partner, the Radical Liberals, found its raison d'etre in demanding institutional change; for Bourgeois parties, labour market reforms provided a well-suited target for routine negotiations over the Budget
- it enabled the party to *avoid what could be worse*: to maintain high compensation and long duration of benefits, the Social Democrats were forced to give in on tightening the system
- the Social Democrats were *not so afraid to* tighten up, because the labour movement maintains considerable control over street-level implementation, and because low unemployment meant that the risks of becoming excluded from unemployment benefits was smaller.

Among these explanations, the considerable degree of control over the implementation stage should not be underestimated. It is a part of the story that the unemployed do not always consider activation as an advantage for their employment chances; but a large majority have always welcomed activation anyway (Hansen et al, 2001). In practice, education and job training in the public sector predominate; by January 2000, 35,000 out of 57,000 full-time activated in the (state) Job Office activation system were taking part in education; 11,000 were in public job training; 3,000 were receiving guidance, and some 8,000 were involved in various other programmes. If this should be considered 'workfare', it is a 'workfare light' version.

Conclusions: economic sustainability and implications for citizenship

The Danish experience shows that the European welfare state, with generous social protection and high economic equality, is perfectly sustainable in a global and highly competitive economy. To what extent this is an effect of the new activation strategies remains uncertain. 'Sound' economic policies appear to be at least as important. The Danish combination of low employment protection and high protection during unemployment may contain drawbacks but ensures a very flexible labour market while at the same time preventing poverty. High emphasis on vocational training means that the number of unskilled workers has declined even faster than the number of unskilled jobs (Ministry of Finance, 2000). So what is left that can be credited to activation strategies? Danish activation programmes have been carefully evaluated on many occasions and with different methods (Madsen, 1999; Larsen, 2000). Usually they conclude that most programmes have significant but small effects. As is the case in other countries, it is uncertain whether they could pass a cost-effectiveness test (Martin, 2000), even in a situation of economic prosperity. Not least, the principle of putting an unemployed person on an activation programme after one year out of work has been very costly. This implies that welfare expenditures could explode in a recession (as in Sweden in the 1990s), while at the same time leading to exclusion from the unemployment benefit system, if the system is not adjusted in accordance with the business cycle[9].

Still, there is no doubt that the activation strategy – and a labour market policy concerned with preventing bottlenecks more generally – has contributed positively to declining unemployment. However, the activation strategy also has considerable implications for citizenship. Following a widely used distinction between two types of citizenship (see Chapter Three), these implications may be considered along two dimensions: citizenship *rights and duties*; citizenship as full *participation* in social and political life. Both the strategies of the 1970s/1980s and of the 1990s were aimed at avoiding marginalisation and maintaining full citizenship, but via different means. The strategy of the 1970s and 1980s was to avoid loss of citizenship by maintaining the unemployed in the unemployment benefit system, avoiding economic marginalisation and stigmatisation, and maintaining equal social rights for the employed and unemployed. This was visible in the:

- prolonged duration of entitlement to benefits
- easy access to the system
- high level of benefits that enabled people to maintain a decent standard of living
- principle that wages during job training should follow collective agreements
- principle of regaining entitlement to benefits, and hence an income, while in job training, as is the case when employed
- strong emphasis, up until 1999, on the principle of giving the

unemployed leave arrangements that equalled those received by the employed.

Although the Danish system has remained quite generous, the active line of the 1990s has violated most of the rights referred to above: duration of benefits has been shortened; access to the system has been restricted; the wages of job trainees no longer follow collective agreements; the unemployed do not gain new entitlements while on activation; and from 1999 the access of unemployed to leave has been restricted. Only the high compensation level has been maintained, along with what remains, by comparative standards, a relatively long duration of benefits after all. As compared to other countries, the tightening of arrangements in Denmark is by no means exceptional (Kalish et al, 1998). The individual plans of action that emphasise the dialogue between the unemployed and the employment officer have strengthened the rights of the unemployed, empowering them, in the cases when this is implemented as planned.

However, in terms of citizenship, there is another important rationale of the active line of the 1990s: it has increasingly been influenced by a communitarian notion of citizenship regarding employment as a more or less indispensable source of full citizenship. From this perspective, activation is an improvement, since people who are excluded from the labour market are believed to also be marginalised in other arenas of social action, to become stigmatised, or even to 'un-civic' attitudes. From a communitarian perspective, renewed stress on duties in return for rights is welcomed. This is also what distinguishes the new conception of citizenship from the conception embodied in traditional full employment policies before the 1970s. Although this normative debate cannot be reduced to empirical questions, it is obvious that it rests on many assumptions about the relationship between unemployment and citizenship that can be put to a critical empirical test. So far, this has rarely been done. Whatever information is available, however, indicates that economic security is an extremely important determinant of well-being and participation, probably even more important than employment as such (see, for example, Andersen, 1996; Halvorsen, 1999; Gallie and Paugam, 2000, 2001a).

Notes

[1] In international statistics based on International Labour Office (ILO) definitions, people are only considered unemployed if they are actively job-seeking and able to take a job, but panel data indicate that this has little or no effect on re-

employment (Bach 1999; Larsen 2000; Andersen 2001b). Students seeking a second job constitute a fair share of the unemployed according to ILO definitions. Because of such problems, national data series are preferred.

[2] Virtually all adults receive a wage or a transfer income from the state. Universal students' allowances complete the picture. It is estimated (Andersen, 1999) that only 1½% of the adult population does not receive an income of their own (housewives and others).

[3] In contrast to Keynesianism, which regarded unemployment as an effect of market imperfections (to be corrected by political regulation), the philosophy of structural unemployment regards unemployment as an effect of the fact that markets are not allowed to function independently because of political regulations.

[4] Like Belgium, Sweden and Finland, Denmark follows the so-called 'Ghent system' based on voluntary membership in heavily state-subsidised unemployment insurance funds attached to the trade unions.

[5] For the purpose of the argument here, we shall not discuss any definitions of basic income, which has many different meanings (Christensen, 2000). Also, not everybody could gain access to the unemployment benefit system, although for some people on social assistance this represented a choice since needs-testing could yield a larger benefit. Some 98-99% of all adults in Denmark receive an income of their own, either a labour income or some transfer from the state. If we count in students (who receive a universal students' allowance), about 65% of the adult population received, in the mid-1990s, their main income from the state, either as public employees or via benefit support (Andersen, 1999).

[6] As mentioned previously, Keynesianism was also revived a little. The Social Democrats never abandoned entirely the idea of steering aggregate demand. One of its first actions was to 'kick-start' the economy by a minor tax relief and by new types of loans for homeowners. The government also (but more than intended) increased public consumption (by some 20% in fixed terms 1992-1999). Still, this does not signify any return to the economic philosophies of the 1970s. For instance, unlike in the 1970s, public debt is not considered only a matter of bookkeeping but a matter of real concern.

[7] To this comes maternity leave which since the mid-1980s is four weeks before birth and 24 weeks after birth. Many collective agreements ensure full wage rather than maximum unemployment benefits during maternity leave.

[8] Often as a necessity, since the guarantee for childrearing does not always include children aged six to 12 months.

[9] As part of the compromise over the 2000 Budget, it was agreed that there could be more than four weeks between offers of activation in the 'active period', and that it would now be possible not to activate 58- to 59-year-olds.

References

Andersen, J.G. (1991) 'Vælgernes vurderinger af kriseårsager', in E. Petersen et al, *De trivsomme og arbejdsomme danskere. Krisen og den politisk-psykologiske udvikling 1982-90*, Aarhus: Department of Psychology/Aarhus University Press, pp 61-80.

Andersen, J.G. (1993) *Politik og samfund i forandring*, Copenhagen: Forlaget Columbus.

Andersen, J.G. (1996) 'Marginalisation, citizenship and the economy: the capacity of the universalist welfare state in Denmark', in E. Oddvar Eriksen and J. Loftager (eds) *The rationality of the welfare state*, Oslo: Scandinavian University Press, pp 155-202.

Andersen, J.G. (1997a) 'Beyond retrenchment: welfare policies in Denmark in the 1990s', paper prepared for the ECPR Round Table on 'The survival of the welfare state', Bergen, 18-21 September, Ålborg: Department of Economics, Politics and Public Administration, Ålborg University.

Andersen, J.G. (1997b) 'The Scandinavian welfare model in crisis? Achievements and problems of the Danish welfare state in an age of unemployment and low growth', *Scandinavian Political Studies*, vol 20, no 1, pp 1-31.

Andersen, J.G. (1999) 'Changing labour markets, new social divisions and welfare state support: Denmark in the 1990s', in S. Svallfors and P. Taylor-Gooby (eds) *The end of the welfare state? Responses to state retrenchment*, London: Routledge, pp 13-33.

Andersen, J.G. (2001a) 'Coping with long-term unemployment: economic security, labour market integration and well-being', paper presented at ESE/EURESCO Conference, Helsinki, 20-25 April, (forthcoming in *International Journal of Social Welfare*).

Andersen, J.G. (2001b) 'How much should the unemployed be searching and available for a job?', revised version of paper presented at COST A13 Workshop, Ljubljana, 8-9 June.

Andersen, J.G. and Christiansen, P.M. (1991) *Skatter uden velfærd. De offentlige udgifter i international belysning*, Copenhagen: Jurist- og Økonomforbundets Forlag.

Anderson, J.G., Halvorsen, K., Jensen, P.H., Johannessen, A., Kangas, O., Olufsson, G. and Øverbye, E. (1998) *Unemployment, early retirement and citizenship: Marginalisation and integration in the Nordic countries*, CCWS Working Papers No 4, Åalborg: Department of Economics, Politics and Public Administration, Åalborg University.

Avisårbogen, Copenhagen: Avisårbogen.

Bach, H.B. (1999) *Længerevarende ledighed – jobsøgning og beskæftigelseschancer*, Copenhagen: Socialforskningsinstituttet.

Christensen, E. (2000) *Borgerløn. Fortællinger om en politisk ide*, Århus: Hovedland.

Commission on Structural Labour Market Problems (1992) *Rapport fra Udredningsudvalget om arbejdsmarkedets strukturproblemer*, June, Copenhagen.

Economic Council (Det økonomiske Råd) (1988) *Dansk økonomi*, June, Copenhagen: Det økonomiske Råd.

Gallie, D. and Paugam, S. (eds) (2000) *Welfare regimes and the experience of unemployment in Europe*, Oxford: Oxford University Press.

Government (Arbejdsministeriet m.fl.) (1989) *Hvidbog om Arbejdsmarkedets Strukturproblemer*, Copenhagen: Government.

Government (1999) *Strukturovervågning – International Benchmarking af Danmark*, Copenhagen: Ministry of Finance.

Halvorsen, K. (1999) *Arbeidsløshet som sosialt problem*, Oslo: Oslo College.

Hansen, H., Lind, J. and Høller, J.H. (2001) 'Aktivering som inklusion', in J.G. Andersen and P.H. Jensen (eds) *Marginalisering. Integration, velfaerd*, Åalborg: Åalborg University Press.

Ibsen, F. (1992) 'Efter Zeuthen-rapporten', *Samfundsøkonomen 1992*, no 6.

Jensen, P.H. (1999) *Activation of the unemployed in Denmark since the early 1990s: Welfare or workfare?*, CCWS Working Papers No 1, Åalborg: Department of Economics, Politics and Public Administration, Åalborg University.

Jonasen,V. (1998) *Dansk Socialpolitik 1708-1994: Menneske, økonomi, samfund – og socialt arbejde*, Aarhus: Den sociale højskole i Aarhus.

Kalish, D.W., Aman,T. and Buchele, L.A. (1998) *Social and health policies in OECD countries: A survey of current programmes and recent developments*, OECD Labour Market and Social Policy Occasional Papers No 32, Paris: OECD.

Larsen, C.A. (2000) 'Det danske mirakel set fra jorden', MA thesis, Ålborg: Department of Economics, Politics and Public Administration, Ålborg University.

Larsen, F. and Stamhus, J. (2000) *Active labour market policy in Denmark*, Working Paper, Ålborg: Department of Economics, Politics and Public Administration, Ålborg University.

Madsen, P.K. (1999) *Denmark: Flexibility, security and labour market success*, Employment and Training Papers No 53, Geneva: ILO.

Martin, J.P. (2000) *What works among active labour market policies: Evidence from OECD countries' experiences*, OECD Economic Studies No 30, Paris: OECD.

Ministry of Finance (1998) *Availability criteria in selected OECD countries*, Working Paper No 6, Copenhagen: Ministry of Finance.

Ministry of Finance (1999) *Finansredegørelse 1998-99*, Copenhagen: Ministry of Finance.

Ministry of Finance (2000) *Finansredegørelse 2000*, Copenhagen: Ministry of Finance.

Ministry of Labour (1998) *Status for arbejdsmarkedsreformerne. 2005-udvalget om videreførelse af arbejdsmarkedsreformerne*, København: Ministry of Labour.

Ministry of Labour (1999) *Arbejdsmarkedsreformerne. Et statusbillede*, København: Ministry of Labour.

Ministry of Labour (2000) www.am.dk/arbejdsmarkedet/Noegletal/januar_2000.htm

OECD (Organisation for Economic Co-operation and Development) (1998) *Employment outlook*, Paris: OECD.

OECD (1999) *Historical statistics 1960-1997*, Paris: OECD.

OECD (2001) *Employment outlook*, Paris: OECD.

Olesen, S.P. (1999) *Handlingsplansamtaler: Intentioner og aktører*, CARMA Arbejdstekst No 1, Åalborg: CARMA, Åalborg University.

Pierson, P. (1998) 'Irresistible forces, immovable objects: post-industrial welfare states confront permanent austerity', *Journal of European Public Policy*, vol 5, no 4, pp 539-60.

Statistics Denmark, *Statistikbank*.

Torfing, J. (1999) 'Welfare with welfare: some reflections on the Danish case', *Journal of European Social Policy*, vol 9, no 1, pp 5-28.

van Kersbergen, K. (2000) 'The declining resistance of welfare states to change?', in S. Kuhnle (ed) *Survival of the European welfare state*, London: Routledge, pp 19-36.

Appendix: Danish labour market reform in three stages: a detailed overview

Decision	Coming into force from	Reform
June 1993	January 1994	Labour market reform I • Duration of receiving unemployment benefits fixed to a maximum of seven years (four + three years, the latter being an 'active period') • Only possible to regain entitlements after six months of non-supported ordinary employment • Early activation for vulnerable groups • Decentralisation of active labour market policy to 14 regions • Individual plans of action for long-term unemployed • Improved leave-of-absence schemes (parental leave, education leave, sabbaticals) • Age limit for early retirement allowance lowered from 55 to 50 years of age
November 1994	April 1995	Labour market reform I: 'check up' (compromise on 1995 Budget) • Right and duty to activation after four years of unemployment ('active period') • Tightening of the rules of availability of the unemployed (aggravated sanctions by refusal; intensified control of disposal; effective quarantine) • Extended rights to unemployment benefits for 50- to 59-year-olds • Permanent parental and education leave; sabbatical leave closed by 1999 • Rate for parental leave gradually lowered from 80% to 60% of maximum unemployment benefits

Appendix: contd.../

Decision	Coming into force from	Reform
December 1995	January-July 1996	Labour market reform II (compromise on 1996 Budget)

- Duration of receiving unemployment benefits lowered to five years (two + three years)
- Right and duty to full-time activation after two years
- Entitlement to unemployment benefits presuppose 52 weeks of ordinary employment in a three-year period (previously 26 weeks)
- Unemployed people below the age of 25 must participate in some education after 26 weeks, or they will receive only one-half of previous unemployment benefits
- Duty to accept work outside own trade after six months
- 'Passive' availability for a job during education
- Demand of travel to work time limit increased to a maximum of four hours a day (previously three hours)
- 'Pool jobs' available for the vulnerable unemployed
- Transitional allowance abolished
- Stronger sanctions follow if an individual refuses to participate in the activation programme

Decision	Coming into force from	Reform
November 1998	January 1999	Labour market reform III (compromise on 1999 budget but negotiated with unions and employers' associations)

- Duration of receiving unemployment benefits lowered to four years (one + three)
- Right and duty to full-time activation after one year
- Abolishing of the longer right to unemployment benefits for 50- to 54-year-olds
- Right and duty to activation for all young unemployed people after six months
- Duty to accept work outside own trade after three months
- Right to education leave limited for unemployed
- More goal-directed education for the unemployed
- Registration at the unemployment office required from the first day of unemployment

Appendix: contd.../

Decision	Coming into force from	Reform
November 1998	January 1999	Labour market reform III. Particular compromise on early retirement allowance and pensions (compromise on 1999 budget; not negotiated with the interest organisations; adjusted in later settlement of January to April 1999; finally accepted in April 1999).

- Pension age lowered from 67 years to 65 years
- Introduction of earmarked contribution to Early Retirement Allowance (in addition to ordinary fee to unemployment insurance fund; voluntary for members of unemployment insurance fund)
- Right to ERA after 25 years of contribution (previously 20 years)
- Individualised programme, including payments to family in case of death
- Standard rate of ERA lowered from 100% to 91% of maximum unemployment benefits
- Larger set-off in other pensions (45-60%)
- By postponing ERA until the age of 62, the rate is 100% of unemployment benefits and set-off in other pensions is lowered
- Cash premium of DKr103,200 for early retirement insured on later retirement for those who abstain from using their right to early retirement

Sources: Statistisk Tiårsoversigt: Økonomisk-politisk kalender; Ministry of Finance (1999); Ministry of Labour (1998, 1999, 2000); Avisårbogen; Jonasen (1998)

FIVE

New institutional forms of welfare production: some implications for citizenship

Willem Trommel and Bert de Vroom

Although citizenship may be affected directly by changing labour markets, this chapter concentrates on the unintended effects of policy change. New welfare policies may start as a mere effort to raise the efficiency of welfare production, in reaction to changing labour market conditions. However, we will show that these types of reform may have moral implications in the longer run.

The chapter focuses on the numerous reforms that have been implemented in the Dutch social security system[1]. Often, welfare state reform is studied as a question of retrenchment. The central focus is then on the ways in which policy changes restrict the level of social protection. However, we find that actual welfare state changes (at least in the Netherlands) are not primarily a matter of more or less social rights. More important is a radical change in the institutional production of welfare, especially in the ways in which citizens, (private) organisations and state agencies are involved in the actual realisation of welfare. So we argue for an institutional approach to welfare state reform that concentrates on changes in the *institutional logic* of welfare production. We will discuss this approach in greater detail in the next section.

As the Dutch case demonstrates, many of the institutional reforms concern the issue of control. In order to discipline the behaviour of clients, firms and administrative agencies, organisational structures and policy programmes have been redesigned. In the third and fourth sections of this chapter we will present a detailed analysis of this process, as it has developed during the 1990s. It is shown that the ambition behind this process of change was to create a more efficient system of welfare production without damaging the level of social protection. Some authors have referred to this as an important element of 'the Dutch miracle' (this term was coined by Visser and Hemerijck (1997), who argued that the Dutch had learned how to fight unemployment while maintaining a reasonable level of social protection). However, whether this miracle has actually been realised remains to be seen.

Our analysis shows that the level of protection has largely remained in tact. However, this is only part of the story. As the institutional logic of welfare production has changed, new ideas on the social rights and duties of citizens have emerged. This brings us to the central question of how the new institutional forms of welfare production generate new normative ideas on social rights and duties and what this means for the concept of social citizenship. These questions will be dealt with in the fifth section.

At first sight, the Dutch reforms might seem to indicate a shift towards a more liberal idea of citizenship, emphasising the need for greater individual responsibilities and a retreat of state intervention. However, we will argue that this would be a misconception. Rather, in several respects, by expanding the scope and intensity of social policy intervention, the welfare state is intruding deeper into the lives of people. We will consider whether this indicates a new type of citizenship, as has been suggested by Giddens et al (2001). In the final section we will summarise our conclusions.

Character of welfare state change: retrenchment versus restructuring

In the macro-sociological approach to welfare state change much emphasis is put on external factors such as economic or technological change. Previously, such factors were assumed to cause state growth, but today it is normally argued that economic and technological forces induce a process of state *shrinkage*. For example, it is argued that globalisation undermines the regulating powers of the state that used to keep the national welfare state in place. Also, technological innovations are assumed to stimulate the replacement of state solutions by market solutions.

Feigenbaum et al (1999, p 26) argue that these hypotheses on state shrinkage are far too deterministic and overlook conditional factors such as changing political ideas and institutional structures. Alternatively, they believe that state shrinkage might be seen as determined by the internal dynamics in the institutions of the state. For instance, welfare states may unintentionally cause a decrease in social solidarity or they may develop new (political and institutional) forces that counterbalance the external pressures towards state shrinkage.

In our view this conditional approach is a promising one that deserves further attention and elaboration. One of the first studies into the institutional aspects of '*retrenchment*', Paul Pierson's book *Dismantling the welfare state?* (1994), is a good starting point since he defines the process of restructuring. Pierson concludes that strategies aimed at retrenchment of the welfare state are in most cases doomed to fail, because existing institutions, policies and interests will halt them. Although we like his study, in particular his attempt to reveal conditional explanatory factors, we will also criticise his inclination to overemphasise the argument of institutional path-dependency. Using the Dutch case of welfare state restructuring we will try to refine the conditional institutionalist approach.

Limited possibilities of retrenchment: policy feedback

Pierson states that traditional explanations of welfare state expansion that refer to the relative power of organised labour and organised capital cannot be applied to explain retrenchment. Once particular welfare state programmes have been established, Pierson argues, these programmes as such create new interests and new interest groups. Briefly, following the argument of Schattschneider (1935, p 288; quoted in Pierson, 1994, p 39), "new policies create a new politics". From this perspective, *policy feedback* from developed welfare state institutions and programmes becomes the crucial variable in explaining welfare state change.

This approach raises three central questions:

• What is Pierson's definition of retrenchment?
• What are the key institutional structures?
• How can those institutional variables be linked to welfare state changes?

We will now present a critical discussion of Pierson's answers to these questions.

Taking his point of departure in Titmuss' distinction (Titmuss, 1974) between 'institutional' and 'residual' welfare states, Pierson simply defines retrenchment as "the process of shifting social provision in a more residualist direction" (1994, p 15). However, he is not very precise at this point. He makes no distinction between *provisions* and *entitlements*. Dahrendorf (1999, pp 11-12) and Sen (1981) define entitlements as "socially defined means of access", or "entry-tickets", whereas provisions are those 'things' to which you are entitled, "the whole range of material and immaterial choices which may be opened up by entitlements". Both dimensions should be taken into account in an analysis of welfare state change, since the overall availability and combination of entitlements and provisions give a better picture of life chances, and as such of the quality of social citizenship.

Pierson's interpretation of retrenchment is framed in the language of 'more' or 'less'. However, there is also the possibility of rearranging provisions and entitlements so that retrenchment in some areas is compensated by the expansion of other provisions or entitlements. The potentials for such 'programmatic compensation' are much larger in welfare states with comprehensive and universalistic programmes and in welfare states with a political-institutional design based on bargaining and exchange[2]. Pierson's framing of retrenchment in this respect seems biased by his selection of cases (the 'liberal welfare state regimes' of the UK and the US) and by his one-dimensional approach to retrenchment.

To specify changes, Pierson distinguishes between *systemic* and *programmatic retrenchment* (1994, p 15). Programmatic retrenchment refers to "direct attacks on social programs" and is, according to Pierson, "generally limited" (p 4). Systemic retrenchment refers to contextual changes that may have an indirect, long-term effect on social provisions. Pierson identifies four types of such contextual changes (pp 15-17):

- reducing funds to the welfare state by constraining the flow of revenues to future administrations
- a policy-induced change in public opinion, weakening popular attachments to public social provision and stimulating public preferences for private provisions
- modifications to political institutions (institutional design), changing the way decision-making about the welfare state is carried out, and thus potentially changing policy outcomes
- the weakening of pro-welfare state interest groups.

These dimensions are more 'contextual' than 'systemic', so we prefer the former notion when referring to Pierson's four dimensions. Below we will add a third type of change ('institutional change'), which refers especially to the reforms in the organisation and implementation of welfare programmes.

As far as institutional design is concerned, Pierson argues on the basis of his empirical findings in the UK and the US that "bureaucratic capacity and autonomy ... have limited implications for the politics of retrenchment" (Pierson, 1994, p 38). So Pierson explores a number of other variables put forward by the 'new institutionalist' approach: policy learning; interest formation; lock-in effects; information. From his comparative research, Pierson draws a strong conclusion with regards to the explanatory power of learning: "reform initiatives did not percolate up from agencies dissatisfied with the workings of current programs" and "lessons learned from specific features of past policies played very little part in the formation of (...) governments' programs" (Pierson, 1994, p 49).

Since policy learning does not contribute much to an explanation of change, Pierson proceeds with stressing the importance of the other institutional feedback factors: interest formation, lock-in effects and the role of information, which he believes all have a "substantial impact" on retrenchment politics. His central argument is that previous policy choices generate resources and incentives that help to structure the development of relevant interest groups. This generates 'lock-in effects', which means that public social programmes generate extensive networks of commitments, making it almost impossible to introduce fundamentally new policies or to modify existing programmes. Finally, the structure of existing programmes determines the availability of information and as such restricts the possibilities of change.

In our view, Pierson's negative conclusions about the possibilities of welfare state change are partly an artefact of his explanatory concepts. We argue that Pierson's model and conclusions are biased by his Anglo-American perspective and empirical setting (UK and US). His account of the institutional system concentrates too much on the policy-making structure and governmental capacity, neglecting the ways in which welfare state programmes are organised, governed and implemented. His conclusions (for instance about learning) are based on findings in two 'liberal' welfare states. However, in other societies or policy domains with a more developed intermediary structure between state and citizen the possibilities of policy learning may be much larger. This is at least what is claimed in the debate in continental Europe (Marin and Mayntz, 1991; Benz, 1994; Hoekema et al, 1998). We argue that the capacity for welfare state change is higher than Pierson's study suggests. This can be made visible by introducing some new elements in the explanatory model and by shifting the empirical focus to other welfare state types.

From retrenchment to restructuring: an alternative analytical model

As we have shown, Pierson pays little attention to the 'institutional structure' of welfare states. With the notion of institutional structure we mean the distribution of power between the actors concerned: the way policy fields are organised and governed and the way programmes are implemented. For continental, often corporatist welfare states, this institutional structure is an important element of the political compromise on which these welfare states are founded. This compromise is embodied in a specific institutional structure of welfare state programmes, in a specific organisation of the administration, implementation and governance programmes (van der Veen, 1996). Bearing in mind the reality of continental welfare states, we suggest a number of adjustments to Pierson's concepts and model:

- Pierson's notion of retrenchment is limited to changes (reductions) in programmes. We suggest that a distinction should be made between *provisions as well as entitlements*. This opens up the possibility of observing and classifying more complex changes in welfare state programmes. Also, this will enable us to discuss the implications of reform in terms of citizenship.
- Change should not only be conceptualised in terms of 'more or less', but also in terms of *qualitative changes*, which can be better conceptualised as provisions and entitlements.
- Change can manifest itself in different dimensions. Pierson makes a distinction between programmatic and systemic change. However, his notion of systemic change mainly refers to contextual changes. Therefore, we suggest a threefold distinction between *programmatic, contextual and institutional change*.
- Our notion of institutional structure is broader than Pierson's notion of institutional design, and encompasses the *implementation, administration and governance* of welfare programmes.
- Processes of *policy learning* should not be neglected. The institutional structure of continental, corporatist welfare states might be more conducive to policy learning than the Anglo-Saxon ones.

In the next section we use these concepts to analyse the changes in the Dutch system of social security that have been made during the last decade.

Reform of the Dutch social security system

In the period 1975-85 the use of social security schemes exploded in the Netherlands. During the first five years of this period the number of disability benefits doubled and in the second five years the number of unemployment benefits almost tripled. In the 1980s this initiated a political discussion about the future of the social security system. In 1987 a Social Security Reform was implemented, but in retrospect this was only the modest beginning of a much more fundamental process of changes in the 1990s.

To what extent do these changes reflect a process of retrenchment? In order to answer this question we will first summarise the major policy changes[3]. As we shall demonstrate below, developments in Dutch social policy can only be understood correctly if we make a distinction between different levels, in this case between policy programmes on the one hand and policy implementation and organisation on the other.

Social security programmes

The Dutch welfare state was a slow starter but a late bloomer. Until the mid-1950s, the protection of the social security system was below the European average (Flora and Heidenheimer, 1982, p 55). However, in the following decades a rapid growth of programmes and a strong improvement of benefit conditions took place. A universal and generous system developed, based on three pillars:

- The oldest and most important pillar consists of the insurance programmes for employees. These programmes cover the risks of sickness, disability and unemployment. This system is regulated by public law and offers wage-related benefits. Participation is mandatory and based on solidarity between the different economic sectors.
- The second pillar consists of national insurance programmes. The most important one is the old age pension system that guarantees a minimal income level to all citizens aged 65 and older.
- The third pillar consists of social provisions on the level of the social minimum. The most important provision is the 1963 Social Assistance Act, which functions as the lowest safety net in Dutch society.

The issue of cost was central in the policy debate of the 1980s. Hence, the 1987 reform concentrated on restricting provisions and entitlements: both in the workers' compensation schemes and in the social assistance programmes where stricter eligibility criteria were implemented and benefit levels were cut. For instance, the benefit level in the workers' compensation schemes was reduced from 80% to 70% and it was decided that people with partial disability could no longer claim a full benefit[4]. However, in spite of these measures the number of disability (and unemployment) transfer recipients did not decrease. This caused a major political crisis and led to a further restriction of rights. In 1993, both the level and duration of disability benefits were reduced substantially.

In the meantime, the central policy issue shifted from cost reduction to (political) control. No longer was the problem exclusively defined as a combination of external factors (economic crisis) and too much generosity in provisions. Political actors became aware that the financial problems were partly due to a lack of strict entitlements: precise rules, well-defined obligations and effective supervision. A Parliamentary Inquiry showed that employers, employees and administrative agencies had too much discretion in using the various social programmes. Among other measures this resulted in a much sharper legal definition of the (administrative and labour market) *duties* of employers and benefit recipients. For instance, it was decided that unemployed workers had to accept jobs below their level of qualification. It also became a legal obligation for employers to use the services of occupational health organisations[5].

Gradually, the issue of control caused a shift in policy style: from a traditional emphasis on rights and duties to an increasing interest in (financial) *incentives and disincentives*. New policies focused on the strategic motives of employees and employers and on instruments that would incite them to active and activating labour market behaviour. Again, the biggest changes took place in the workers' compensation schemes. The 1913 Sickness Benefit Act (ZW) was dismantled and privatised in two steps. First, in 1994, financial responsibility for employers was introduced during the first six weeks of sickness absence. Then the risk was fully privatised in 1996, although since then employers are legally obliged to pay 70% of the wage during the first year of sickness absence[6]. Employers must now turn to private insurance companies if they choose to insure themselves against this risk.

In 1998, similar measures were introduced in the 1966 Disability Benefit Act (WAO). Although employers can still choose to join the public disability scheme, they are confronted with premiums that rise with the number of occupational-disabled in the firm[7]. By giving the employer more responsibility for sickness and disability the incentives for firms to develop a policy for health and safety and sick leave are strengthened. Finally, sticks and carrots were also introduced to influence the behaviour of beneficiaries. In 1995, a new legal framework was implemented that specified the financial penalties in case a beneficiary would not fulfil his (administrative and labour market) duties[8]. In the social assistance schemes both positive and negative (financial) incentives were created to stimulate active labour market behaviour.

The most far-reaching measures were directed at the workers' compensation schemes: benefit levels were cut, eligibility criteria were sharpened and private responsibilities were enlarged to promote active labour market behaviour. However, it is too simple to conclude that the developments described above have diminished the income security of workers. First, some highly effective compensating mechanisms were developed. For instance, when the sickness payments were cut in 1987, most firms decided to supplement the benefit. When both the level and duration of disability benefits were limited in 1993, these measures were 'repaired' in nearly all industrial sectors by means of collective bargaining. Finally, when the 1913 Sickness Benefit Act was privatised in 1996, a legal compensation was realised by introducing a law on wage payment in case of sickness. Apart from these compensating mechanisms a second development became increasingly relevant during the 1980s, namely the construction of early exit programmes for older workers (Trommel, 1995). The most important one was the so-called VUT (voluntary early retirement scheme), which in most cases was designed and financed at the sectoral level by collective agreements.

Fewer changes were realised in the national insurance schemes. However, one important exception must be named, that which concerns the 1959 Benefit Act on Widows and Orphans. In this scheme the level of protection was drastically reduced in 1996 via the introduction of a stringent means-test and by excluding specific age groups from the insurance.

Policy implementation and organisation

The daily administration and implementation of the workers' compensation schemes has traditionally been the responsibility of the social partners, executed by bipartite sectoral industrial insurance boards. The administration and implementation of the social assistance schemes has always been in the hands of municipal agencies. In the early 1990s, both types of organisations were criticised for operating like 'benefit factories'. After the Parliamentary Inquiry of 1993, several instruments were introduced to stimulate a more activating administrative policy. This led to a reduction of the discretionary powers of the industrial insurance boards, and financial incentives designed to stimulate a more restrictive supply of benefits. A similar approach was introduced in the field of social assistance administration: the municipalities were confronted with a new budget policy that made them partly responsible for the expenditures.

Still, the political discontent over the functioning of the industrial insurance boards continued. Gradually, nearly all political parties agreed that more far-reaching measures were needed to establish a controlled and more activating implementation of social security programmes. A major structural reform was implemented that should serve three goals:

- improve the control and monitoring of administrative organisations
- reduce the role of unions and employers' associations in administrating social insurance
- create a market for administrating social insurance.

The process of reform started in 1994 when the Social Insurance Council (the SVR) was dismantled. This organisation controlled and monitored the administration and implementation of social security legislation and was dominated by representatives of unions and employers associations. The SVR was replaced by an independent organisation that became responsible for supervision and control (Ctsv). Also, in 1994 a new organisation was set up to coordinate and steer the implementation process (TICA/LISV)[9]. In 1997, the industrial insurance boards were dismantled and the administrative parts of the organisations became private firms (Uvi's). The LISV became the principal of these privatised organisations and was responsible for concluding contracts. The unions and employers' associations were given a modest role advising the board of the LISV.

By introducing independent control and monitoring systems (via the Ctsv and LISV) and by creating a quasi-market for administrating social insurance it was hoped that the implementation process could be better controlled and that the administration would become more self-controlled because it now had an incentive to operate more efficiently and effectively. However, the Dutch government began to fear that the social partners would still be too influential within this quasi-market of social security administration. By 2000, this resulted in a new decision being taken on the administrative structure of the system. In the near future the Uvi's will be transformed into (quasi-)governmental organisations. This seems to be a final step in reducing private interests in the field of administration. On the other hand, market competition remains to be stimulated to a large extent in the field of labour exchange and reintegration. Commercial activities in this area are increasing rapidly.

Institutional change of the Dutch welfare state

Programmatic change

On close inspection, the Dutch case shows few examples of programmatic retrenchment. It is true that the benefit levels in social insurances have been cut, but to a large extent this was neutralised by collective bargaining and company policy. It is also true that a (partial) privatisation of social risks has been realised, for instance in the 1913 Sickness Benefit Act, but this had no effect on the entitlements of employees, since employers became legally obliged to offer decent sick pays. (Private) programmes for early exit from the labour market have been developed, which partly opened up new ways of income security and partly functioned as an extra compensation to the reduced benefit conditions in the disability schemes. The only straightforward case of retrenchment has been the radical change in the 1959 Act on Widows and Orphans. The public programme for these groups has been minimised without any form of compensation.

Programmatic changes in Dutch social security have led to little retrenchment; the reduction of the 'replacement rate' is limited. In most cases, compensatory mechanisms neutralised the effects of retrenchment in public programmes. This compensation is the result of company- or sector-wide supplementary insurance that has been agreed on in collective labour agreements. The changes made to the system of social security should therefore not be described in terms of retrenchment. What has happened is that entitlements remained by and large intact, so has the level of provision, but financing has become more of a mix of public and private social programmes. The intention of this shift of the dimension of entitlements and provisions is to restrict the use of provisions. Because employers and administrative agencies are more directly financially responsible, they will try to reduce sick leave and occupational disability.

Contextual change

What then about *contextual* (systemic) retrenchment? If we consider the four dimensions mentioned by Pierson, again we do not find much evidence of this. In the Dutch system of social security a process of defunding is hardly possible: the system makes it hardly possible to reduce the contributions involved[10]. There is no evidence of a policy-induced change in public opinion; several studies show that there is still large support among the Dutch population for the social security system (Social and Cultural Planning Agency, 1998). Pierson's weakening of pro-welfare state groups is not easily applicable to the Dutch case. Although the unions and employers' associations have been accused of fraudulent use of social security programmes, which weakened their position, they had and still have an institutionalised position in the decision-making process. Perhaps the weakened position of unions and employers' associations made change possible, but at the same time their continuing participation in the decision-making process limited the possibilities for drastic retrenchment measures. Finally, Pierson suggests that future cut-backs might be induced by changes in the decision-making system. This level might be relevant, due to the (partial) privatisation of risks in the Netherlands. Today, companies and industrial actors have more freedom of choice with respect to the ways in which they want to cover specific risks, but not whether they want to arrange coverage, since this is still a legal obligation.

In sum, Pierson's account of systemic change does not apply to the social security reforms in the Netherlands. What is missing is what we have called the level of implementation, administration and governance of social security.

Institutional change: the activating paradigm

In the Dutch case many changes have taken place in the way in which social programmes are organised, administered and controlled. In our view, these are also systemic changes, since they refer to the context in which social programmes are effectuated. That is why we introduced the distinction between contextual and institutional changes. However, we do not think that these changes necessarily produce programmatic cut-backs. Whereas Pierson focuses on retrenchment alone, we think it is not *a priori* given that institutional change indicates future cut-backs. To judge possible programmatic effects, we need to have a better understanding of the 'logic' of institutional change.

So let us review the Dutch case from this perspective on institutional change. Two major categories of change can be distinguished. The first refers to the increasing efforts to reduce the use of social programmes by means of financial incentives and disincentives. It is not the entitlement that is at stake here, but its actual utilisation, the way it is provided. Entitlements have become embedded in a system of instruments that affect the decision to claim these rights. The second category of changes refers to the transformation of administrative agencies. This transformation is not directed at reducing entitlements, but at improving efficiency with respect to the administrative handling of entitlements.

Both types of change indicate a *fundamental* shift in institutional logic. First, the introduction of incentives and disincentives reflects a (partial) break from the idiom of social rights and duties. Utilisation of programmes is no longer exclusively seen as the consequence of circumstances beyond the person's control, but also as an individual decision that can be influenced by (financial) policy instruments. The image of the individual in policymaking shifts from rule-following to rational-economic. Second, the reform of the administration means a break from a tradition that was dominated by interest representation. By dismantling the administrative role of unions and employers' associations, a more neutral and business-like approach to policy implementation is stimulated. Here the image of organisations in policymaking changes into a more economic direction.

The shift to greater individual and corporate responsibilities in the field of social security, the efforts to increase efficiency in its administration and the adoption of market principles in the field of labour exchange and reintegration all point to the emergence of a so called *activating paradigm* in social policy. Citizens are held responsible for their 'employability', which also includes new duties with respect to (a healthy) lifestyle, investment in training and so on. Next to these new duties we also witness the emergence of new rights as an important element in the activating paradigm, such as the right to childcare facilities and part-time work.

Implications for citizenship

From institutional to ontological to normative change

Most changes in the Dutch social security system have taken place at the institutional level, in particular with respect to the organisation, administration and control of programmes and programme use. These changes had only a limited effect on entitlements because of a number of compensatory mechanisms, but they had a profound impact on the provision of these entitlements. The provision has become embedded in a complex structure of incentives directed at administrative agencies, employers and employees. These changes have a fundamental character, because they imply profound transformations in the images of the individual and organisation.

Why fundamental? To answer this question we refer to the notion of policy paradigms introduced by Sabatier and Jenkins-Smith (1993). They make a distinction between three dimensions in a policy paradigm: an upper, instrumental dimension, a policy core and a deep core. These dimensions are related, and refer to beliefs about the working of instruments, the content of policy problems and to values concerning the approach to policy problems, distributive justice and the distribution of power and responsibilities. Many of the changes that have been implemented in the Dutch social security system should be placed in the 'deep core' of the policy paradigm. In this deep core Sabatier and Jenkins-Smith distinguish between ontological and normative principles. Ontological principles pertain to images of people and organisations. It is exactly in these notions that changes have been carried through in the Netherlands. The change in images of the individual and organisations (as reflected in the activating paradigm) has consequently influenced the policy core and the instrumental dimension.

Now what about the normative principles? It can be argued that by avoiding a fundamental discussion on the normative functions of social security, its institutional reform was made possible and legitimate. Implicitly, it was assumed that the existing ideas on distributive justice and the related social rights and duties would stay intact. As our analysis shows, this has to a large extent been the case. However, this does not imply that the institutional changes are without moral and/or normative consequences. In fact, it would be rather unlikely. Both the 'economisation' of the concept of the individual and the redistribution of responsibilities within the institutional system give rise to new ideas on the moral obligations of the citizen and the state.

We will now evaluate these ideas from the perspective of citizenship. Elsewhere we have characterised the Dutch reforms as a process of 'managed liberalisation' (van der Veen and Trommel, 1999). This may suggest that the social dimension of citizenship is weakening and/or shifting into a more liberal direction. However, as we will show, this would be a misleading perception, since we have also seen that there are vital tendencies towards new and more extensive forms of institutional intervention in social life.

Social dimension of citizenship

In most European welfare states, such as the Dutch one, the social dimension of citizenship is well developed. This emphasis on the social dimension of citizenship has been translated in extensive social rights with respect to paid work and income security (Dahrendorf, 1999). Labour participation is seen as a precondition for citizenship, which implies that the social-political community has the right to regulate the labour market (for instance with respect to entrance and exit).

This view on citizenship means that the political process produces collective rules on the exchange between work and welfare. For instance, older people must leave the labour market and receive pension benefits in return, so that problems of decreasing productivity and a declining health status are prevented and the job opportunities for younger workers are improved. Inclusion in the labour market for specific groups implies the exclusion of others, which is compensated by means of social rights to welfare. The value of inclusion in paid labour is not absolute; a fair degree of social equality (based on work *and* social security) is more important.

In contrast with this view stands the liberal concept of citizenship. This concept is associated with the idea of negative freedom – the absence of obstacles that limit individual choice (Berlin, 1969). It is based on a political theory of limited government and defines civil right as the right to be treated as an individual, irrespective of personal characteristics such as race, age and sex. Liberal citizenship includes the freedom to participate in private business, but there is no social right to work. Neither does there exist a collectively arranged exchange between work and welfare. The basic principle is that people, irrespective of their age or race, may (or must) earn a living within the labour market.

Although a more moderate liberal view does exist, based on the notion of positive freedom, this does not include social rights as a precondition for citizenship. It is recognised that state policies may sustain individual life chances, for instance by legal measures against age discrimination within the labour market. However, such interventions are not rooted in a collective account of social needs and only acceptable for as far as they help the individual to take responsibility in life.

New directions

At first sight, you might argue that the dominant tendency in Dutch welfare state reform is towards a more liberal view on citizenship. Take the following observations:

• the emergence of a more economic and calculative image of the individual
• the increasing emphasis on individual responsibilities with respect to work and welfare
• a shift to corporate (firm-level) responsibilities and provisions
• a tendency towards activating policies (supported by a new social movement fighting age discrimination).

These observations suggest a withdrawal of the state from the domain of labour regulation and social protection. This would mean that the right to work and welfare are no longer guaranteed and that the social dimension of citizenship declines. However, a number of objections can be raised against this interpretation.

In our analysis of the Dutch case we have shown that several compensatory mechanisms counterbalance the policy trend towards residualisation. This is in line with Clayton and Pontusson (1998), who argue that social citizenship is not (necessarily) the product of the welfare regime alone.

The shift towards greater individual responsibilities is a limited one. That is to say, only to the extent that individuals are capable of influencing the risks they face, they will be confronted with larger financial responsibilities. In this respect, Giddens (1994, p 152) speaks of *manufactured* risks to identify the situations in which individual (lifestyle) choices have an impact on the risks people face and the responsibilities they have to bear. This is an institutional categorisation of individual responsibility, which differs largely from the philosophical account of responsibility in the liberal concept of citizenship.

The decentralisation of responsibilities in the social security system should not be mistaken for a retreat of the state or a decline of institutional control. On the contrary, the new forms of welfare production rest on a variety of (new) institutional mechanisms. Individual behaviour with respect to labour force participation, welfare consumption and lifestyle is more closely inspected and disciplined by means of strict surveillance and financial incentives. New types of policy instruments are being developed to support the social and cognitive capacities of citizens to care for themselves. This refers to what Giddens (1994, 1998) has called the "social investment state". Although still in their infancy, new policies can be observed that intend to 'empower' citizens as 'self-designing' creatures who take responsibility for their own future. Finally, this suggests that structural changes in the deep core of the policy paradigm are emerging.

These changes concern the morality of the modern citizen. During the periods of welfare state growth, policymakers assumed that people were socialised within all sorts of cultural and religious settings, which guaranteed a strong work ethic in society. Today, this assumption is no longer taken for granted. Instead, it is believed that the individual's morality can and must be constructed through institutional mechanisms that do not only affect incentives to work, but also influence related issues such as a healthy lifestyle and a prudent planning of your own future (for example, by continuous investment in your 'employability'). In other words, the modern welfare state tries to develop into a powerful educational force that can counterbalance the forces of detraditionalisation.

This means new duties are entering the concept of citizenship. People are forced to act as 'clever people', making life choices that reduce (traditional) welfare consumption both in the short- and long-term. On the other hand, this also implies the emergence of new social rights, with respect to empowerment (training in life skills, cognitive capacities), activation (employability, lifelong learning) and participation (childcare facilities, parental leave schemes).

The Dutch case indicates the arrival of new dimensions in the concept of citizenship. The most crucial are:

* institutional construction of individual morality
* new rights and duties with respect to healthy behaviour, employability, prudent life planning ('life politics')
* stronger individual responsibilities where possible ('manufactured risks')
* stronger institutional control, not only through state agencies, but also by means of (quasi-)markets and new partnerships between government and civil society.

A third way?

In the previous explanation, elements of the political programme that has been labelled 'the third way' by Anthony Giddens and others (Giddens, 1998, 2000) are evident. Giddens argues that third way politics imply a radical renewal of classical social democracy ('the old left'). We do not intend to recap the extensive discussion that has been held on the subject in the past few years. Rather, we want to stress some points that are related to the Dutch case and the interpretation of it.

Normative changes in the Netherlands are still in their infancy and far from stable, which is partly due to the fact that they are the (unintended) outcome of institutional reform, rather than the driving force behind it. As yet, a strong political movement behind the normative renewals is lacking and it is only recently that third way rhetoric has been applied to the institutional changes in the system. We must be careful in interpreting the current tendencies as a definite and irreversible transition.

From this consideration a second one follows, concerning the quality of the implemented reforms. The continuation of normative change largely depends on the actual performance of the new modes of welfare production. Thus far, the reforms have been successful. The use of benefits has decreased, the social security costs have been reduced and the participation in paid labour has increased. However, it is very difficult to judge to what extent these results can be ascribed to policy change and/ or to a general restoration of the economic climate. It remains to be seen how the new system will react to a situation of decline and what then the normative effects will be.

Which brings us to a third point of reflection, concerning the issue of social equality. Several studies have shown that the new institutional system tends to promote various practices of 'risk selection' within firms (Andriessen et al, 1995). As employers become more and more responsible for the costs of social security, they will be more selective in their hiring and firing policies. In a situation of economic decline, this could easily lead to the exclusion of people with a suspicious health status and/or a limited employability. In this context, a new wave of liberalisations is no longer hypothetical, for instance with respect to the legislation on minimal wages and wage protection. The new system may still develop in a liberal direction; this is more likely now than it was a decade ago. In the end the strong emphasis on inclusion may go at the cost of social equality.

Exactly on this point Steven Lukes (1999) has criticised the advocates of third way politics. He argues that the concept of inclusion is a misleading one, obscuring the crucial question in social policy, that of social equality. Given the Dutch experiences, we do not agree with the resoluteness of Lukes' argument. Still, we must be strongly aware of the dangers that are inherent in policies that make an absolute value out of participation into paid labour.

Conclusions

Throughout this chapter we have argued that welfare state change is not (only) a matter of more or less welfare, but above all a problem of institutional change. We discussed Paul Pierson's political approach to welfare state change and argued for much more attention being given to the actual forms of welfare production. Consequently, in our analysis of the Dutch social security reforms we focused on crucial changes in the *institutional logic* of welfare production. From this analysis we concluded that more than a decade of major reforms did no serious harm to the average level of social protection. However, it did produce new institutional mechanisms of welfare production.

These do have implications for citizenship, beginning with the emergence of a much more economic image of the individual. New normative notions develop that do not fit the classical concepts of liberal, social liberal or social democratic citizenship. A central element in this process of normative change is the institutional production and control of individual responsibilities with respect to life choices and lifestyle. We discussed some of the new social rights and duties that come with such institutional innovations as 'life politics' and the social investment state.

Although these normative changes do reflect some of the programmatic elements in what Giddens and others have named third way politics, we emphasised the unintended, tentative and unstable character of the changes. In particular, it is still unclear how the new forms of welfare production will behave during periods of serious economic decline. Under poor economic conditions the strong emphasis on inclusion (in paid labour) might trigger a much stronger wave of liberalisation than we have witnessed so far. In that case, the Dutch would still be confronted with less social protection and greater social inequality. The 'miracle' would turn out to be a 'fairy tale' after all. However, at present this danger is still limited and we expect that the realised changes in the organisational and institutional dimensions of the welfare state will gain strength as carriers of the new normative beliefs.

Notes

[1] Parts of this contribution (sections 2-4) are rewritten versions of an earlier published work (cf van der Veen et al, 2000).

[2] This has also recently been acknowledged by Pierson (1998).

[3] For a detailed analysis of changes see van der Veen and Trommel (1999).

[4] In 1972 it had been decided that people with partial disability could apply for a full benefit if they were not able to find a part-time job. It was argued that their partial unemployment was also due to their handicap (the so-called 'verdisconteringsartikel').

[5] This was regulated by the Amendment to the Working Conditions Act (ARBO, 1994).

[6] Here we refer to The Act on the Enlargement of Wage Payment During Sickness (Wulbz, 1996).

[7] The Act on Differentiation of Contributions and Market Competition in the Disability Schemes (Pemba, 1998). This Act concerns the first five years of disability. The employer can also choose to insure this risk with a private company or to pay the (legal) benefit himself.

[8] The 1995 Act on Penalties, Measures and Reclamation Social Security.

[9] After a probationary period this Institute acquired a permanent status in 1997, when its name was changed to the National Institute for Social Insurance (LISV).

[10] The rights of clients are legally guaranteed, which implies that expenditures cannot be cut by means of defunding; a yearly collection of premiums covers the total costs.

References

Andriessen S., Veerman, T.J. and Vijgen, J. (1995) *Risicoselectie op de Nederlandse arbeidsmarkt (Risk selection on the Dutch Labour Market)*, Zoetermeer: Ctsv.

Benz, A. (1994) *Kooperative Verwaltung. Funktionen, Voraussetzungen und Folgen*, Baden-Baden: Nomos Verlag.

Berlin, I. (1969) *Four essays on liberty*, Oxford: Oxford University Press.

Clayton, R. and Pontusson, J. (1998) *The new politics of the welfare state revisited*, San Domenico: European University Institute.

Dahrendorf, R. (1988) *The modern social conflict*, London: Weindfeld and Nicolson.

Feigenbaum, H., Henig, J. and Hamnett, C. (1999) *Shrinking the state: The political underpinnings of privatisation*, Cambridge: Cambridge University Press.

Flora, P. and Heidenheimer, A. (1982) *The development of welfare states in Europe and North-America*, New Brunswick: Transaction Books.

Giddens, A. (1994) *Beyond left and right*, Cambridge: Polity Press.

Giddens, A. (1998) *The third way*, Cambridge: Polity Press.

Giddens, A. (2000) *The third way and its critics*, Cambridge: Polity Press.

Giddens, A. (2001) *The global third way debate*, Cambridge: Polity Press.

Hoekema, A.J., van Manen, N.F., van der Hijden, G.M.A., van der Vlies I.C. and de Vroom, B. (1998) *Integraal Bestuur*, Amsterdam: Amsterdam University Press.

Lukes, S. (1999) 'A last word on the third way', *The Review: Journal of the Market Foundation*, March.

Marin, B. and Mayntz R. (eds) (1991) *Policy networks: Empirical evidence and theoretical considerations*, Frankfurt: Campus/Westview.

Pierson, P. (1994) *Dismantling the welfare state?*, Cambridge: Cambridge University Press.

Pierson, P. (1998) 'Irresistible forces, immovable objects: post-industrial welfare states confront permanent austerity', *Journal of European Public Policy*, vol 5, no 4, pp 539-60.

Sabatier, P. and Jenkins-Smith, H. (1993) *Policy change and learning*, Boulder, CO: Westview Press.

Sen, A. (1981) 'Ingredients of famine analysis: availability and entitlements', *The Quarterly Journal of Economics*, vol 96, p 433.

Schattschneider, E.E. (1935) *Politics, pressures and the tariff*, New York, NY: Prentice-Hall.

Social and Cultural Planning Agency (1998) *Social and cultural report 1998*, 'sGravenhage: SCP.

Titmuss, R. (1974) *Social policy*, New York, NY: Pantheon.

Trommel, W.A. (1995) *Korter Arbeidsleven (Shorter working life)*, 's Gravenhage: Sdu.

van der Veen, R. (1996) 'Solidarity: the development of the welfare state in the Netherlands and the United States', in H. Bak (ed) *Social and secure? Politics and culture of the welfare state: a comparative inquiry*, Amsterdam: V.U. Uitgeverij.

van der Veen, R.J. and Trommel, W.A. (1999) 'Managed liberalisation of the Dutch welfare state', *Governance*, vol 12, no 3, pp 289-310.

van der Veen, R., Trommel, W. and de Vroom B. (2000) 'Institutional change of welfare states: empirical reality, theoretical obstacles', in H. Wagenaar (ed) *Government institutions: Effects, changes and normative foundations*, Amsterdam: Kluwer.

Visser, J. and Hemerijck, A. (1997) *The Dutch miracle*, Amsterdam: Amsterdam University Press.

SIX

Unemployment, welfare policies and citizenship: different paths in Western Europe

Jørgen Goul Andersen and Knut Halvorsen

One of the characteristics of the 'new politics of welfare' (Jordan, 1998) is the emphasis on work as an indispensable precondition of citizenship, at the expense of the traditional emphasis on social rights and equality. To some extent, these attempts to redefine citizenship also represent an effort to make virtue out of necessity. In most countries, political actors have learned from the negative experiences of the 1970s and 1980s when rights-oriented and labour-force reducing welfare policies were used to combat unemployment. Even the strongest adherents of generous social protection have to acknowledge that economically unsustainable welfare policies do not leave much room for discussing ideals of full citizenship.

However, this has left a certain notion of economic determinism in social theory – sometimes even more so in sociology and political science than in economics. The question is whether globalisation and technological change (the extent of which will not be debated here) constitute such strong constraints for welfare policies that only one broad path is possible, with the consequence that a new doctrine of full citizenship compatible with economic realities has to be formulated. This chapter will explore, on the basis of recent European experiences, whether there is such a pressure for convergence, or whether several possible pathways are open – pathways with quite different implications for the ideals of full citizenship.

When OECD's new Jobs Strategy was published in 1994 (OECD, 1994), unemployment seemed an insurmountable problem in nearly all European countries, calling for structural reforms that could adapt these welfare states to new demands of 'flexibility' in a globalising economy. The job-generating capacity of the American economy in the 1980s and 1990s stood in sharp contrast to declining employment rates in Europe, where countries seemed faced with a trade off between equality and employment, at best, or caught in 'Eurosclerosis' at worst. Although the OECD strategy recommended a mixture, with more socially orientated elements in line with European traditions, the neoliberal cure stood almost as an imperative. Except for a few countries with very 'special economies', such as Norway, Switzerland and Luxemburg, all countries seemed to face the same problems. Even Sweden's heralded 'third way' of active labour market policy had failed dramatically.

However, by 2000, the situation looked rather different (see Table 6.1). In some countries, such as the Netherlands, Ireland, the UK and Denmark, unemployment rates declined significantly in the second half of the 1990s, and in 2000, even Sweden joined this group. To this may be added the above-mentioned group of countries with 'special economies' – Norway, Switzerland and Luxemburg – as well as Austria and Portugal, which maintained relatively low unemployment throughout the 1980s and 1990s but were more or less forgotten in the overall picture. This puts even the 'special economies' in a new perspective: perhaps they are not that special after all. It emerges that among the small, open economies in Western Europe, only Belgium, Finland and Greece have maintained high unemployment rates. Turning to the big central European countries, Spain, France and Italy have maintained high unemployment but with significant improvements in Spain and France. Finally, Germany, which used to be the strongest economy in Europe, was hit by mass unemployment in the 1990s; however, whether this should be ascribed to structural problems of its welfare/labour market system, or to temporary problems created by German unification remains an open question.

Considering the unusually tight economic policies in most European countries in the 1990s, set up to meet the convergence criteria of the Euro, the unemployment record of the European welfare states, as compared to the US, is perhaps not that bad after all. By 2000, unemployment among EU countries was down to 8.2%, and this fall continued in early 2001 when the figures for April 2001 revealed a (weighted) EU average of 7.6%, while the American figures had increased to 4.5%, from the all-time low of 4.0% in 2000. This is the smallest difference between the US and Europe for nearly a decade. Besides, the sharp contrast between the American success and European failures has been blurred by the success of many small European countries in the second half of the 1990s. By 2000, countries with unemployment rates around or below 5% outnumbered those with high unemployment, although it must be underlined that the most successful countries do not count very much in economic importance. However, it nevertheless

Table 6.1: Unemployment in Western Europe, 1980-2001 (standardised unemployment rates in %)

	1980	1985	1990	1991	1992	1993	1994	1995	1996	1997	1998	1999	2000	April 2000
Portugal	–	8.7	4.6	4.0	4.2	5.7	7.0	7.3	7.3	6.8	5.2	4.5	4.1	4.0
Greece	–	–	6.4	7.0	7.9	8.6	8.9	9.2	9.6	9.8	10.7	–	–	–
Spain	10.5	21.7	16.3	16.4	18.4	22.7	24.1	22.9	22.2	20.8	18.8	15.9	14.1	13.1
Italy	5.6	8.3	9.0	8.6	8.8	10.3	11.2	11.6	11.7	11.7	11.8	11.3	10.5	9.9
France	5.8	10.1	9.0	9.5	10.4	11.7	12.3	11.7	12.4	12.3	11.8	11.2	9.5	8.5
Belgium	9.3	10.4	6.7	6.6	7.2	8.8	10.0	9.9	9.7	9.4	9.5	8.8	7.0	6.8
Netherlands	6.1	8.3	6.2	5.8	5.6	6.6	7.1	6.9	6.3	5.2	4.1	3.4	3.0	2.4
Luxemburg	2.6	–	1.7	1.7	2.1	2.6	3.2	2.9	3.0	2.7	2.7	2.4	2.4	2.4
Germany	–	7.2	4.8	4.2	4.5	7.9	8.5	8.2	8.9	9.9	9.4	8.6	7.9	7.7
Austria	–	–	–	–	–	4.0	3.8	3.9	4.4	4.4	4.5	4.0	3.7	3.7
Denmark	–	–	7.7	8.5	9.2	10.1	8.2	7.3	6.8	5.6	5.2	5.2	4.7	4.7
Sweden	2.0	2.9	1.7	3.1	5.6	9.1	9.4	8.8	9.6	9.9	8.3	7.2	5.9	4.9
Norway	1.7	2.7	5.3	5.6	6.0	6.1	5.5	5.0	4.9	4.1	3.3	3.2	3.5	–
Finland	5.3	6.0	3.2	6.7	11.6	16.4	16.7	15.3	14.6	12.6	11.4	10.2	9.7	9.1
Ireland	6.2	–	13.4	14.8	15.4	15.6	14.4	12.3	11.7	9.9	7.5	5.6	4.2	3.8
UK	–	11.5	7.1	8.9	10.0	10.5	9.6	8.7	8.2	7.0	6.3	6.1	5.5	5.1
Switzerland	–	–	–	2.0	3.1	4.0	3.8	3.5	3.9	4.2	3.5	3.0	–	–
EU15	–	–	–	8.3	9.2	10.7	11.1	10.7	10.8	10.6	9.9	9.2	8.2	7.6
US	7.2	7.2	5.6	6.8	7.5	6.9	6.1	5.6	5.4	4.9	4.5	4.2	4.0	4.5

Source: 1980-89: OECD (1999c); 1990-97: OECD (2000a); 1998-2000: OECD *Main economic indicators*, available on http://www.oecd.org/media/new-numbers/index.htm

Entries are standardised unemployment rates, unemployment as a percentage of the civilian labour force (OECD, 1999d, p vi)

raises the question about what should be explained – the successes or the failures? In the German case, it is not even obvious whether the country should be considered a success or a failure – until 1992 Germany was among the low-unemployment countries. Finally, if we manage to sort out the successes and the failures, the question is whether there are any common denominators to these two groups of countries, respectively.

It is far beyond the scope of this chapter to provide answers to all these problems. Our main purpose is to ask whether the questions should be reformulated, considering the uncertainties above. The questions and the answers so far typically stem from three different sources:

- economic theory
- systematic macro- or micro-level empirical analyses in relation to economic theories
- in-depth case studies, or country comparisons based on a 'most similar' design.

Below, we briefly summarise these theories and hypotheses into a 'standard interpretation' guided by economic theory (but surfacing in other social sciences as well), and 'institutional interpretations', which often seek to formulate alternatives.

'Standard interpretation'

To put it crudely, much economic theory has switched from seeing unemployment as a market imperfection that should be cured by political means, to seeing unemployment as a sign of political or institutional 'disturbance' of the smooth functioning of markets (Sandmo, 1991). This change in perspective derives from several sources but not least from the recognition that globalisation and rational expectations make a difference: in the sheltered economy of the nation state, much regulation was possible (at worst with slightly negative consequences for economic growth); in a globalised economy[1], inflexible European labour markets and generous welfare states come under severe pressure. Below, we give a short and crude presentation of the 'standard interpretation', which has guided policies in Europe since the early 1990s[2].

According to this interpretation, the problem of globalisation is not only one of *aggregate* unemployment that could be solved by sustained economic growth, facilitated, for example, by wage moderation. Rather, unemployment is *structural*, not (only) in the sociological sense that it hits particular groups, but in the economic sense that it is a 'natural' unemployment under prevailing institutional conditions. Structural unemployment may stem from several sources[3], but the most important factor is the mismatch between the demand and supply of low-skilled jobs. With high minimum wages, there is a mismatch between wages and productivity for many unskilled and other low-productive labourers. As a consequence, these groups tend to be marginalised within the labour market. Even if economic growth leads to increased demand for labour power, these groups are not brought back into employment because their productivity is too low to justify high minimum wages. Rather, employers start competing for better-skilled labourers. This leads to wage drift and thus to higher inflation and deteriorating competitiveness. In a situation with fixed currency rates, there is no escape from this (and if there were, fear of devaluation among investors would immediately lead to higher interest rates). An economic upswing turns into a new recession as soon as unemployment comes down to the level of structural unemployment. In economic analyses, structural unemployment is simply defined as the lowest unemployment rate that is compatible with stable prices or stable wages[4]. European welfare states face a trade off between employment and equality; they cannot have both. As dependency ratios are already high, and will be much higher in the future due to ageing populations, they do not really have a choice: structural change is mandatory.

So, if this is the diagnosis, what are the solutions? Basically, there are three possible solutions to the mismatch problem (which are summarised as part of Figure 6.1):

- *More wage flexibility:* This means 'less compressed wage structures', or more precisely, lower de facto minimum wages. This would increase demand for low-skilled labour power, not least in low-productive services, which are often underlined as an indispensable job generator. Lower minimum wages presuppose that people are willing to work for a lower wage and will lower their 'reservation wage'. In turn, this presupposes less generous social protection. The problem here is that this may increase inequality to an unacceptable level. However, so the argument runs, this can be compensated via the tax system, for example by a tax credit or equivalent arrangement for people in employment[5].
- *Higher productivity:* For the labour movement, this is an attractive alternative since it avoids the trade off between equality and employment by means of activation of the unemployed, and by means of education. This is also where European countries may hope for a comparative advantage, as compared to the US, because of a stronger tradition of vocational training.

Figure 6.1: 'Standard interpretation': a map of structural reforms

Problem	Solution	This pre-supposes
Mismatch between wages and productivity for low-skilled workers	Wage flexibility: less compressed wage structures (lower reservation wages)	Less generous social protection
	Higher productivity	Activation of unemployed Education/qualification
	Subsidise low-productive services	
Otherwise stimulate smooth functioning of markets	Flexible employment protection Flexible working time Avoid distortions/disincentives of tax/welfare system More strict works test/workfare	
	Match demand/supply of types of qualifications)	

- *Subsidies for low-productive services:* As mentioned above, it is possible to provide an indirect subsidy for low-paid work via the tax system, such as deductions or a negative income tax for the employed. However, labour-intensive services may also be subsidised directly, or via lower value-added tax (VAT) for particular types of services. Again, this is a 'functional alternative' to lowering minimum wages.

Briefly, these are the basic options to correct the wage inflexibility problem. However, according to the 'standard interpretation' there are also other types of inflexibility that impede the smooth functioning of markets. This includes inflexible employment protection (which makes employers reluctant to create new jobs), inflexible working time, and distortions/disincentives within the tax/welfare system. As in the case of more wage flexibility, this is basically a task of *deregulation*. To these problems are often added the need for control (works test) of the unemployed, and a problem of mismatch between the types of qualifications that are demanded and supplied on the labour market.

Apart from the matching of qualifications and subsidising services (see Figure 6.1), the options above are exactly the elements included in the OECD Jobs Strategy, which adds 'sound' macroeconomic policies, technological innovation and entrepreneurship as general measures to improve growth (Table 6.2).

The 'standard interpretation' implies that the capacity of the welfare state to alleviate unemployment problems is reduced. It can act in conformity with the market by providing activation and qualification but the 'politics against markets' part of social protection and regulation is an aspect of the unemployment problem itself and should be cured by deregulation and more flexibility. To a large extent, this view has also been accepted by sworn supporters of the welfare state (Esping-Andersen, 1996, 1999) whereas prominent sociologists (Gilbert, 1995; Giddens 1998, 2000) have at the same time accepted that a side-effect of social protection may even be the development of a 'dependency culture' among recipients that passes on from one generation to another (Murray, 1984; for criticism see, for example, Dean and Taylor-Gooby, 1992).

Institutional theories

Institutional theories seek to draw lessons from cross-national variations in institutions and policies. Some of these theories may be in full accordance with the 'standard interpretation' above. For instance, theories focusing on the number of 'veto points' in political systems may simply take the necessary solution more or less for granted and try to explain why some countries have been able to adapt while others have not (Pierson, 1998; Ferrera and Rhodes, 2000). A second group of institutional theories may test or specify the predictions of the 'standard interpretation' above;

Table 6.2: OECD Jobs Strategy

Growth policy/qualification	Deregulation/flexibility
Non-inflationary macroeconomic policy	More flexible wages (lower minimum wages)
More technological innovation	More flexible working time
More fostering of entrepreneurship	More flexible employment protection
Higher skills/education and training	Reform unemployment system (and interaction with tax system)
Active labour market policy	Product market competition

Source: OECD (1999a, p 142)

for example, test the importance of employment protection rigidity for unemployment. Finally, a third group of institutional theories, which seek explanations of successes and failures from case studies, or from country comparisons, may implicitly rest on other interpretations of the causes and nature of unemployment. Occasionally, such theories may be rooted in some mutation of Keynesianism, or they may be concerned mainly with competitiveness or with the growth of the service sector, implicitly assuming that these parameters are at the heart of the unemployment problem[6]. In this section, we leave aside the first type and concentrate on theories that test and specify, or implicitly challenge, the 'standard interpretation' above.

The most well-known theory specifying the problems of globalisation and structural unemployment is Esping-Andersen's (1990, 1996, 1999) distinction between three ideal-typical welfare (state) regimes: Liberal, Conservative and Social Democratic. A Liberal welfare regime is defined by its emphasis on the market and a (deliberately chosen) limited role for the welfare state, which should act in conformity with the market. The Conservative performance-achievement orientated welfare state is based on social contributions and a high level of protection (income replacement), especially for male breadwinners[7]. Finally, the Social Democratic welfare states are based on universal, all-encompassing protection and a high provision of public service for working families. These ideal types find their most close empirical counterparts in the Anglo-Saxon, Continental European, and Scandinavian countries, respectively.

From the perspective of the 'standard interpretation', the *Liberal model* is equipped to meet the new challenges, including the provision of low-skilled service jobs, but with the risk of producing a 'low wage/low productivity equilibrium' (Esping-Andersen, 1999) with a large group of 'working poor'; critics would add the risk of producing an 'underclass' among the most weak unemployed. The *Social Democratic* model, with its generous social protection, may impede the creation of low-skilled service jobs in the private sector, but up to some limit of public sector overload this is compensated by growth in public services. Finally, the *Conservative* ideal type reinforces insider/outsider divisions both in a sociological and an economic sense, and limits the creation of service jobs both in the private and the public sector. To protect breadwinners, this welfare model tends to stimulate early retirement to a degree where employment rates become very low. During recessions, this model may impose higher social contributions on employers and aggravate the problems. Following Esping-Andersen and the 'standard interpretation', this model faces particular difficulties – although it is acknowledged that it tends to produce a highly productive labour force.

If we interpret the trends and the rates of unemployment in 2000 as more than random fluctuations – and there are strong reasons to do so as the figures of some countries have broken out of the 'normal' intervals of the business cycles for more than two decades – this theory is to some extent confirmed: the US and UK are both managing well in terms of unemployment; and the Scandinavian countries have largely recovered (with the exception of Finland which is improving but has developed an enormous dependency on one single firm: Nokia). By 2000, the unemployment problems seemed to be concentrated in the Continental European welfare states. However, at the same time, there are significant variations among these countries[8].

To account for some of these variations, and to test the 'standard interpretation', a number of institutional parameters have been tested in econometric models[9]. In such tests, institutional parameters are tested one by one in isolation. These include, for example, contribution-based versus tax-financed benefits, employment protection, and centralisation of wage negotiations (proxy for corporatism). The results are surprisingly weak. It is shown that contribution- versus tax-financing of benefits (proxy for welfare state model) does not have any systematic impact on aggregate unemployment but affects its distribution, since it tends to reinforce insider/outsider divisions, with higher frequency of long-term unemployment and youth unemployment (Calmfors and Holmlund, 2000; OECD, 1994). Roughly the same can be said about employment protection legislation (Bertola et al, 1999; OECD, 1999b, p 88), which may lead to less external flexibility but give more incentives to internal flexibility[10]. It seems that both decentralised wage formation and strong, centralised corporatism may be beneficial to employment (Calmfors and Holmlund, 2000). Also, such analyses typically report only small effects of *levels* of unemployment benefits but somewhat larger effects of *duration*, while the effect of activation is usually positive but otherwise rather uncertain (Martin, 2000; van Oorschot, 2000; Larsen, 2000). Finally, there seems to be no clear association between service employment and overall employment/unemployment (OECD, 2000a, pp 79-128). Among the few significant correlations found, the OECD notes an association between a composite measure of the implementation of the OECD Jobs Strategy and employment/unemployment performance (OECD, 1999a, p 157).

However, many of the recommendations that follow from the 'standard interpretation' have not been followed. In the case of lower minimum wages, the OECD even notes that this has, on average, moved in the 'wrong' direction (1999a, p 152). The third group of theories that seek to explain success and failure from case studies and country comparisons is often orientated towards identifying solutions that allow both flexibility and social security (sometimes labelled 'flexicurity'). In the Danish case, success is often explained by a particular combination of liberal employment protection and generous unemployment protection (see: Chapter Four in this book; Andersen and Christiansen, 1991; Madsen, 1999). This may well be so, but it seems dependent on (Danish) contextual factors: as mentioned above, the degree of systemic correlation between unemployment benefits and employment/unemployment is small, and there is no systematic effect of employment protection on *aggregate* employment/unemployment (see above); only the *distribution* of unemployment (such as long-term unemployment) seems affected (Calmfors and Holmlund, 2000). If this is the case, it is uncertain whether there is a lesson to be learned for other countries.

Corporatism is a key factor in recent attempts to explain the 'Dutch miracle' (Visser and Hemerijck, 1997), or the differences between the Netherlands and Austria on the one hand, and Belgium and Germany on the other (Hemerijck et al, 2000b; Hemerijck et al, 2000a; Hemerijck and Visser, 2000; see also Bonoli et al, 2000, Chapter 7). This echoes Scharpf's (1991) classical explanation of why some countries were more successful than others in combating unemployment in the 1970s and early 1980s. However, this explanation implicitly seems to rest on the assumption that the key problem of globalisation is *competitiveness* (rather than structural unemployment), and that *wage moderation* is the key instrument: wage moderation is exactly the main policy goal that corporatism is 'designed' to obtain. This is explicitly acknowledged by Hemerijck et al (2000b, p 228) who endorse the interpretation of the Dutch Central Planning Bureau when they write that "wage moderation has been the single most important weapon in the Dutch adjustment strategy [...] *two-thirds of job growth between 1983 to 1996 should be attributed to wage moderation*". They conclude that "looking back on twenty-five years of policy adjustment, one is struck by the ongoing importance of wage restraint for maintaining competitiveness [...]. Apparently there were no alternative policy options in economies exposed to international competition" (Hemerijck et al, 2000b, p 252).

However, from the point of view of the 'standard interpretation', wage moderation is basically a dependent variable which, due to wage drift, is almost impossible to obtain if structural unemployment is high. Corporatism is likely to be part of the problem rather than part of the solution (van Oorschot, 2000). Wage moderation does have beneficial effects, but solidary wage policy and compressed wage structures tend to be its corollary[11]. This would aggravate structural unemployment problems, according to the standard interpretation. Parallel arguments pertain to generous social protection. If corporatism really is efficient, this tends to challenge the 'standard interpretation' of unemployment, unless it can be proved that corporatism facilitates agreement on structural reforms, such as on more flexibility[12].

To sum up, there are a large number of plausible institutional explanations of successes and failures, based on case studies and country comparisons. However, with a few exceptions, they appear to be at odds with systematic studies. This need not mean that the conclusions are wrong, only that conclusions cannot be generalised as advice for other countries: stripped of the particular institutional context in individual countries, most of these factors do not appear to be very efficient.

Testing the 'standard interpretation'

As pointed out in Holmlund and Calmfors (2000), the 'standard interpretation' (as we have called it) rests on a combination of 'strong' theoretical arguments and uncertain empirical findings. We would even argue that, with few exceptions, empirical findings are inconclusive: taking the core argument about wage flexibility in Europe as an example, it is not convincing that countries with low minimum wages and high wage dispersion fare better in terms of unemployment. True, the UK and the US have high and increasing wage dispersion along with improved unemployment, and Austria has maintained a high income inequality throughout the period (see Table 6.3). However, the equally successful Scandinavian countries and the Netherlands are found at the other end of the scale. Besides, wage dispersion should increase employment among the low-skilled. Yet the ratio between unemployment of low-skilled and high-skilled workers is 4:1 in the 'flexible' US labour market as compared to less than 2:1 in the EU countries (calculated from OECD, 2000a). When it comes to active labour market policies, conclusions are equally vague: such policies seem beneficial but have nowhere proved very efficient (not even in Sweden, see Furåker, 2000), and a number of countries such as Austria (and until the early 1990s Germany!) have managed quite well with 'passive' policies.

The OECD (1994) has itself provided much evidence against the assumptions behind its Jobs Strategy: liberal employment protection, lower taxes and improved incentives do not have convincing effects across countries. The question is whether anything at all seems to work across

Table 6.3: Earnings dispersion in selected OECD countries

	9th decile/5th decile ('how rich are the rich')			5th decile/1st decile ('how poor are the poor')		
	1979	1986	1995	1979	1986	1995
Italy	150	143	160	196	175	175
France	194	196	199	167	162	165
Germany	–	164	161	–	158	144
Netherlands	–	162	166	–	155	156
Austria	178	180	182	194	193	201
Denmark	152	155	–	141	142	–
UK	165	178	187	169	174	181
US	–	–	210	–	–	209

Source: OECD *Economic Outlook 1996*, quoted in Bertola et al (1999)

countries. We may distinguish between three broad groups of strategies (see Chapter Four):

• strategies addressing the alleged 'structural' problems of the labour market
• competitiveness strategies
• Keynesian/work sharing strategies.

Tentatively, it appears that a few points can be made.

As to 'structural' strategies, the arguments about wage flexibility and employment protection flexibility are not clearly confirmed, but we do not find much data that speak against a positive association between work-time flexibility and employment. As to social protection, the level of unemployment benefits only seems to play a minor role, whereas duration has more significant effects (but it is disputed whether it should be considered an advantage that the unemployed take more time to find an appropriate job). Next, there may be much doubt about the cost-effectiveness of activation, but few would claim that it is entirely without an effect. The same holds for education, not least for the amount and quality of education at the lower levels. In Denmark, the number of unskilled labourers has been reduced even faster than the number of unskilled jobs (Ministry of Finance, 2000).

Unlike the 'structural' strategies, there is nothing really new about competitiveness strategies. It may be more than sheer coincidence that small, open economies have generally fared well around the millennium. These countries have always been exposed to strong competition from abroad and may find it easier to manoeuvre in a globalised economy. If *competitiveness* is the real challenge of globalisation, wage moderation is more important than (reducing) wage compression. If that was the case, it also seems more convincing to present corporatism as an institution with potentially positive employment effects – and as a socially responsible alternative to strong decentralisation. It may be the case that traditional strategies of competitiveness (rather than strategies addressing the alleged 'structural' labour market problems) are the appropriate answer to the challenges of globalisation.

Only the traditional set of strategies of stimulating aggregate demand by means of public deficits, or sharing available labour by means of early retirement, do seem to have counterproductive effects, at least for small countries acting alone. What *does* seem to pay are 'sound' macroeconomic policies: at least they seem to have been characteristic of nearly all the 'successes'[13] – including even Germany, until reunification – whereas strong deficit budgeting seems to have led to serious problems (Ludwig-Mayerhofer, 2000). This generalisation even includes Sweden, which issued a partly unfinanced tax reform at the worst thinkable moment in 1990, hoping that 'dynamic effects' of better incentives would finance it in the long run (Furåker, 2000).

Many routes to improved unemployment but with different effects on citizenship

Apart from 'sound' economic policies, it seems difficult to find many common denominators for the employment 'successes' in Europe – or for the 'failures'. Austrian corporatism, market-orientated reforms in Britain, the Dutch mixture of both, Danish 'flexicurity', and Swedish active labour market policy do not have much in common but they all seem to work in their respective contexts. There does not seem to be one single route to improved employment (as implied by the 'standard interpretation'), but many different routes. This is indirectly confirmed by analyses of the relationship between bargaining centralisation and unemployment, which usually reveals a U-shaped association: very low and very high centralisation work equally well (Calmfors and Holmlund, 2000). Even more flexible employment protection does not seem to have uniform effects on employment and unemployment, but they do seem to affect the *structure* of unemployment – the less flexibility there is, the more long-term unemployment, insider/outsider divisions and so on.

However, such parameters are highly important from a citizenship point of view. More generally, various strategies that are equally productive in relation to unemployment may have highly divergent effects on citizenship.

Spain and Italy not only have a high unemployment rate, but also a high incidence of long-term unemployment of 12 months or more (see Table 6.4).

Long-term unemployment, on the other hand, is low in Scandinavia and the Anglo-Saxon countries, characterised by frequent but short spells of unemployment. In Scandinavia, this is partly an effect of activation, but the figures also reflect a high movement in and out of the category of unemployed, due to a flexible labour market.

The other side of the coin is the protection of male breadwinners. A rule of thumb used to be that unemployment among prime age men was nearly the same – and small – in all countries: it was unemployment

Table 6.4: Long-term unemployment as percentage of labour force, and employment/unemployment among prime age men, 1999 (%)

	Long-term unemployed (12 months or % more) of labour force	Unemployment among prime-age men (25-54)		Unemployment among 35- to 44-year-old men	Employment among prime-age men (25-54)	
	1999	1990	1999	1991	1990	1999
Greece	5.8	3.2	5.7	–	91.3	89.0
Portugal	1.9	2.2	3.4	1.8	92.1	89.8
Spain	8.2	9.3	9.2	7.5	85.5	84.2
Italy	6.9	3.9	6.9	1.8	90.2	84.3
France	4.6	5.9	9.0	5.0	89.8	85.7
Belgium	5.2	4.0	6.1	4.6	88.5	86.2
Netherlands	1.4	5.0	2.1	3.9	88.8	91.5
Germany	4.5	4.7	7.3	4.7	86.9	87.0
Austria	1.2	–	4.5	2.5	–	89.6
Denmark	1.1	7.5	3.7	7.9	87.4	89.3
Sweden	–	1.3	6.5	1.9	93.5	84.5
Norway	0.2	4.7	2.6	4.0	88.0	89.4
Finland	3.0	2.5	7.9	8.0	90.6	83.4
Ireland	3.0	11.8	5.7	16.0	81.1	86.4
UK	1.8	5.6	5.4	6.7	89.5	86.7
Switzerland	1.4	.8	2.2	.7	97.0	95.1
EU15	4.4	5.3	6.9	4.9	88.8	86.3
US	0.3	4.6	3.0	7.6	89.1	89.0

Source: OECD (2000a); OECD (1994, pp 166-8)

Table 6.5: Relative poverty rates in households where head of household is unemployed, 1988 (%)

Denmark	3
Netherlands	23
Belgium	28
France	35
Italy	36
EU12	38
Germany	44
UK	48

Source: European Commission (1995)

among all the other groups – women, the young and the elderly – that produced the differences in aggregate unemployment figures. To some extent, this remains true. By 1990, most EU countries maintained a very low unemployment among 25- to 54-year-old men, around the same level as in the US. The same holds for employment rates, which may sometimes be a better indicator, due to the high American incarceration rates (Buchele and Christiansen, 1999). However, by 1999, even though aggregate unemployment is only a little higher, unemployment among prime age men in the Continental European welfare states has typically increased to some 50%, whereas in Scandinavia and the UK it follows the general trend in unemployment. As the age brackets are a bit too broad because of education and early retirement, we have also presented unemployment rates for men in the 35-44 age group in 1991. This illustrates the differences between welfare states even more clearly. Unemployment rates for this group were very low in most Continental European welfare states at that time – and much lower than in the US; in Italy, the figure was only 1.8%. To conclude, until recently the Continental European welfare states managed to fulfil what was traditionally their main goal: to protect male breadwinners. This may also help to explain the low incidence of social unrest, even in periods of high unemployment. However, this pattern seems to have deteriorated somewhat during the 1990s.

Another indication of the different paths is the incidence of (relative) poverty among the unemployed. Table 6.5 shows figures from a detailed study that is based on 1988 data but probably still captures the basic differences. It emerges that the proportion of unemployed households falling under the relative poverty level was only 3% in Denmark but 48% in the UK. These two extremes (together with the Netherlands, which after Denmark had the next lowest rate) are among the countries with the best unemployment record around 2000. It comes as no surprise that the UK has experienced a steep increase in the fear of unemployment among its people whereas Denmark has the lowest level, in spite of low employment protection (Madsen, 1999). Again, lower minimum wages and social protection do not appear to be a precondition of improved employment – it is one among several possible routes that can be followed – but they do have consequences for citizenship.

Notes

[1] 'Globalisation' is a buzzword that is rarely defined. Here, it simply means increasing and unrestricted movement of capital and commodities across borders. It may be argued that 'globalisation' is nothing new, since this was also a significant trend before the First World War (Krugman, 1996). But even if the 'globalisation curves' may be U-shaped, this only reminds us that globalisation is to a large extent a *politically* determined process, and this does not change the fact that there has been a change since the mid-20th century. Also, if globalisation is recurrent from the half century before the First World War, it may be noted that this was also a period of deregulation. Even for countries where most of the curves are rather flat, as in the case of foreign trade as a percentage of GDP for some small economies, liberalisation of capital movements and the growth of an 'expectation economy' clearly impedes the use of traditional macroeconomic steering instruments (Bonoli et al, 2000, Chapter 3). However, the constraints of globalisation are often exaggerated; for instance, for small open economies used to acting within a balance of payment constraint, a strong emphasis on competitiveness is not all that new.

[2] For a full account see for example, OECD, 1994; Calmfors and Holmlund, 2000.

[3] This may also include high levels of frictional unemployment, due to unnecessarily long unemployment periods in the transition from education to work, from leave to work, from one job to another and so on.

[4] Labelled NAIRU or NAWRU, respectively: Non Accelerating Inflation (Wage) Rate of Unemployment. It is estimated on the basis of econometric analyses of the relationship between unemployment and inflation.

[5] This is an indirect subsidy which may, however, have the side-effect of increasing the de facto marginal tax rate. If welfare benefits and services are means-tested,

this may lead to interaction problems with quite perverse incentives as combined marginal tax ratios approach 100%.

[6] A more complete account of the possibilities may be derived from the classification of possible strategies given in Chapter Four. One type of – largely theoretical – interpretation could be added: those who maintain that what we are seeing now is the end of the Full Employment Society, and that we have to distribute wealth independently of people's involvement in formal work, for example, by some type of citizens' income (Offe, 1996; Gorz, 1999; Vobruba, 1999).

[7] Many authors distinguish between an extremely family-oriented Mediterranean version and a Central European version (Ferrera, 1996; Kuhnle and Alestalo, 2000).

[8] Many other implications relating to such issues as labour force participation do not fit well either; but this is outside the scope of this chapter.

[9] Often propositions can also be tested by time series, or in micro-level analyses. See, for example, Tema Nord, 1999, p 572.

[10] From a citizenship perspective, this is very important, since the threat of long-term unemployment is more alarming than aggregate unemployment as such.

[11] However, Austria seems to form an exception, since corporatism has not prevented high wage dispersion; also, in the Netherlands this seems to some extent to have been the case (Hartog, 1999).

[12] One of the preconditions is that governments at all want to invite associations to negotiations. In the Danish case, the trade unions did not participate in the preparation of labour market reforms, except in 1998.

[13] There may be a problem of causality here: high unemployment leads to budget deficits and high employment leads to a surplus. However, it also seems that countries that deliberately seek to limit state debts have better unemployment records in the long run.

References

Andersen, J.G. and Christiansen, P.M. (1991) *Skatter uden velfærd. De offentlige udgifter i international belysning*, Copenhagen: Jurist-og Økonomforbundets Forlag.

Bertola, G., Boeri, T. and Cazes, S. (1999) *Employment protection and labour market adjustment in OECD countries: Evolving institutions and variable enforcement*, Employment and Training Papers No 48, Geneva: Employment and Training Department, ILO.

Bonoli, G., George, V. and Taylor-Gooby, P. (2000) *European welfare futures: Towards a theory of retrenchment*, London: Polity Press.

Buchele, R. and Christiansen, J. (1999) 'Do employment and income security cause unemployment?', in J. Christiansen, P. Koistinen and A. Kovalainen (eds) *Working Europe: Reshaping European employment systems*, Aldershot: Ashgate, pp 33-56.

Calmfors, L. and Holmlund, B. (2000) *Den europeiska arbetslösheten*, NOU 2000:21, En strategi for sysselsetting og verdiskaping, Vedlegg 4, Oslo: NOU.

Dean, H. and Taylor-Gooby, P. (1992) *Dependency culture: The explosion of a myth*, London: Harvester Wheatsheaf.

Esping-Andersen, G. (1990) *The three worlds of welfare capitalism*, Princeton, NJ: Princeton University Press.

Esping-Andersen, G. (1996) 'After the golden age? Welfare state dilemmas in a global economy', in G. Esping-Andersen (ed) *Welfare states in transition: National adaptations in global economies*, London: Sage Publications, pp 1-31.

Esping-Andersen, G. (1999) *Social foundations of postindustrial economies*, Oxford: Oxford University Press.

European Commission (1995) *Employment in Europe 1994*, Brussels: European Commission.

Ferrera, M. (1996) 'The southern model of welfare in social Europe', *Journal of European Social Policy*, vol 6, no 1, pp 17-37.

Ferrera, M. and Rhodes, M. (2000) 'Recasting European welfare states: an introduction', in M. Ferrera and M. Rhodes (eds) 'Recasting European welfare states', *West European Politics*, vol 23, no 2, special issue.

Furåker, B. (2000) 'Unemployment and welfare state arrangements in Sweden', paper presented at seminar in COST A13 Working Group Unemployment, Brussels, 3-4 November, Gothenburg: Department of Sociology, University of Gothenburg.

Giddens,A. (1998) *The third way:The renewal of social democracy*, Cambridge: Polity Press.

Giddens, A. (2000) *The third way and its critics*, Cambridge: Polity Press.

Gilbert, N. (1995) *Welfare justice: Restoring social equity*, New Haven, CT: Yale University Press.

Gorz,A. (1999) *Reclaiming work: Beyond the work-based society*, Cambridge: Polity Press.

Hartog,J. (1999) *The Netherlands: So what's so special about the Dutch model?*, Employment and Training Papers No 54, Geneva: Employment and Training Department, ILO.

Hemerijck,A., Manow, P. and van Kersbergen, K. (2000a) 'Welfare without work? Divergent experiences of reform in Germany and the Netherlands', in S. Kuhnle (ed) *Survival of the European welfare state*, London: Routledge, pp 106-27.

Hemerijck, A., Unger, B. and Visser, J. (2000b) 'How small countries negotiate change: twenty-five years of policy adjustment in Austria, the Netherlands, and Belgium', in F.W. Scharpf and V.A. Schmidt (eds) *Welfare and work in the open economy, Vol II: Diverse responses to common challenges*, Oxford: Oxford University Press, pp 175-263.

Hemerijck,A. and Visser, J. (2000) 'Change and immobility: three decades of policy adjustments in the Netherlands and Belgium', *West European Politics*, vol 23, no 2, special issue on 'Recasting European welfare states' edited by M. Ferrera and M. Rhodes, pp 229-56.

Jordan, B. (1998) *The new politics of welfare*, London: Sage Publicaions.

Krugman, P. (1996) *Pop internationalism*, Cambridge, MA: MIT Press.

Kuhnle, S. and Alestalo, M. (2000) 'Introduction: growth, adjustments and survival of European welfare states', in S. Kuhnle (ed) *Survival of the European welfare state*, London: Routledge, pp 3-18.

Larsen, C.A. (2000) 'Employment miracles and active labour market policy – summarizing the Danish effect evaluations', paper presented at Nordic Research Seminar 'Unemployment, early retirement and citizenship', 8-10 December, Aalborg: Department of Economics, Politics and Public Administration, Aalborg University.

Ludwig-Mayerhofer, W. (2000) 'System description of unemployment and (un)employment policies: Germany', paper presented at seminar in COST A13 Working Group Unemployment, Brussels, 3-4 November, Munich: Department of Sociology, Ludwig-Maximilians University.

Madsen, P.K. (1999) *Denmark: Flexibility, security and labour market success*, Employment and Training Papers No 53, Geneva: Employment and Training Department, ILO.

Martin, J.P. (2000) *What works among active labour market policies: evidence from OECD countries' experiences*, OECD Economic Studies No 30, Paris: OECD.

Ministry of Finance (Finansministeriet) (2000) *Finansredegørelse 2000*, Copenhagen: Ministry of Finance.

Murray, C. (1984) *Losing ground: American social policy 1950-1980*, New York, NY: Basic Books.

OECD (Organisation for Economic Cooperation and Development) (1994) *The OECD jobs study: Evidence and explanations, Part I: labour market trends and underlying forces of change; Part II: the adjustment potential of the labour market*, Paris: OECD.

OECD (1999a) *Economic outlook, June 1999*. Paris: OECD.

OECD (1999b) *Employment outlook, June 1999*, Paris: OECD.

OECD (1999c) *Historical statistics 1960-1997*, CD-Rom version, Paris: OECD.

OECD (1999d) *Quarterly Labour Force Statistics*, no 4, Paris: OECD.

OECD (2000a) *Employment outlook*, June 2000, Paris: OECD.

OECD (2000b) *Main economic indicators*, available at http://www.oecd.org/media/new-numbers/index.htm#Standardised Unemployment Rates.

Offe, C. (1996) 'Full employment: asking the wrong question?', in E. Oddvar Eriksen and J. Loftager (eds) *The rationality of the welfare state*, Oslo: Scandinavian University Press.

Pierson, P. (1998) 'Irresistible forces, immovable objects: post-industrial welfare states confront permanent austerity', *Journal of European Public Policy*, vol 5, no 4, pp 539-60.

Scharpf, F. (1991) *Crisis and choice in European social democracy*, Ithaca, NY: Cornell University Press.

Sandmo, A. (1991) 'Presidential address: economists and the welfare state', *European Economic Review*, vol 35, nos 2-3, pp 213-39.

Tema Nord (1999) *Dagpengesystemene i Norden og tilpasning på arbeidsmarkedet*, Copenhagen: Nordisk Ministerråd.

van Oorschot, W. (2000) 'Work, work, work. Labour market participation in the Netherlands. A critical review of policies and outcomes', paper presented at seminar in COST A13 Working Group Unemployment, Brussels, 3-4 November, Tilburg: Department of Sociology, Tilburg University.

Visser, J. and Hemerijk, A. (1997) *The Dutch miracle*, Amsterdam: Amsterdam University Press.

Vobruba, G. (1999) 'The end of the full employment society: changing the bias of inclusion and exclusion', in P. Littlewood (ed) *Social exclusion in Europe*, Aldershot: Ashgate.

SEVEN

Youth unemployment, welfare and political participation: a comparative study of six countries

Torild Hammer

The concept of citizenship provides a fruitful approach to an analysis of individual actors in countries with different welfare regimes. This chapter will study the relationship between welfare regimes and political participation among unemployed youth, based on nation-wide representative samples of unemployed youth in six Northern European countries. The point of departure is Marshall's analyses of citizens' rights as conditions for full civil, political and social citizenship (1992). Marshall saw the liberal democratic welfare state as the basis for citizens' rights. By guaranteeing citizens civil, political and social rights, the welfare state ensures the individual's integration in society and enables everybody to participate in social and political life. If such rights are not developed, this leads to social marginalisation and low participation.

This Marshallian understanding of citizenship is sometimes described in the literature as passive or private citizenship, because citizens' rights are claimed without any requirements of responsibility and duties. In a review of the literature, Kymlicka and Norman (1994) show how this has been criticised. Citizens should not only have 'passive' rights but also bear a responsibility for an active citizenship, which implies self-provision and political participation. Whereas Marshall claims that citizenship rights guaranteed by the welfare state are a condition for participation, critics argue that the welfare state creates passive citizens and a dependency culture, which does not increase opportunities for the 'underclass', quite the contrary (Murray et al, 1990). An effective welfare state should involve citizens in common responsibility and duties. Welfare dependency may involve a 'learned helplessness' and a retreat from political and public life. By the same token, Habermas claims that social marginalisation expresses a "particular clientalisation of the citizen role" (1992, p 11).

This chapter analyses the relationship between the citizens' social rights and political participation among unemployed young people. There are different welfare regimes for unemployed youth in different countries. The question is whether and how different welfare arrangements are related to political orientation and participation among unemployed youth. To answer these questions, we shall use data from a comparative survey of unemployed youth conducted in Scotland and in the five Nordic countries from 1996 to 1998.

Throughout the European Union (EU), rates of unemployment among young people tend to be higher than among the general population and there is a serious risk of marginalisation and exclusion (European Commission, 1994). In 1998, the rate of youth unemployment within the EU was around 20%, more than twice the rate experienced by adults (9%). In other words, about 40% of the unemployed were less than 25 years old, although this age group comprises only 20% of the total labour force. This increase in youth unemployment has occurred despite a demographic decrease in youth and an increased level of education participation within most member states. The EU countries have eight million young unemployed people, and 50% of them are long-term unemployed – unemployed for more than one year (OECD, 1998). Different countries have handled these problems in different ways, both regarding labour market measures and welfare policy. An interesting question is what type of consequences different welfare arrangements have for unemployed young people and their citizenship. It has been shown, on the basis of Euro-barometer data, that young unemployed people across Europe show more distrust towards the political system than young people in employment (Bay and Blekesaune, 2001). This distrust is especially high among unemployed youth in Britain and particularly low in Scandinavia. A reasonable explanation could be the different welfare policy directed at the young unemployed in the different countries. Unemployment benefits have been withdrawn from young people below 18 years in Britain. This is important since about 30% of the cohort leave education at 16 years of age. The New Deal programme implies that all young people must be in training or education to receive benefits. The ideal of 'workfare' (work for welfare) has been implemented in Britain as in most West European countries during the last decade (Lødemel, 1997). British researchers have questioned the withdrawal of benefits for young unemployed people as a withdrawal of citizenship rights (MacDonald, 1997).

According to Marshall's argument, social rights should be a condition for active political participation. As the Scandinavian countries have the most generous welfare arrangements, we should expect a higher political activity among unemployed youth in these countries than in countries with more residual welfare arrangements, such as Britain. In Britain, the unemployed youth receive Jobseekers' Allowance – a flat-rate benefit that is rather low compared to the level of benefits in the Scandinavian countries. They are not entitled to any other support except housing benefits, if they are not living with their parents.

In contrast, young unemployed people in Scandinavia who have previous work experience, receive unemployment benefits that typically cover from 60-90% of their previous income. Those among unemployed youth who do not have any work experience are entitled to social assistance, which is much lower. Social assistance is means-tested and not related to previous income.

In all the Nordic countries, there has been an increase in social assistance recipients during the last decade (Eardley et al, 1996a). Young people below the age of 25 constitute the highest proportion of recipients. Growing unemployment and, to a lesser extent, the growth of lone parenthood, are probably key factors explaining this increase, the majority of recipients being single males and lone parents (females) (Eardley et al, 1996b). The levels of social assistance benefits in the various Nordic countries are about the same (Carle and Julkunen, 1998), and rather generous compared with other OECD countries.

The level of support from social assistance in Scandinavia is about the same as received by those on Jobseekers' Allowance in Britain. According to Marshall's argument we would expect a higher political participation among those in Scandinavia who are entitled to unemployment benefits, and a lower level of activity among those who receive only social assistance that is residual in all Scandinavian countries. We would also expect a lower level of political activity among Scottish young unemployed people in general compared to the other countries. However, according to those who criticise Marshall's argument it could be the other way around. Generous welfare provision may create welfare dependency, which may be associated with political passivity and alienation.

Previous findings

Comparative research on social assistance in the Nordic countries has documented differences between the countries, both regarding social security systems (Bradshaw and Terum, 1997) and long-term social assistance clients (Fridberg, 1993). However, research from our study based on the same comparative data as we use in this chapter concludes that young unemployed social assistance recipients differ from other unemployed youth in much the same way across the Nordic countries. They had longer periods of unemployment, more financial hardship, more health problems, felt more isolated, had lower work involvement and more problems in coping with unemployment. They also had a lower probability of re-entering employment compared with other unemployed youth (Hammer, 2001). In other words, the social assistance clients were more socially marginalised and more marginalised with regard to labour market participation. It seems reasonable to assume that social assistance clients may be more politically marginalised than other unemployed youth. Previous findings show that young long-term unemployed people had a lower political participation than those experiencing shorter periods of unemployment (Carle, 2000). They also show that social assistance clients were unemployed for longer periods than other unemployed youth. The social assistance clients also had a lower level of education compared with other unemployed young people. We know that all types of political activity increase with the years of schooling (Togeby, 1989), and this was also the case in our study across countries (Carle and Julkunen, 1998).

When we study political participation it is important to differentiate between regular and irregular channels. Participation such as voting in elections and participation in trade unions or political parties can be characterised as regular activities, while activities such as participation in demonstrations, boycotts, wildcat strikes, occupation of empty buildings or signing petitions are examples of irregular political activities. Previous research from the Nordic countries has shown that the level of irregular activities is higher among young people than older and slightly higher among women than men (Togeby, 1989).

In accordance with previous research we will expect lower levels of political participation in all types of political activity among unemployed social assistance clients compared with unemployed youth who receive more generous unemployment benefits across countries. The next question is whether such political marginalisation expresses alienation or opposition. Alienation would imply a mistrust of political authorities and could be expressed by active objections to participate in regular political activity such as voting in elections and probably less interest in politics. On the other hand, political opposition could be expressed through participation in irregular political activity and objections to regular political participation. If unemployed social assistance clients are more politically marginalised, another interesting question is whether there is a basis for political mobilisation in this group. What type of attitudes do they have towards regular and irregular political activity? What are their political orientations? Are they concentrated on the Left- or Right-wing politics, or are there tendencies towards political polarisation?

The other important question is whether there are different levels of political activity and different political orientations in different countries that can be related to different welfare regimes.

The data set

The surveys in our study of unemployed youth carried out in 1996 to 1998 were initially based on postal questionnaires with additional strategies used to minimise bias due to skewed response rates. Those who failed to respond to the initial questionnaire after having been sent a reminder, we interviewed by telephone. These measures were necessary in a study of unemployment and exclusion, since young people without work have been found to be less likely to respond (Dodds et al, 1989). National register data from the unemployment register has been coupled to the surveys enabling us to analyse attrition as well as the reliability and validity of the survey data.

In Sweden, the sample consisted of 3,998 young people (18- to 24-year-olds) with a response rate of 63%; in Finland, 2,386 with 73% response rate; Iceland, 2,280 with 60%; Denmark, 1,540 with 76%; Norway, 2,000 with a response rate of 56%; Scotland 1,500 with 55% response rate. Attrition analyses based on registration data in Norway showed no skewed attrition based on information about education level, duration of unemployment, work experience, proportion without relevant work experience or education, proportion receiving unemployment benefits, age, gender and county. In Sweden, register data showed no biased attrition. In the other countries permission was not given to couple the survey to register data. However, country specific attrition analyses have found the data to be representative. The Nordic report from the project gives a detailed analysis of each country (Carle and Julkunen, 1998). Measurements and indices used in this chapter can be found in the Appendix.

Results

If we first look at participation in irregular and regular political actions among social assistance recipients, we find the same results across countries (in Scotland, we have used as the social assistance cohort those who have received housing benefits). Surprisingly, in all countries the social assistance clients report a higher level of irregular political activities but a lower level of regular activity than other unemployed youth. Table 7.1 presents mean values of the index for irregular and regular political participation by country.

Table 7.1 shows that social assistance clients participate in more irregular political activity than other unemployed youth[1]. The tendency is the same in all countries, but only significant in Finland and Scotland. The total across all countries shows that this is significant. As previously discussed, we would have expected a lower level of political activity, because we know from previous research that social assistance clients experience longer periods of unemployment and possess a lower level of education, factors that are clearly correlated with a low level of activity. However, with regard to regular political activity the tendency is more in line with what we expected with a lower level of activity among the social assistance clients, but only significant in Finland and Sweden. We know from previous research that females have a higher level of activity in irregular political actions. We found the same results here across countries. However, when we look at the activity level of social assistance clients, the pattern is the same for both genders.

If we run the same analysis for those receiving unemployment benefits

Table 7.1: Irregular and regular political activity by receiving social assistance or not, by country

		n	Irregular activity (mean)	Regular activity (mean)
Finland	Receiving social assistance	340	0.15	0.30
	Not receiving	1,347	0.12**	0.32*
Iceland	Receiving social assistance	100	0.22	0.41
	Not receiving	1,151	0.21	0.44
Norway	Receiving social assistance	200	0.22	0.35
	Not receiving	882	0.20	0.39
Sweden	Receiving social assistance	349	0.23	0.36
	Not receiving	1,948	0.22	0.39*
Denmark	Receiving social assistance[†]	10	0.24	0.40
	Not receiving	1,127	0.20	0.40
Scotland	Receiving housing benefit	105	0.29	0.28
	Not receiving	690	0.21***	0.26
Total	Receiving social assistance	1,566	0.21	0.33
	Not receiving	6,680	0.19***	0.39***

* $p<0.05$

** $p<0.01$

*** $p<0.001$

[†]The small number of social assistance clients is caused by the biased sampling in Denmark

compared with other unemployed youth across countries, we do not find any differences at all between the groups.

If we look at the general level of activity across countries we do not find significant differences. The only exception is the level of irregular political activity in Finland, which is clearly lower than in the other countries. However, this difference is not due to different welfare arrangements or unemployment among youth in Finland. Previous research has found that the level of this type of political activity is lower in Finland among young people in the general population compared with the other Nordic countries (Togeby, 1989).

Table 7.1 shows that social assistance clients (and in Scotland those who receive housing benefit) have a higher irregular political activity and a lower regular political activity than other unemployed youth across countries. However, this could be explained by the fact that these clients are older and more of them have left their parents and live alone compared with other unemployed youth. It is possible that political activity increases with age and independence. If we run regression analysis with political activity as a dependent variable, we find that the effect of receiving social assistance or housing benefit remains significant even when taking age, gender and living alone or not into account.

The higher level of participation in more irregular political actions could be explained by left-wing radical political orientation among the social assistance clients. Table 7.2 shows the proportion who claim they are not interested in politics along with mean values on a Left–Right scale by country (range 1 to 5). We have also here differentiated between social assistance clients and other unemployed youth. Denmark has been excluded in all further analysis because of a very small number of social assistance clients.

Table 7.2 shows that social assistance clients tend to have a more Left-wing political orientation in all countries, but only significantly so in Finland, Sweden and Scotland. More of them also state that they are not interested in politics or have no political opinion, but this is only significant in Finland, Norway and Sweden. This picture is interesting since we have shown in the previous table that social assistance clients have a higher level of irregular political activity. There seems to be a polarisation. On the one hand, they are less interested in politics, but those who have a Left-wing orientation have a higher level of activity than other unemployed youth. This activity level is only high with regard to irregular political actions; with regular politics, it is the other way around. The picture is not of alienated unemployed youth, but rather political opposition. Could this type of opposition reflect a mistrust in the political

Table 7.2: Political orientation (Left–Right position on scale from 1 (Left) to 5 (Right) and interest among social assistance clients and other unemployed youth by country[†]

| | | Left–right scale | | |
		n	Mean	% with no interest
Finland	Receiving social assistance	121	3.0	64
	Not receiving	588	3.3**	55**
Iceland	Receiving social assistance	53	2.9	45
	Not receiving	685	3.1	40
Norway	Receiving social assistance	106	3.0	45
	Not receiving	577	3.1	33***
Sweden	Receiving social assistance	216	2.5	36
	Not receiving	1,325	2.8**	29**
Scotland	Receiving housing benefit	62	2.3	49
	Not receiving	313	2.6*	53

* $p<0.05$

** $p<0.01$

*** $p<0.001$

[†] The respondents were asked to place themselves on a scale from left to right; alternatively, they could tick a box stating 'no interest in politics'

system and a clear reluctance to participate in actions through established political channels? Table 7.3 shows the index for those who could not imagine that they would participate in regular political actions by country.

There is a tendency for social assistance clients to have negative attitudes towards more regular channels of politics. If we look at irregular political activity, it is again the other way around; as expected, they are less negative to such activity in all countries. Those who are negative to such actions have a more right-wing political orientation.

The next question is whether those social assistance clients who claim they are not interested in politics are also negative to political activity in general. Are these people who could be mobilised politically or is their political passivity an expression of mistrust and alienation?

Table 7.4 shows that even among those who say that they are not interested in politics, young social assistance clients are more positive towards irregular political actions than other unemployed youth ($F = 30.1$, $DF = 1$, $p<0.001$). If we look at those who had received housing benefit, the picture is just the same in Scotland.

Previous research on social movements, which focuses on irregular or regular political actions, has tried to explain such actions by two types of hypotheses or theories. According to the mobilisation theory, groups

Table 7.3: Participation in regular political actions among social assistance clients and other unemployed youth in all countries (*n*=8,296) (%)

	Reluctant to do		Have already done	
	Social assistance clients	Others	Social assistance clients	Others
Vote in elections	9.2	5.2***	75	80***
Attend political meetings	52	52	9	11
Attend union meetings	35	30***	9	15***
Attend other organisation meetings	32	28*	14	17***

Table 7.4: Types of political action that appeal to those young unemployed people who claim to have no interest in politics, all countries (mean values)

	Irregular activity	Regular activity
Receiving social assistance (*n*=758)	0.38	0.31
Not receiving (*n*=2,581)	0.33***	0.29

*** p<0.001

who participate in such irregular actions are those who oppose the regular political democracy or who feel that their interests are not represented through regular political channels (the politically poor) (Olsen and Sætren, 1980). However, empirical research seems to support the other theory, that irregular political actions are primarily used by those who are also active in regular politics. They are not 'politically poor', but rather young people with individual recourses, political knowledge and high education (Olsen and Sætren, 1980; Togeby, 1989). However, the findings presented here seem to support the mobilisation theory. Social assistance clients have low education, long-term unemployment, poor mental health and financial problems, and still have a higher irregular political activity than other unemployed youth. Another explanation could be that young unemployed social assistance clients are more strongly integrated in youth cultures characterised by political opposition to regular democracy and a higher political engagement in irregular political actions. Social assistance clients have a marginal position both socially, economically and with regard to the labour market in all of the Nordic countries.

Table 7.5 shows the relationship between regular and irregular political activities among social assistance clients and other unemployed youth, when gender, age, education, financial problems and duration of previous unemployment are taken into account. The table shows a strong relationship between regular and irregular political activity both among social assistance clients and other unemployed youth, revealing similar results for both groups and across countries.

As shown in Table 7.5, those who are active in irregular political actions also tend to be more active in regular political action; the picture is the same both among social assistance clients and other unemployed youth. The next question is whether those who receive social assistance have a higher level of irregular political activity when we control for their participation in regular political activity.

To be female, have higher education and financial problems also has a positive effect on the propensity to participate in irregular political activity. Further analysis shows that even when such factors are controlled for, social assistance clients have a significantly higher irregular political activity than other unemployed youth. However, it is those with a left-wing political orientation in particular who have a high level of activity. Those among the social assistance recipients who have a right-wing orientation

Table 7.5: Ordinary least square regression: the relationship between regular and irregular political activities among social assistance clients and other unemployed youth controlled for gender, age, education and marginalisation (dependent variable: index irregular political activity)

	Social assistance clients		Others	
	Beta	**SE**	**Beta**	**SE**
Female	0.08	0.01**	0.08	0.01***
Age	0.03	0.003	−0.04	0.001**
Education	0.15	0.01***	0.09	0.002***
Unemployment experience (months)	−0.04	0.000	−0.02	0.000
Financial problems	0.08	0.02**	0.07	0.01***
Regular political activity	0.42	0.03***	0.41	0.01***
Constant	0.03		0.01	
R square	0.23		0.20	

Beta: standardised regression coefficients; SE: standard error

** p<0.01

*** p<0.001

have a lower level of activity than other unemployed youth. Table 7.6 shows that this is the case when also controlled for social background, financial problems, regular political activity and duration of unemployment. Social assistance recipients have a higher irregular political activity. However, there is an interaction effect showing that those among the social clients who have a right-wing political orientation have a lower activity than other unemployed youth. The table also shows that whether unemployed youth are entitled to unemployment benefits or not has no significant effect.

Interestingly, the duration of unemployment has no significant effect on political participation. A Swedish study found a curvilinear relationship between duration of unemployment and political participation (Alm,

Table 7.6: OLS regression: the impact of receiving social assistance and unemployment benefits on irregular political activity (dependent variable: index irregular political activity; pooled sample, *n*=8,002)

	Beta	SE
Female	0.06***	0.004
Age	–0.04**	0.001
Education	0.11***	0.002
Unemployment experience (months)	–0.01	0.000
Financial problems	0.05***	0.008
Regular political activity	0.39***	0.008
Social assistance receipt	0.12***	0.009
Unemployment benefits	0.000	0.004
Living alone	0.02	0.005
Political opinion	–0.10***	0.002
Social assistance*political opinion	–0.08***	0.006
Iceland	0.12***	0.007
Norway	0.09***	0.007
Sweden	0.14***	0.006
Denmark	0.04**	0.007
Scotland	0.15***	0.008
Constant		0.13
R square	0.24	

Note: Reference group = Finland

** *p*<0.01

*** *p*<0.001

1998). However, this study did not differentiate between regular and irregular political activity. The time spent in unemployment was measured within one year, implying censoring of the data on unemployment duration. The long-term unemployed may react differently.

Previous results from our study have found that political participation tends to decrease with the duration of long-term unemployment (Carle and Julkunen, 1998).

As expected, the strong association between regular and irregular political activity remains the same, even controlled for different welfare arrangements for unemployed youth such as those receiving unemployment benefits or social assistance.

Discussion

Previous research has found that unemployment is related to political marginalisation.

Bynner and Ashford (1994) found that unemployed youth were less interested in politics and were less likely to vote in elections compared with youth in employment. Data based on the Euro-barometer surveys show that unemployed youth have less trust in the political system (Bay and Blekesaune, 2001). These findings have also been confirmed by studies carried out on the UK. In a study of 1,294 17- to 18-year-olds, Banks and Ullah (1987) found that unemployed youth were more politically disaffected than those in employment. Bynner and Ashton (1994) found similar results. However, these studies are restricted to the UK. In the comparative study based on all EU countries, Bay and Blekesaune (2001) found that such differences between unemployed youth and those in employment were especially strong in the UK compared with other European countries. That unemployment goes hand in hand with mistrust in the political system is to be expected. The important question is whether there is a basis for political mobilisation of this group. Research seems to indicate that this is not the case among unemployed youth. In countries with very high youth unemployment, such as Southern Europe, unemployed youth reported no more interest in politics than those in employment, compared with countries with a lower youth unemployment rate (Bay and Blekesaune, 2001). However, unemployed youth in Europe have a stronger left-wing orientation compared with employed youth (Bay and Blekesaune, 2001).

In our comparative study, we have focused on different groups of unemployed youth and whether their political marginalisation may be related to financial marginalisation. As discussed in the introduction, there are different theoretical arguments with regard to the relationship between different welfare models and political participation or marginalisation. On the one hand, Marshall argues that a generous welfare state ensures that all citizens may participate politically on the same level. This view can also be supported by those who argue that the lower level of political activity among unemployed youth compared with those in employment may be related to social and financial marginalisation. Employment has in itself important integrative functions in our society and being unemployed may also be related to social marginalisation, which is clearly associated with economic hardship (Hammer, 2000).

On the other hand, others argue that generous welfare provision may imply political marginalisation and a clientalisation of the citizen role. Esping-Andersen (1993) claims that a new social class of clients appears to develop, provided by public transfer. Habermas takes this argument further and describes the client's role as passive and private, implying that this group has less political participation than others (Habermas, 1992).

In our study, we have tested these different arguments empirically by analysing political participation among unemployed youth. Unfortunately, we can so far only compare two different welfare regimes, those of Scandinavia and Britain. We have looked at different welfare arrangements in these countries, analysing the political participation among the unemployed youth in Scandinavia, who are entitled to generous unemployment benefits, and comparing this with those receiving the flat-rate Jobseekers' Allowance in Scotland. The results show that the unemployed youth in Scandinavia do not have a higher level of political participation than those in Scotland who received a much lower level of support. In each country there are also no differences in political participation between those who received unemployment benefits and those who did not.

The results do not support any relationship between political and financial marginalisation. We would have expected that those who received benefits in countries with a generous compensation level would have a higher political participation.

The other argument, that welfare dependency may be related to political withdrawal and passivity, had some support in the data. Social assistance clients in all of the Nordic countries as well as those receiving housing benefits in Scotland, reported less interest in politics, less political participation through regular political channels and a higher reluctance to participate. However, social assistance recipients had a higher participation in irregular political activity if they had a left-wing political orientation, compared with other unemployed youth across countries.

Generally, social assistance clients reported a stronger left-wing orientation than other unemployed youth. These results are interesting, since a lot of research of political marginalisation would indicate otherwise. Previous research has documented that both irregular and regular political activity is higher among young people with higher education and experiencing a shorter period of unemployment. Since social assistance clients in all of the countries have lower education, a higher rate of school drop-out and longer duration of unemployment than other unemployed youth, we would have expected different results. However, social assistance clients also reported a higher degree of financial hardship than other unemployed youth, which probably mobilises this group politically. Those who reported financial problems had a significantly higher participation in irregular political activities than other unemployed youth. The lower participation in regular political activity among social assistance recipients combined with a higher participation through irregular political channels also indicate political opposition and a distrust in the formal political system.

In conclusion, different welfare models and protection systems in different countries were not related to the level of political participation among unemployed youth. However, we did find evidence of a relationship between welfare dependency and political disinterest and passivity. Contrary to expectations, we found higher political activity in groups dependent on welfare who had a Left-wing political orientation, but such activity had different channels than via the formal political system.

Acknowledgements

The study has been funded by The Nordic Council of Ministers, The EU's Fourth Framework Programme on Targeted Socio-Economic Research and the European Commission's Youth Research Programme 'Youth for Europe'. It is part of a broader comparative study: 'Youth unemployment and marginalisation processes on the Northern European periphery' and 'Youth unemployment and social exclusion in Europe', coordinated by the author.

The Norwegian Research Council has provided national funding. Visit the project homepage on the Internet at http://www.isaf.no/nova/fou/ Hammer/Unemployment.htm

Notes

[1] The distributions across the group are the same in Table 7.1. In other words, it is not a small active group that causes the different level of political activity.

References

Alm, S. (1998) 'Arbetsløshet en demokratifråga? Om arbetsløshet och politisk deltagande', in J. Palme and S.Å. Stenberg (eds) *Arbetsløshet och Velferd*,Velferdsprosjektet Report No 11, Stockholm, pp 193-216.

Banks, M.H and Ullah, P. (1987) 'Political attitudes and voting among unemployed and employed youth', *Journal of Adolescence*, no 10, pp 201-16.

Bay, A.H and Blekesaune, M. (2001) 'Youth, unemployment and political marginalisation', *International Journal of Social Welfare*, in press.

Bradshaw, J. and Terum, L.I. (1997) 'How Nordic is the Nordic model? Social assistance in a comparative perspective', *Scandinavian Journal of Social Welfare*, no 6, pp 1-10.

Bynner, J. and Ashford, S. (1994) 'Politics and participation: some antecedents of young people's attitudes to the political system and political activity', *European Journal of Social Psychology*, no 24, pp 223-36.

Carle, J. (2000) 'Political activity in the context of youth unemployment. Experiences from young people in six Northern European countries', *Nordic Journal of Youth Research*, vol 8, no 7, pp 16-39.

Carle, J. and Julkunen, I. (eds) (1998) 'Unemployed youth in Scandinavia: a comparative perspective', *Nord*, no 14, Copenhagen: The Nordic Council of Ministers.

Dodds, S., Furlong, A. and Croxford, L. (1989) 'Quality and quantity: tackling non-contact attrition in a longitudinal survey', *Sociology*, vol 23, no 2, pp 275-84.

Eardley, T., Bradshaw, J., Ditch, J., Gough, I. and Whiteford, P. (1996a) *Social assistance in OECD countries: Synthesis report*, Department of Social Security Research Report No 46, London/Paris: HMSO/OECD.

Eardley, T., Bradshaw, J., Ditch, J., Gough, I. and Whiteford, P. (1996b) *Social assistance in OECD countries: Country reports*, Department of Social Security Research Report No 46, London/Paris: HMSO/OECD.

Esping-Andersen, G. (1990) *The three worlds of welfare capitalism*, Cambridge: Polity Press.

Esping-Andersen, G. (ed) (1993) *Changing classes: Stratification and mobility in post-industrial societies*, London: Sage Publications.

European Commission (1994) *European social policy*, White Paper, COM(94) 333, 27 July.

Fridberg, T. (eds) (1993) *On social assistance in the Nordic capitals*, København: Nordisk Ministerråd.

Habermas, J. (1992) 'Citizenship and national identity: some reflections on the future of Europe', *Praxis International*, vol 12, no 1, pp 1-19.

Hammer, T. (2000) 'Mental health and social exclusion among unemployed youth in Scandinavia: a comparative study', *International Journal of Social Welfare*, no 9, pp 53-63.

Hammer, T. (2001) ' Unge arbeidsledige sosialklienter i de nordiske land', *Tidsskrift for Velferdsforskning*, vol 7, no 2, pp 120-34.

Kymlicka, W. and Norman, W. (1994) 'Return of the citizen. a survey of recent work on citizenship theory', *Ethics*, no 104, January, pp 352-81.

Lødemel, I. (1997) *Pisken i arbeidslinja. Om iverksetjing av arbeid for sosialhjelp*, FAFO Rapport No 226, Oslo: Fafo Institute for Applied Social Science.

MacDonald, R. (1997) *Youth, the 'underclass' and social exclusion*, London: Routledge.

Marshall, T.H. and Bottomore, T. (1992) *Citizenship and social class*, London: Pluto Press.

Murray, C.A. et al (1990) *The emerging British underclass*, London: IEA Health and Welfare Unit.

OECD (1998) *Employment outlook*, Paris: OECD.

Olsen, J.P. and Sætren, H. (1980) *Aksjoner og demokrati*, Bergen: Universitetsforaget.

Togeby, L. (1989) *Ens og Forskellig. Gresrodeltagelse i Norden*, Århus: Politica.

Appendix: Measurements and indices

The measurements and indices used in this chapter are as follows.

Economic difficulties during the previous year, indexed from 11 items

- During the last 12 months, which of the following have you had to give up due to lack of money:
  - warm meals
  - essential clothes for yourself or your family
  - paying rent and bills on time
  - visiting the cinema, theatre or concerts
  - inviting friends to your home
  - visiting relatives or friends living in other towns
  - buying birthday or Christmas presents
  - holidays away
  - newspapers
  - hobbies or other recreational activities
  - visiting pubs or restaurants.

Scored from often (1) to never (3), the index is coded as a dummy for each question: often=1, range 0 to 11, Cronbach alpha=0.85, mean=2.4, standard deviation=2.7.

Number of years of education, continuous variable

Age, year of birth, continuous variable

Job-seeking strategy, indexed from six items

- Thinking about your current or last period of unemployment, can you indicate which methods you used to try to find a job:
  - replied to advertisements
  - through an employment agency
  - contacted employers yourself
  - through friends
  - through family
  - looked at advertisements in the newspapers.

Scored yes=1, no=0, range 0 to 6, Cronbach alpha=0.57.

Unemployment duration, measured as total months of unemployment ever

Financial support during the last year, measured by dummy variables

- supported by parent
- supported by a partner
- received social assistance
- received housing benefits
- received unemployment benefits
- jobs in the grey economy.

Political actions, measured by involvement in several pre-specified political actions on three levels

- had actually engaged in a stated political action
- could be willing to carry out a stated action
- could absolutely not imagine carrying out a stated action.

The following actions are divided into regular and irregular political actions:

- Irregular political activities:
  - signing a petition
  - taking part in boycotts
  - taking part in legal demonstrations
  - taking part in wildcat/illegal strikes
  - occupying buildings or factories
  - wearing a badge to show support for a cause

- Regular political activities:
  - voting in elections
  - attending meetings organised by a political party
  - attending meetings organised by the trade union
  - attending meetings organised by other organisations.

We have constructed one additive index of irregular actions and one index for regular political actions, both range 0 to 1.

Political interest, measured by dummy variable yes/no

Political orientation, measured by a five-point scale from Left- to Right-wing sympathy

Political attitudes, measured by seven statements (items) on a five-point scale

Do you strongly agree (1) to strongly disagree (5) with the statement 'What kind of society do you think we should be working towards?':

- a society with more private enterprises and a market economy
- a society that takes care of the environment even if this implies lower economic growth
- a society that utilises advanced technology, such as computers and robots
- a society of law and order
- a society of equality with small income differentials
- a society of equality between men and women
- a society of equality between ethnic groups.

EIGHT

Ethnicity, racism and the labour market: a European perspective

Gary Craig[1]

What difficulties face people entering the labour market, seen from the particular perspective of ethnicity? This chapter will examine the experience of those – including younger people of labour market age – who enter the European Union (EU) and associated states from outside the EU, and are typically identifiable by skin colour, culture and first language distinct from that of the majority 'host' population[2].

Given the many differing national legislative, socioeconomic and political contexts that will be covered here, it is necessary to define certain key concepts. The term 'ethnicity' is used to denote the primary ethnic origin of people – defined in terms of ancestry, culture and language (Fenton, 1999) – regardless of their status as legal citizens (or not) of particular nation states. We also refer to 'ethnic minority' or 'minority ethnic group' to mean people – a numerical minority – of different ethnicity from the host country. These are referred to in differing national literatures as 'foreigners' or 'immigrants' and we borrow these terms without any pejorative connotations – although to use the term 'immigrant' for someone who may have been settled for 30 years or more is misleading. The term 'ethnic minority' is also used in some countries to refer to small indigenous minorities.

The chapter begins with general remarks about the demographic characteristics and origins of ethnic minorities in a sample of European countries. This is followed by a review of the ethnicity data publicly available in these countries, grouped roughly into those of greater and smaller minority populations. Although this sample is not strictly representative – given it is the data that were less difficult to obtain within a limited time-scale – there seems no reason to believe that the conclusions drawn from this review are not equally apposite to those countries not represented here. Some concluding comments highlight general policy issues and gaps in our knowledge.

Unfortunately, the quality and comparability of current data on ethnicity from differing countries is highly variable – although universally poor – making international comparisons fragile. The editors comment in their introduction that "solid knowledge about labour market change, its interrelationship with welfare policies and, in particular, its joint impact on citizenship appear quite rudimentary and fragmented". The increasingly politically and socially sensitive dimension of 'race' and ethnicity, and the rapid growth in the numbers of refugees and asylum-seekers, a result of conflicts on the margins of Europe, makes accurate data even more difficult to obtain.

Consequently, this chapter raises more questions than answers, pointing to the need for much greater – and more culturally sensitive – research and policy debates and interventions in relation to ethnicity and the labour market. Much of the discussion is concerned with general issues of labour market access for minority ethnic groups, although specific data is alluded to in relation to the experience of young people.

Citizenship and settlement patterns

The minority ethnic composition of each European state has developed as a result of differing combinations of elements. Many countries have significant indigenous ethnic minorities such as the Saami of Northern Scandinavia, the Roma of East and Central Europe, and the Basque of Northern Spain and Southern France; most of these minorities appear to experience discrimination and victimisation no less than immigrant minorities. However, immigration of comparatively contemporary types is the route by which most minorities have become established. This has been shaped by a number of factors, the most obvious of which is the imperial or colonial history of the state. The following nation states have each experienced substantial recent immigration from former colonies: the UK (from Bangladesh, Pakistan, India, Sri Lanka, Hong Kong, much of sub-Saharan Africa, Malaysia, Singapore and most of the Caribbean); the Netherlands (Netherlands Antilles, Surinam and Indonesia); Belgium (Kinshasa, Rwanda and Burundi); France (West, Central and North Africa, Guyana and SE Asia); Portugal (Angola, Guinea Bissau and Mozambique) and, to a lesser extent, Italy, Spain and Germany.

Some of this immigration was facilitated initially by notions of shared citizenship, but much was promoted for economic reasons. Labour shortages after the Second World War, in particular in poorly-paid sectors of reconstructing European economies, led to significant immigration from former colonies. Many of these colonies were very poor relative to the former imperial powers; there were strong 'push' factors at work as well. As demand for this type of labour weakened, and domestic political pressure, often stirred up by racist formulations, strengthened to halt or reduce immigration, this immigration slowed considerably and was increasingly limited to allowing wives and children of those already resident in the 'host country' to enter[3]. In some countries, such as the UK and France, there were attempts – resisted politically from the left – to seek the repatriation of even legal immigrants as western economies came under pressure from the 1970s OPEC 'oil shocks' (Weill, 1997). Many commentators have argued that the increasingly restrictive immigration policy developed by these and other countries has itself contributed to racism (discrimination against people of differing ethnicities on either an individual or a systematic basis) and racial violence.

However, demand for labour was not met solely by supply from former colonies. In many cases, labour was supplied predominantly from countries that were either physically close by (for example, migration from the former Yugoslavia and Turkey into Austria), or that had, by western European standards, underdeveloped economies and low wage structures. The migration of Greek and Turkish men to relatively well-paying German car factories was typical of this phenomenon. As some of these formerly 'underdeveloped' economies have themselves 'developed', they have in turn become 'receiving' as opposed to (or as well as) 'sending' countries: thus Italy, in the period after the war, lost many of its young men to more northern European labour markets but, in recent years, has gained men from North Africa (Tunisia and Libya) and women from Latin America. Italy admits between 50,000 to 80,000 immigrants each year, most Latin American immigrants primarily being women employed as domestic workers and North African immigrants being men self-employed or as construction workers[4]. In some countries, former emigrants have returned to their country of origin. In EU member states with a substantial foreign population, two thirds (or more in some cases) come from (mainly) the former Yugoslavia, Turkey, East and Central Europe. The UK and France are notable exceptions to this pattern, for historical reasons.

Some EU countries, such as Greece, Spain, Italy, Portugal and Finland, have very small ethnic minority populations. However, ironically, Jean-Pierre Chevenement, the former French Interior Minister (*The Guardian*, 29 March 2000), and others have argued that Western European countries may need to *increase* immigration to cope with the effects of demographic change. The UN Population Division estimates that the population of the 15 EU countries and those bidding for membership would fall by about 15% to 628 million in the next 50 years leaving a labour deficit in many areas of the labour market. The UK is considering relaxing immigration controls to permit entry of skilled professionals to certain identified professions where there are labour shortfalls.

However, given the structural position of most immigrants in local labour markets and despite particular local features (for example, Germany arguing for the immigration of 20,000 IT specialists from India, and Ireland requiring up to 200,000 skilled workers to meet booming labour demand during the next seven years) it is highly probable that the great proportion of these immigrating workers will find employment in less-skilled, low-paid and insecure sectors of these economies.

A final important phenomenon has been the recent growth in numbers of refugees and asylum-seekers seeking political sanctuary in European states from the civil wars and violence that have characterised several parts of Africa, Asia and the eastern margins of Europe itself. The flow of refugees to particular national destinations may in part have been shaped by notions of the responsibility of former colonies, but appears also to be influenced by opportunity, by the perceived 'generosity' of the host's national regime towards immigrants, and by the refugees' (and their 'brokers' – the criminal syndicates that have developed to facilitate illegal immigration, often under appalling and murderous conditions) sense of the ease in which differing countries may be entered. This responsiveness may be perceived in differing ways.

The British and German right-wing media portray their countries as relatively easy for refugees to enter and, once there, relatively easy in which to remain (either because of lax national rules – or tacit acceptance into citizenship – or the ease with which people can 'disappear' from official surveillance). Alternatively, some, particularly the Scandinavian countries, are seen as having been politically and economically more generous in their attitudes to refugees in the past. These states have fairly diverse minority populations with little past connection with the countries in question and thus no historical citizenship obligations.

Local attitudes towards the civil, political and social citizenship rights of minority ethnic groups – and their specific rights within the labour market – are shaped by a combination of these factors, most of all by the history of the establishment of these populations, their past connection with the host country, their size relative to the 'host' population and the manner of their arrival, as much as by any formal legal status they have. Their legal status depends on local political culture, whether it has a multicultural approach, as in the UK or the Netherlands, or is what Heckmann (1999) describes as a "culturally unifying, universal model", as is the case in republican France. While formal civil and political rights for minorities – such as the right to vote – are relatively uniform across the EU, within labour market mechanisms, discrimination and racism are much more apparent, and are a result of the complex interplay of local factors. In a period of increasing globalisation of economic activity, of communication and of political responses, it is true also that local responses are increasingly shaped by global trends, of which increasing racism is the most dismal, as Wallace et al (2000) note in relation to the impact of global electronic communication on young people.

Economic recession across the EU during the last 10 years has led to growing calls for controls on immigration and for repatriation of existing 'foreigners'. This has lent support to xenophobic campaigns in populist media and to racist violence against religious, ethnic and cultural minorities in countries that between them have very different cultures and histories of immigration. These include the UK (MacPherson, 1999), Finland (Virtanen, 1998), France, the Netherlands, Greece (ECRI, 2000b), Hungary and Germany. The growth of racist violence makes the position of immigrants even more precarious both in relation to the labour market, because minority ethnic groups tend to occupy jobs within the service sector which make them more physically exposed, and outside the labour market, because of difficulties of accessing social protection systems.

Data and data problems

The information on which this chapter draws is based on three main sources:

• country correspondents identified through networking
• (limited) data from transnational organisations such as the International Labour Office and the Organisation for Economic Cooperation and Development
• material provided by individual academics and officials.

Three general observations can be made at this point.

The first is that there are significant differences between national jurisdictions, because of culture and history, in the way in which the issue of ethnicity is treated in labour market policy formulation. In the UK, for example, there is growing pressure to identify members of minority ethnic groups through, for example, ethnic monitoring of administrative records (rarely done at present), underpinned by more sophisticated counts through the decennial censes, to show the extent to which minority groups are the subject of discrimination. Currently, large-scale surveys to establish discrimination within the labour market are severely hampered by the lack of adequate data, a problem in all states but particularly acute within some.

A second, related, point is that the effectiveness of statistical recordkeeping regarding ethnicity – even where statistics are collected – is at best inadequate and in many areas, quite abysmal. This is one aspect of what has come to be known in the UK, since the violent death of the black youth Steven Lawrence and the subsequent official enquiry into his murder, as 'institutional racism' (MacPherson, 1999). The consequence of these two problems is that comparative work in this area is extraordinarily difficult: it will not properly be possible until national jurisdictions (perhaps supported by directives from the EU[5]) develop effective administrative recordkeeping. Records are also inadequate in the sense that, in most countries, data that is kept usually refers to minorities resident legally within those jurisdictions (but may not differentiate between immigrants and indigenous minorities). However, in some states (Greece is one example), there are thought to be more illegal immigrants than there are legal ones. In many countries there are both legal and illegal immigrants in significant numbers who are not recorded in any administrative data. The 'young disaffected' feature particularly strongly among this group (Chatrik et al, 2000). As a result, this can only be a sketchy discussion of what should become a very significant policy issue for the EU – and more widely – the removal of racial discrimination within labour market structures and practices[6].

Thirdly, the source of more reliable data varies widely between differing countries; the perspectives and structural position of writers differs widely, as do the particular interests that they were pursuing and the questions that sources have taken for granted when analysing the issue. One key research and policy task is for the compilation and analysis of data to be aligned across Europe. The brief and uneven review of evidence from a number of European countries provided below emphasises just how difficult this task of comparative work is at present. This difficulty is also reflected in some of the transnational, or comparative literature (Melvyn, 1998; NOVA, 1999; OECD, 2000), most of which hardly acknowledges the dimension of ethnicity in their analyses. It is clear from many national commentaries that the issue of ethnicity is not yet seen as worthy of serious attention (Threlfall, 2000).

Poverty, ethnicity and exclusion

The continuing general 'colour-blindness' of many of the organisations represented in these reports is alarming when, on the one hand, most analyses of poverty and government responses to it, point to the importance of paid work as possibly the most important route out of poverty, while, on the other hand, the few analyses of race and poverty available show in parallel a strong association between poverty and membership of particular minority ethnic groups. The literature shows clearly, for example, that in the UK, Pakistani, Bangladeshi and African-Caribbean groups – and particularly young men – feature disproportionately among the poorest in society (Modood et al, 1997; Craig, 1999). Similarly, recent exploratory research shows that 'foreign' immigrants (including recent flows of refugees and asylum-seekers) – who constitute approximately 10% of Germany's population – are more vulnerable to poverty and marginalisation (Riphahn, 1999), as measured by participation in social assistance programmes. A review of social protection in several European countries notes that among the five million or so poor, excluded people and the 3.9 million unemployed in France, "several groups seem to be more vulnerable, especially young people ..." (Hirsch, 1997, p 33), among whom minority young people will be disproportionately represented. Riphahn's findings are all the more striking since for those with no permanent residence rights "social assistance receipt is connected with a risk of expulsion" (1999, p 5). The numbers of those on social assistance are likely to understate the extent of poverty among minority ethnic groups.

The European Anti-Poverty Network's (EAPN) review of poverty and racism demonstrates that the "reality [for immigrants] of most of the member countries of the European Union is one of increased poverty, a greater number of poor people, and a form of racism which seeks the culprits, designates immigrants, migrants and refugees as those responsible for insecurity, unemployment and all the evils of the city" (EAPN, 1999a, p 7). This form of racism is developing on a national and transnational basis and has led, for example, to arson attacks and the murder of Turkish migrants in German streets and hostels, attacks in which UK white nationals were implicated. Even countries traditionally viewed as liberal and tolerant now witness the growth of influential racist political movements; one such is the Danish People's Party, which argues for repatriation of immigrants and has popularity ratings as high as 15%.

The EAPN lists a number of ways in which racism specifically affects the opportunities of minority ethnic groups in the labour market:

- migrants frequently suffer from having the least training, the least appropriate skills and as a result are seriously over-represented in unemployment statistics throughout the EU
- immigrants and refugees may be blamed if they do find work ('they have taken a job from a local person'), or blamed if they do not work ('living off the welfare benefit system')
- much of the available work for ethnic minorities is with poor pay, includes shift work, part-time and temporary work without protection and security
- ethnic minorities, refugees and travellers may find work, but in illegal or particularly arduous conditions, or in the informal ... economy
- where there is a problem of illegality within the work-force and among ethnic minorities and migrants, local populations within Europe blame the illegal or migrant workers for bringing down wages and creating unemployment among the host population
- in some cases (eg refugees in Greece) there is evidence that certain categories of the population do have work permits and pay social security contributions but do not receive the same legal rights and allowances as the rest of the population (EAPN, 1999a, pp 18-19).

The position of minority ethnic groups is also often made more precarious by their lack of language skills and knowledge of local welfare arrangements. This lack of social and cultural capital impacts on their health, social security, education and housing prospects. The EU has begun to acknowledge the difficulties faced by minority ethnic groups and "within the context of the European Employment Strategy ... explicitly set ... the target of intensifying efforts to deal with the employment problems of ethnic minorities" (Stille, 1999). Stille's paper, which provides a useful overview of the position of minority ethnic groups across the EU, argues that:

- labour market problems facing the first generation of immigrants are significantly greater than those facing second and third generations
- most ethnic minority populations have a younger age profile than the 'host' population
- many countries have both sent and received migrants but 'push' factors, such as the collapse of the Soviet Union, have become more dominant in recent years
- minority ethnic groups tend to have lower participation rates, lower employment rates than those of host nationals, and lower rates of self-employment (but again there are significant exceptions)

- minority ethnic groups tend to have lower levels of qualifications (although this is not always the case; for example, in the UK, there is a clear divide between the education attainment and labour market experience of Indian and Chinese minorities on the one hand and Pakistani, Bangladeshi and African Caribbean groups on the other), more limited experience of formal education and work in occupations, usually in the service sector, requiring lower levels of skill, and paying lower wages
- unemployment rates tend to be higher for minority groups than for host nationals, although there may again be significant differences in some countries between differing minorities.

Ethnicity and local labour markets

Countries with relatively lower levels of ethnic minority residents

Denmark

In a study of unemployment and unemployment policies in Denmark, Andersen (1999, p 6) observes that "the Danish labour market has a low capacity to integrate foreign citizens on the labour market, in particular foreigners from countries outside the EU region". While the proportions of those registered unemployed in 1998 (at a time of relatively high unemployment overall) were 5% and 7% for men and women of Danish origin respectively and 10% and 11% for men and women of other EU country origin, for minorities from all other countries outside the EU (representing less than 3% of the total Danish population), the rates were 25% and 31% respectively (see also Schultz-Nielsen, 2000). These disparities followed a period of policy change that began to emphasise activation policies, including lower minimum wages and improved productivity through education and job training. A youth allowance had already been introduced in the early 1990s "requiring early activation as a condition for receiving social assistance" (Andersen, 1999, p 18).

Although changes such as improved education and job training were probably less helpful to migrant workers than to those of Danish origin, Andersen acknowledges the connection between policy changes and the serious unemployment situation facing Denmark's minority ethnic groups. He notes that both first and second generation immigrants have high unemployment rates but suggests only that "insufficient lack of knowledge of the Danish language is often believed by public authorities to be a part of the problem" (Andersen, 1999, p 25). Immigration to Denmark by non-Danish nationals peaked in 1995 and has fallen back considerably since then. Denmark receives about half the applications for asylum as are received by each of Norway and Sweden.

Finland

The largest minority ethnic group in Finland consists of the indigenous Saami, about 40,000 of whom live in north Finland (as well as in Sweden, Norway and Russia). Minority ethnic groups from outside Europe constitute a very small proportion of Finland's minority population, about 2% of the total population, mainly from Somalia, Iran, Iraq, Vietnam, Morocco and Turkey; in the two last-named countries, the large majority were single men. Nevertheless, the data show these minorities to be in a very marginal position. Pitkanen et al (1999, p 61) state that "the average unemployment rate for immigrants rose at the beginning of the 1990s [at the time of a deep economic crisis] from 10% to 55%" towards the end of the decade; some groups, such as those from former Yugoslavia suffered unemployment rates as high as 67%. Those employed tended to work in the service sectors or in low-skilled manufacturing jobs, with only one-third of those working having permanent contracts. Pitkanen et al's study suggested that a lack of language skills was a barrier to work, with demand for language training exceeding supply: "[T]he immigrant's path to employment is a long one. It takes normally two years until the immigrant achieves the language and vocational skills required in the Finnish labour market" (1999, p 62). Their action research study provided vocational testing, second language training and new programmes in vocational training, which together had a measurable impact on helping immigrants into work. A separate study confirmed findings that even where immigrants had professional skills and resources, it was difficult for them to obtain first jobs on the basis of these qualities: "the fact is that no work experience gained abroad is very much appreciated here" (Forsander and Alitilppa-Niitano, 2000, p 4).

Minorities who came to Finland as refugees during the 1990s faced an even more difficult labour market situation, when unemployment rates stood at least 70% of the population, and the experience was of longer periods of unemployment, and a "hardening of attitudes towards foreigners" as Finland had adjusted to recession (Valtonen, 1999, p 7). They also had to cope with substantial net immigration since the 1980s as a result of emigrants returning from Russia and Sweden. This resulted in a shift away from humanitarian approaches to refugees to ones incorporating stronger concerns with employability. Valtonen reports barriers to employment for non-national immigrants including a lack of language skills, various forms of discrimination in employment interviews, and a lack of acceptance of overseas work experience or qualifications, all of which undermine the vocational training and support being given to immigrants.

Valtonen also observes (2000, p 5) resistance from employers to employing immigrants even at "the outer edge of the labour market at the first 'gates'". Analysing the position of immigrants in terms of Marshall's notion of social citizenship (1963), she concludes that the addressing of social rights, such as meeting basic needs and providing for participation, as well as providing for engagement in the labour market, does not empower immigrants in that "participation in the central labour market sphere is still elusive ... this approach cannot ... deal with structural barriers of discrimination and resistance that block immigrants' access to employment" (Valtonen, 2000, pp 6 and 9). Youth unemployment rates in Finland have, meanwhile, consistently been among the highest in EU countries (Helve, 1999).

Norway

During the early 1970s, Norway briefly encouraged immigration as a way of coping with labour shortages. In 1975 it was restricted largely to those entering with the status of refugee (on humanitarian grounds) or those seeking family reunification. A relatively small proportion (5%) of the Norwegian population of 4.5 million is of immigrant status, although the proportion in Oslo is three times that at 15%. First generation immigrants outnumber second generation immigrants by a ratio of about 10 to 1. The major countries of origin outside the EU are Pakistan, Vietnam, former Yugoslavia and Turkey. Andersson (2000, p 3) comments that "... in spite of this relatively low share of immigrants ... questions concerning the integration of immigrants have been in the centre of the public agenda in the 1990s", a debate that has taken place in the context of increasing restrictions on immigration, and has been affected by the tenor of political debate in which a populist right-wing party (FRP) has focused on the 'immigrant question'. This has doubtless contributed to what Andersson characterises as a "high and relatively stable degree of resentment towards immigrants".

Unemployment rates are high among minorities – about four times the national average at 11% – and housing discrimination against these minority groups is marked. Andersson argues that Norway, like Sweden, has moved to a problem-focused, case-centred approach rather than thinking more structurally in terms of policy responses, an approach that has not effectively been challenged by academic researchers, despite considerable evidence of structural racism. This racism has been noted by the Council of Europe, which reported that, despite recent efforts to combat racism and discrimination, such

> problems ... persist and are particularly acute in the field of access of employment, housing and access to goods and services. High levels of voter support for populist parties using racist discourse is also a matter of concern ... there still seems to be a lack of recognition of the possibility that Norwegian identity may also encompass other forms of identity than the traditional one. (ECRI, 2000e, p 4)

In relation to labour market access, there has been concern that Norwegian employers do not recognise qualifications, education and experience gained outside of the country. New arrangements are being implemented to support immigrants via induction programmes, financial support and education. However, the evidence suggests that employers, including the government itself (which employs only 2% of its workforce from minorities), engage in racist and discriminatory practices. Norway's indigenous Saami and migrant gypsy Roma have both been the subject of harassment in the past, although the organised levels of this have reduced. The Saami's cultural and linguistic rights are now incorporated into Norwegian law.

United Kingdom

Britain's ethnic minority population, about 5% of the total population in 1991 although probably nearer 7% now, is dominated by those originating from countries that were formerly British colonies. Immigration has also been characterised by considerable inflows from 'white' former colonies such as Australia, Canada and South Africa as well as substantial outflows of white Britons to those countries. The British ethnic minority population, as in other EU countries, is concentrated in major urban centres, typically in areas with the highest rates of unemployment, although there are now minority populations in every part of the UK.

Notwithstanding difficulties caused by the failure of most official agencies to engage in ethnic monitoring, the evidence demonstrates that minority ethnic groups are more likely, in some cases very much more likely, to be in poverty and on the margins of society, than the population at large. This is the result of a combination of factors including high unemployment (Pakistani and Bangladeshi rates for both men and women being three to five times as high as for white people throughout the 1990s [Andersen, 1993; Jones, 1993; Sly, 1994]), low levels of economic activity among women, low pay/income (Platt and Noble, 1999), and structural racism. Levels of competence in the English language are generally lower among Pakistani and Bangladeshi groups, especially women (Modood et al, 1997), partly as a result of cultural norms. Their disadvantage continues into labour market age: Pakistanis and Bangladeshis with degrees are as likely to be in poverty as white people with no qualifications (Chahal, 2000). Minority communities are concentrated in inner-city areas where older industrial sectors have borne the brunt of recession and the international restructuring of capital. Racism affects the way in which people are selected for jobs or made redundant (Trades Union Congress [TUC], 1994, 1995; Parekh, 2000). People from minority ethnic groups are more likely to be working in low-paid jobs, partly as a result of more wideranging racial discrimination, and they have more limited access to adequate health and housing provision. Increasing restrictions on the ability of refugees and asylum-seekers to access help from social assistance put them particularly at risk, but the social security system as a whole fails to address the issue of the greater poverty of minority ethnic groups (Craig, 1999). Young black people represent a particularly problematic group since many of them have 'disappeared' from official data, due to structural racism (Chatrik et al, 2000).

Although most minority young people stay on in education post-16 (the earliest school-leaving age), African-Caribbean young men take longer to achieve qualifications than white young people and fewer achieve qualifications at all levels. By the time young men reach the labour market, disadvantage is considerable: when the unemployment rate for young white men was one in eight, for young Africans, African-Caribbeans, Pakistanis and Bangladeshis it was one in three. Young African-Caribbean men were found to be twice as likely to be unemployed as their white counterparts with the same level of education attainment, and more vulnerable to unemployment during recession (Berthoud, 1999). However, people of Chinese or Indian origin were far less likely to be disadvantaged than minority ethnic groups as a whole, having similar rates of education attainment and labour market participation as the white population. Berthoud notes that education and the general economic climate had the greatest impact on young people's chances of appropriate work (1999). Heath and McMahon (2000) demonstrate that class origins and education qualifications (physical and cultural capital) account for just half the overall disadvantage experienced by African-Caribbean and Pakistani people in the labour market. They add that "the barriers to entry that they face in gaining access to particular kinds of work" (2000, p 24), including racism and discriminatory practices, are considerable.

There are also significant differences among women in terms of labour market careers:

> ... while minority ethnic women in non-manual occupations have similar longitudinal occupational profiles to white women, those in manual occupations fare worse than their white counterparts, despite the fact that a larger proportion of minority ethnic women are in full-time employment. (Holdsworth and Dale, 1997, p 435)

Ethnic minority women are more likely to be in paid work because of poverty (although there are variations between groups because of, for example, the impact of religious customs and of the lack of local childcare facilities). However, they are also more likely to be in poorly-paid work and to lose their jobs, because of employers' racist practices.

The 1997 New Labour government began slowly to address the widespread exclusion of ethnic minority people (Social Exclusion Unit [SEU], 2000; Craig, 2001). In relation to labour market issues, it proposes reviewing the treatment of qualifications obtained in other countries, improving the accessibility of services to ethnic minority groups, and promoting race equality through employment programmes and social protection. The mainstream agencies responsible for training and supporting young people into employment, Training and Enterprise Councils (TECs), generally failed to meet their obligations towards ethnic minority groups (Boddy, 1995) and were replaced in 2001 by a network of new agencies, Learning and Skills Councils, which appear to be addressing the educational underachievement of most ethnic minority communities (see, for example, www.lsc.gov.uk/documents).

Countries with relatively higher levels of ethnic minority residents

Austria

Austria has long depended, like Germany, on the use of 'Gastarbeiter' ('guest' workers) to provide a cheap labour force. This approach is now evolving into one similar to that in Switzerland of 'saisonnier' – the seasonal worker. These policies have traditionally been supported by trade unions, which have colluded in the operation of racist employment practices.

Reiter's analysis of young immigrants notes that:

> the unemployment rate of young foreigners and especially the
> unemployment rate of the 15- to 18 year-old foreigners are much higher
> than the unemployment rate of young Austrians. One reason is the
> early entrance of young foreigners to the employment system in general
> and the high quota of foreign workers in sectors with higher
> unemployment risks. (2000, p 1)

A total of 80% of the 'young foreigners' from more than 100 nationalities
present in Austria are from Turkey and former Yugoslavia. A high
proportion have no vocational qualifications and many are in special
schools, as a result of systemic racism, for example through language
difficulties compounded by other factors such as poor housing, which
prevents effective learning. The pattern of immigration has changed over
time: in the 1960s, young single males were brought to work in specific
occupations on limited contracts. Although the government intended
that they should return to their own countries and be replaced by others,
a policy underpinned by refusal of access to full residential, employment
and welfare rights (Baumgartner and Perchinig, 1995), employers
obstructed this 'principle of rotation', wishing to keep experienced workers.
During the 1970s economic downturn, the government limited new
immigration. However, the continued arrival of family members and
enhanced fertility rates means that the immigrant population has continued
to grow. The proportion of the Austrian population of foreign origin is
9% (and about 11% of young people), but their citizenship status remains
uncertain.

> [B]ecause of a missing co-ordination of immigration and access to the
> labour market, foreigners are at risk to be excluded from working life,
> to lose their job and income and, in consequence, to be deported ....
> (Reiter, 2000, p 5)

Reiter's review suggests that these young people face disadvantage at
each of four crucial stages in the transition into work: success at school;
selection on the way to vocational education and training; success in
vocational education; selection into employment. For example, at the
point at which children choose whether to remain in academic education
or move to vocational education, 30% of Austrians go to academic
secondary school, compared with only 14% and 5% of those of Yugoslavian
and Turkish origins resident in Austria respectively. On the other hand,

at all stages in compulsory schooling, the proportion of minorities in special schools is higher, increasing steadily through school careers until it is four times that for Austrian national schoolchildren by the age of 14-15. In relation to apprenticeships, young ethnic minority people perform the function of a reserve for variations in supply and demand; when demand falls, it is ethnic minority young people who are squeezed out.

Disadvantage is also strongly gendered: the proportion of young women from Yugoslavian and Turkish origin remaining beyond compulsory school attendance age is only two thirds that of Austrian female nationals. Within the labour market, the drop-out rate from apprenticeships is three times as high for 'foreign' apprentices. Unemployment rates for young foreign nationals are up to three times the rates for Austrian national young people, and much higher still among foreign young women. The influence of Islamic culture is strong, families often pressing young women – many of whom wish to work – to marry at an early age.

Reiter draws on incomplete statistical data collected from a variety of sources. Strikingly, the official detailed sourcebook on Austrian social security systems (Horndler et al, 1998) again contains no analysis of the dimension of ethnicity, other than a passing reference that "problem groups are increasingly awarded the recognition they deserve" (p 66), such as migrant counselling points.

Belgium

The most comprehensive Belgian data come from an ILO International Migration Paper (Arrijn et al, 1998) commissioned as part of the ILO's programme to "combat discrimination against immigrant workers and ethnic minorities in the world of work". The report "demonstrates convincingly, for the first time, that discrimination against job seekers of foreign origin is widely prevalent despite legislative measures prohibiting [it]". However, the study is limited to an examination of discrimination by individual employers on the grounds of ethnicity.

Belgium's minorities, comprising about 9% of the population, largely comprise immigrants from Morocco and other African countries with substantial, although smaller, numbers from southern European countries such as Greece and Turkey. The ILO study undertook a series of tests, through applications for posts in a range of sectors, across the three Belgian regions, with applicants from both Moroccan and Belgian origin. Discrimination was observed in many ways, for both men and women. This included the distortion of procedures, such as requiring different working conditions, and discrimination in the application of bilingual requirements; applications involving visual contact often enhanced the likelihood of discrimination. The report notes that recruitment criteria involved cultural indicators that "could prove to be very discriminatory"; similar tests in the US for army recruits were modified at the end of the First World War when they were shown to downgrade the intelligence of immigrant applicants.

France

France is one of the countries in which the analysis of data regarding ethnic minority groups is particularly difficult, because, for constitutional reasons, use of the variable of ethnicity is prohibited in official national accounts and statistics. The Board of Statistics (HCI, 1998) reported in a study on integration that "there is no standardised and reliable system which produces statistics regarding migratory processes in France" (p 1); there is therefore no reliable estimate of the 'minority' population within France, although it is among those countries with a relatively higher proportion. France has longstanding and strong ties with its former colonies and a substantial population of people of North and West African, and South East Asian origins, who arrived at a relatively early stage in the immigration process. Thus 60% of Algerian and Tunisian, 27% of Moroccan and 22% of other non-Maghreb African immigrants arrived in France before 1975. Most Asian migration into France occurred later.
However, as Heckmann notes:

> as to the societal definition of the immigration situation, France never understood herself – like the United States – as a country or nation of immigrants. The large recruitment of foreign workers in the 1960s and 1970s was viewed ... as work immigration limited in time. (1999, p 8)

Attempts to repatriate many immigrant workers failed in the face of left-wing political opposition and "temporary migration ... changed into immigration and settlement" (Heckmann, 1999, p 8). French governments, like those in Britain, have long held the view that a precondition for effective settlement of existing immigrants is strict control of further immigration. However, like Britain, but unlike Germany, anyone born in France who wishes to become French can do so if they satisfy certain conditions of residency, that is citizenship is associated with socialisation rather than ethnicity.
The HCI report notes that seasonal workers come to France, mainly to work in agriculture and the hotel industry, for periods limited to eight

months. The number of asylum-seekers increased from 1997 as a result of civil wars. The greatest numbers came from Turkey, former Yugoslavia, Vietnam, the former Zaire and Rumania, another country with which France had historic links. However, the HCI report (2000) provides only an oblique analysis of labour market issues, for example reporting that more than 25,000 young people aged 16-21 were granted French nationality in the first eight months of 1998, thus allowing them full social and employment rights (in principle at least). Ironically, from the perspective of this chapter, these 25,000 then 'disappear' from official data as far as issues to do with their ethnicity are concerned. However, Heckmann (1999) notes that the transition from a predominantly scholastic training system into the labour market causes serious problems. This is particularly reflected in the experiences of young immigrants who suffer very high unemployment rates.

The Council of Europe has monitored the extent of racism and discrimination in France, confirming that these problems are "particularly acute vis-à-vis young people of immigrant background" (ECRI, 2000a, p 4). In relation to the labour market, it notes that, despite the lack of effective statistics, it is nevertheless clear that employment is one of the areas in which the incidence of racial and ethnic discrimination is more widespread. Unemployment rates are three times as high for non-EU citizens as for French citizens (four times among young men of Algerian origin). However, possession of French nationality "does not seem to prevent discriminatory practices" (ECRI, 2000a, p 15). So discrimination based on skin colour is a powerful counter to theoretical notions of citizenship, and to the French principle of equality of all citizens on which the prohibition of ethnic monitoring is founded. The ECRI argues that ethnic monitoring is the most effective tool to counter the 'invisibility' of minorities.

Labour market discrimination emphasises earlier systemic failures (such as the failure of the education system to provide equality of opportunity). However, even where equally qualified young people are considered, and given the higher education aspirations of many immigrant families compared with comparable French families (Brinbaum, 1999), unemployment rates among Algerian young men are still twice the level of their French counterparts. Brinbaum's study shows that North African children are equally disadvantaged in comparison with those originating from southern European countries (such as Portugal), a finding that supports the view that racial discrimination is strongly associated with the physical 'visibility' of minority groups.

Germany

Germany is one country where the recent upsurge in neo-Nazi racist violence against ethnic minority workers and refugees across Europe has been most apparent. Since 1990, a series of attacks on hostels and in public places has led to 20 reported deaths (including 10 deaths in a hostel fire in Lubeck in 1996 for which, in a manner consistent with racist responses to racism, the victims were themselves blamed [Fekete, 2000]) and left many ethnic minorities with serious injuries. One, ironically, was a black Briton attacked in Potsdam in 1996. Koopmans (1999) describes "the migration of foreigners ... [as developing] ... into the most conflict-ridden issue of political mobilisation in 1990s Germany", attributing this level of conflict to Germany's exclusion of foreigners from citizenship, in contrast to its attitude to ethnic Germans returning from other countries.

These 'foreign' immigrants – leaving aside the migration of about 4.5 million people from east to west within Germany in the period prior to the construction of the Berlin Wall and another almost one million following its demolition – were mainly the *Gastarbeiter* recruited in the 1960s and 1970s from southern European countries (especially Greece, Turkey and Italy) and from the former Yugoslavia. They worked mainly in low-skill manufacturing and construction jobs, until recruitment ceased (paralleling the ban in France) in 1973. Since that time, apart from ethnic Germans, most immigration has comprised movements of refugees and asylum-seekers. Immigrant groups have substantially higher levels of unemployment (at 17% in 1996) than native Germans. Their access to the labour market is impeded by elements of institutionalised discrimination, such as the regulation that allows employment offices to match foreign workers with vacancies only if no suitable German worker is available (similar to Austria's policy of *ersatzkraftverfarhen*).

Riphahn's 1999 study demonstrates that younger immigrants have a better chance of accessing the labour market than older ones, that the overall risk of being on welfare has not fundamentally altered from cohort to cohort, and that the "income drop following unemployment yields graver consequences for the economic independence of immigrants, than of natives" (p 23). This suggests that immigrants are highly motivated to remain within the labour market once there, whatever the conditions under which they work. Germany is currently reconsidering its notion of citizenship but, as in France, detailed analysis of the position of ethnic minorities is difficult because of a lack of credible official data. Under present arrangements, citizenship is not obtainable to those 'immigrants' merely born within German territory; conversely, the status of foreigner remains to those who are born within Germany but to foreigners. As a result, even though more foreigners leave Germany each year than enter it, according to recent annual statistics (Koopmans, 1999), the number of foreigners within Germany appears to be increasing because of children born to resident foreigners. In other countries, such as the UK or the Netherlands, as Koopmans points out, these children would not be regarded or recorded as foreigners. Koopmans suggests that the way in which citizenship is currently conceptualised in Germany and reflected in official data encourages the scapegoating of foreigners for economic ills (as reflected in the numbers of racist attacks). This is despite the fact that *Aussiedler* (ethnic German migrants) present much more of a real threat within the labour market to native Germans because of their special treatment – for example, a right to unemployment benefits and pensions as if they had worked and lived all their lives in Germany (Munz et al, 1997). The much higher levels of unemployment in parts of former East Germany provide the state with an opportunity to overlook the systemic difficulties faced by migrant workers.

Hungary

Hungary is currently applying for membership of the EU. The treatment of ethnic minorities within Hungary is highlighted most of all by that of the Gypsy or Roma population. The size of this resident but mobile minority (albeit with links to similar minorities in many other countries) is variously estimated to be from 400,000 to more than one million (between 4-10% of the total population) (Kertesi, 2000). The Roma is a minority ethnic group that experienced discrimination and racial violence for many years under the former state socialist regime and since, both in Hungary (Varga and Versceg, 1991) and in other East and Central European countries (ECRI, 2000c). Although Kertesi indicates that education is having a positive effect on improving the prospects of Gypsies entering and staying within the labour market, it is only in reality making their situation less bad than before. A range of other structural factors continues to make their position marginal. For example, they tend to live in areas characterised as backward in terms of industrial development and entrepreneurship (a circular process since further investment is discouraged), they are affected strongly by discrimination and, as a result, experience much higher levels of unemployment (six times as high as that of the total population in the 1990 census[7]). Kertesi links the issue of structural discrimination to inter-ethnic violence, noting that "as unemployment rates are increasing, more and more unskilled jobs are endangered – the less can the unemployment problem of low educated people be solved at the cost of a discriminated minority" (1995, p 36).

Netherlands

The proportion of ethnic minorities in the Netherlands has increased sixfold during the last 25 years to almost 10% of the Dutch population. This rate continues to increase, despite, as in France and Germany, attempts to ban further immigration in 1974. Because of demographic pressure on land, for much of the first half of the 20th century, the Dutch government strongly encouraged emigration of Dutch nationals. The paradox of strong parallel policies for emigration and immigration appears, in Doomernik's view, "not to have been noted or publicly discussed" (1998, p 54). The most strongly represented among the 1.5 million members of minority groups, are about 20% from Surinam and the former Netherlands Antilles, and about 33% from Turkey and Morocco. Official reports suggest ethnic minorities arrive with relatively poor education attainment and that government policy relating to ethnic minorities has been ineffective in addressing this and other issues of disadvantage. "The ethnic minorities are strongly over-represented among the underprivileged groups of society" (SCP, 1998, p 6); for example, "people of foreign origin make up around 20% of the unemployed, while constituting only 5% of the workforce". Immigrants can become Dutch citizens relatively easily (naturalisation is possible after five years and is automatic for third generation residents).

Veenman has undertaken detailed studies of Dutch ethnic minorities as they make the transition from education to the labour market (Veenman, 1997a, 1999). He finds that, as with Reiter's Austrian study, on every count – school achievement, school-leaving tests, school drop-out, and participation in higher vocational and university education – ethnic minorities do significantly less well than their Dutch counterparts, with those of Turkish and Moroccan origin (those who do not even have the advantage of a knowledge of the Dutch language compared with those from Surinam and the Antilles) doing least well of all. This disadvantage carries over into the labour market with those of Turkish and Moroccan origin spending much longer periods unemployed or working within lower skilled, lower paid work, than either their migrant counterparts or Dutch native workers. Veenman explains this initial disadvantage both in terms of characteristics inherent in arriving migrants – their lack of understanding of Dutch culture and language ('cultural capital') and their lower socioeconomic status – and structural discrimination, particularly through schools and elements of the labour market. Within the labour market, both direct and indirect racial discrimination are at work; this, and the likelihood that immigrants will be located in the most vulnerable industrial sectors and have little education capital to protect them against redundancy, all contribute to their relatively very high unemployment levels.

Veenman's conclusions parallel those of UK studies, that the influence of these various factors is not uniform across the differing ethnic minorities and also that, although, over time, the position of minorities has improved absolutely, it is slipping back, relative to the majority population. However, he notes that the position of second generation immigrants is generally improved compared with their first generation counterparts, particularly as young immigrants have orientated themselves to more skilled work within the service sector. On the issue of citizenship he comments that:

> the opportunity structure is above all characterised by formal equality of rights, which implies that equal outcomes are to be expected for individuals and groups with equal characteristics. But because the characteristics often differ, the formal equality of the opportunity structure implies the occurrence of social inequality .... (1997a, p 7)

In reality, selection processes that depend on a degree of judgement and discretion discriminate against minorities on a structural basis. This happens because it is (wrongly) assumed that rules and procedures should be applied uniformly, regardless of the cultural origin of job applicants, a familiar form of indirect discrimination ('colour-blindness') often underpinned by direct discrimination. Stille notes that at the start of the 1990s, Dutch workers earned about 40% more than Moroccans and Turks: although "... these differences can largely be explained in terms of differences in education, training and work experience, discrimination also offered a partial explanation" (1999, p 8).

Van Hoof's (2000) study of the decline of youth unemployment during the latter part of the 1990s and of the reforms of Dutch vocational training and education suggests that this has been associated with a decline in youth employment (many turning to higher education, for example). However, while debate around the youth labour market both in Denmark and in the Netherlands has focused on labour shortages, youth unemployment "gets associated once more with the situation of marginal groups, in particular from ethnic minorities" (2000, p 4). Veenman believes it is appropriate to describe them as an "ethnic underclass" (1997b, p

211). An alternative way of putting this would be that, even at times of economic upturn, it is ethnic minority young people who are the last to experience the benefits of that upturn in terms of effective labour market participation. The specific reforms that van Hoof discusses in vocational education and training appear to have encouraged more young people into higher education. However, this will not have affected the marginalised minorities significantly and they remain more exposed within the labour market than before.

Conclusions

Methodologically, this chapter points to some of the advantages and difficulties in undertaking comparative research of this type. For example, reports from which the material discussed here was drawn have not been written to a common template and this has presented difficulties in drawing country comparisons. It remains a major task – which has a clear political dimension – to ensure that research across the differing European jurisdictions can draw on comparable data collected in robust ways.

On the other hand, the different policy stances taken by countries both help to illuminate the failings of national approaches to addressing the issue of ethnicity and provide indications of better practice for countries where policy in this area is least well developed. This review also points to the need to exercise care in thinking about ethnicity as a defining variable in the analysis of people's experience. The experience of different minority ethnic groups may be common in relation, say, to the issue of overt and institutional racism; but it is equally true that the experience of specific minority ethnic groups may be very different in relation to aspects of the workings of the labour market, due, for example, to their different pattern of immigration, expectations and cultural assumptions. This is an issue that has been highlighted in other social policy areas, such as housing (White, 1997).

In policy terms, this chapter has identified key questions. The first of these is the overarching problem of the persistence, even the growth of overt racism. The 1997 Treaty of Amsterdam has placed the issue of racism formally on the social and economic policy agendas of the European Commission. The evidence drawn together here, however incomplete, suggests, nevertheless, that there is a substantial research and policy task yet to be achieved across the EU and beyond its boundaries. In the context of increasingly xenophobic responses to immigrants and immigration, the growth of Right-wing populist parties and racist attacks on immigrants in all EU countries, the task of confronting racism and discrimination both within the labour market and outside it is becoming more difficult for national governments to confront – even given the political will to do so (which is clearly not always present).

Stille's paper (1999), summarised earlier, supported by other evidence in this chapter, outlines the many ways in which racism and discrimination affect the opportunities open to ethnic minority workers in, or entering, the labour market. The second policy issue specific to the workings of the labour market is that there are few aspects of the social and economic systems of all EU countries that do not contribute to racism and discrimination, directly or indirectly. Consequently, the proper integration of minority ethnic groups into national labour markets on a socially just basis requires action at all levels and in all sectors; in schools and further and higher education, in the development of training schemes, in recruitment and employment practices, and in on-the-job support and further training, for example.

Third, governments need to recognise that those lacking social and cultural capital enter countries and their labour markets at a profound disadvantage. This disadvantage increases unless it is specifically addressed in ways that are sensitive to the cultural norms of immigrants alongside those of the host country. Heckmann argues that "the inclusion of immigrants in general integration policies is far more important for immigrant integration than any targeted special policies" (1999, p 21). However, the fourth policy lesson is precisely that of the weakness of generalist (non-targeted) labour market policies. These are almost inevitably 'colour-blind' and fail to target the needs of those who do not conform to mainstream cultural norms. At the same time, special measures, such as schemes to improve language skills and vocational training, support self-employment, improve education attainment, support job search, sensitise employers and recruitment agencies to the need to confront racist practices, have not been as effective as they might have been. Stille (1999, p 10) notes that such measures have rarely been systematically monitored for their effectiveness, a further reflection of an inherently racist approach to labour market participation. Such monitoring might, for example, demonstrate the extent to which recent immigrants cause a displacement effect in relation to earlier migrants rather than in relation to the position of host country workers (an argument used to justify chauvinistic attacks on immigrants). It might also differentiate between the needs and experiences of first, second and third generations of immigrants, alluded to above, another area where current research has told us little.

The fifth policy issue relates to the broader question of the meaning of citizenship within EU countries for those immigrating to them. Even effective special measures may fail against the backdrop of increasing societal-wide racism. Evidence from the many European countries discussed here suggests a strong growth in racism and xenophobic responses to immigrants; this evidence considerably underreports the level of physical violence against immigrants (Chahal and Julienne, 2000). The notion of full citizenship, developed by Marshall and others, and discussed in the introduction and elsewhere in this book, is a wideranging one, incorporating social, civil, economic and political rights. The editors of this book suggest in Chapter One that "we have to distinguish, at least, between labour market marginalisation, social marginalisation and political marginalisation ... [and] economic marginalisation" and that "one form of marginalisation does not automatically lead to another". While this may be true at the level of generalisation, there seems little doubt that seen within the perspective of ethnicity, the specific associations between these different forms of marginalisation are very strong. It is equally true that the goal of full citizenship, a key theme of this book, is currently beyond the reach of ethnic minorities in the countries discussed here. The rights that underpin citizenship should not be separated. As the EAPN puts it:

> the worse-off individuals and families are, the more of all their civil, political, economic, social and cultural rights they lose. These situations clearly show how indivisible and interdependent rights are in daily life. (EAPN, 1999b, p 6)

The final major policy issue is that of the implications of the free movement of labour within the EU. These include the transferability of social and healthcare rights and the extent to which this may lead to more complex and layered forms of discrimination against those moving across national boundaries.

There are differences between the life chances of particular groups such as young people, and especially ethnic minority young people, across the various countries discussed here. For example, a review of risk factors tending to push young people towards dropping out from schools shows that the overall level of 'dropping out' in the UK – where the gap between high and low income groups is one of the greatest – is among the highest in Europe (Iacovou, 2000). However, these differences pale into insignificance compared with the common themes identified in this chapter, those of racism and discrimination within the structures associated with the labour market. It is clear that all the countries represented here, whether they have relatively large or small ethnic minority populations, (and probably all of those not represented here) fail Marshall's test of citizenship in relation to their treatment of ethnic minority groups, some by a considerable margin. Ethnic minorities are more or less substantively marginalised throughout Europe.

The evidence available suggests that members of (at least most) minority ethnic groups are more likely to be in poverty, and that their poverty is inadequately addressed by social protection mechanisms. They are more likely than host country nationals to be on the margins of national labour markets in low-paid, casual and low-skilled work, with unsocial hours and poor conditions, and to be more prone to falling out of those markets, particularly at times of national economic difficulty. With some exceptions, the position of ethnic minority young people is likely to be even worse than the general picture presented here in each country for ethnic minorities as a whole. It is also clear that, at least in formal political terms, minority ethnic groups have scant political representation for their views at national or local levels. For ethnic minorities, action at the level of social protection systems will be quite inadequate to address their citizenship deficit. This position can only be changed by the more wideranging action programmes of the type described above at both national and international levels. What is required most of all is strong action from governments – and by social partners such as trades unions (whose record is far from exemplary), and transnational bodies such as the ILO – to confront the directly and indirectly racist behaviours of individuals and the social and economic structures, policies and practices of organisations in most countries. International action will also be necessary to confront the racist and exploitative behaviour of many companies that have been content to make use of immigrants as a pool of low-paid, flexible and mobile labour. Despite growing national resistance to immigration, globalisation will generate increased migration and economic and social inequalities, making such action even more necessary, particularly since these inequalities will bear down most harshly on minorities (Castles and Davidson, 2000).

At the level of the EU, approaches to citizenship still vary enormously, despite what Heckmann calls a "remarkable trend of convergence of citizenship laws" (1999, p 3). These approaches range from the French republican unifying model, through the British and Dutch multicultural approaches (which aim in principle at least to acknowledge and not undermine cultural difference) to the German model, which in all cases does not acknowledge immigrants as citizens. These different approaches are reflected in policy, practice, and in modes of data collection and analysis.

However, it is clear that the 'colour-blind' approaches to citizenship of, for example, France and Germany, in no way protect immigrants from racism. The picture at present across the countries represented here is closer to a conditional 'citizenship' of minority ethnic groups, characterised by marginalisation and exclusion. In the context of growing racism in the political sphere, demands for greater – but specifically targeted – levels of immigration to resolve the crisis facing sectors of the labour market seem more likely to be resolved by offering new waves of immigrants temporary and conditional citizenship, to be abrogated as soon as the need for their labour is gone. To paraphrase the Council of Europe, the ideal of inclusive European citizenship, which might incorporate citizens whose origins lie outside the EU, and which acknowledges the salience of the cultural dimension of citizenship – with its emphasis on difference, diversity and the possibility of multiple identities (Castles and Davidson, 2000) – appears to be a very long way from becoming a reality.

Notes

[1] The author is grateful to correspondents within the CostAction 13 network and beyond, who provided material from a range of sources, often at short notice, and for helpful comments on an early draft from Adrian Sinfield and Herwig Reiter. Any further interpretation of the material sent and used here is the sole responsibility of the author.

[2] The chapter will not examine the experience of the Irish community within the UK, although it is probably the largest UK minority ethnic group. Although this cannot be demonstrated statistically (because 'Irish' has not hitherto been a separate ethnic category within the UK decennial census), this will change when the 2001 census is published.

[3] Immigration policies have been particularly prone to racist interpretations. While the UK, the Netherlands, France and Germany introduced increasing controls on minority ethnic immigration from the 1970s, at the same time in the UK and in the Netherlands substantial numbers of white emigrants were leaving the country, their numbers occasionally exceeding those entering. These facts did not get in the way of the populist media, led by politicians such as UK Prime Minister Margaret Thatcher, claiming that their countries would be 'swamped' by (black) immigration.

[4] A pattern that is challenging to Italy's 'pro-family' social policy.

[5] The EU has recently agreed a directive that enforces the principle of equal treatment, based on Article 13 of the Amsterdam Treaty of June 1997, which allows "appropriate action to combat discrimination based on sex, racial or ethnic origin, religion or belief, disability, age or sexual orientation" (Commission for Racial Equality [CRE], 2000). This will require most member states to rewrite their legislation by the end of 2002 but it will also undoubtedly require much improved administrative recordkeeping in all member states.

[6] The 33rd Session of the UN Commission on Population and Development, held in New York in March 2000, heard from the Director of the UN Population Division that 'international migration' would become the major demographic issue of the 21st century, leading to changes in language, religion, ethnicity and nationality and to "negative public sentiment and xenophobia". Alternatively, he suggested, it might lead to innovation, revitalisation and tolerance. In some countries, which have been moving towards a high dependency ratio of non-economically active to economically active people, immigrants were now being looked to as a source of (possibly cheap) labour to provide caring services for the growing population of older people, which might add to social differentiation within the labour market. Other delegates noted the strong gender dimension of international migration, particularly in relation to women being drawn into the sex industry.

[7] The unemployment levels among the Roma are uniformly much higher in all countries where they reside; Hungary's figure is relatively less troubling than those of Slovakia where it is 80% in some Roma communities, and around 100% in a few Roma areas, compared with 4-36% regional unemployment rates as a whole.

References

Andersen, H. (1993) *Ethnicity and gender in the West Midlands labour force*, Birmingham: West Midlands Low Pay Unit.

Andersen, J.G. (1999) 'Work and citizenship: unemployment and unemployment policies in Denmark, 1980-1999', paper prepared for Research Symposium on Social Democracy, Brussels, 23 September.

Andersson, M. (2000) *All five fingers are not the same*, Bergen: IMER.

Arrijn, P., Feld, S. and Nayer, A. (1998) *Discrimination in access to employment on grounds of foreign origin: The case of Belgium,* Geneva: ILO.

Baumgartner, G. and Perchinig, B. (1995) 'Vom Staatsvertrag zum Bombenterror: Minderheitenpolitik in Osterreich seit 1945', in R. Seider et al (eds) *Osterreich 1945-1995*, Vienna.

Berthoud, R. (1999) *Young Caribbean men and the labour market*, York: York Publishing Service.

Boddy, M. (1995) *TECs and racial equality*, Bristol: SAUS Publications.

Brinbaum, Y. (1999) 'Family-educational aspirations: another approach to the school-to-work transition for immigrants' children', in *Transitions and mobility in the youth labour market*, proceedings of a workshop held at NOVA, Oslo, 2-5 September, pp 11-24.

Castles, S. and Davidson, A. (2000) *Citizenship and migration*, Basingstoke: Macmillan.

Chahal, K. (2000) *Ethnic diversity, neighbourhoods and housing*, York: Joseph Rowntree Foundation.

Chahal, K. and Julienne, L. (2000) '*We can't all be white!*': *Racist victimisation in the UK*, York: York Publishing Service.

Chatrik, B., Coles, R., Craig, G., Hylton, C. and Mumtaz, S. (2000) 'The disappeared: how many are there and where have they gone?', paper for the Youth Research Conference, University of Keele, 3 September.

Craig, G. (1999) 'Poverty, "race" and social security', in J. Ditch, *An introduction to social security*, London: Routledge.

Craig, G. (2001) 'New Labour and "race"', in G. Fimister (ed), *An end in sight?*, London: Child Poverty Action Group.

CRE (Commisson for Racial Equality) (2000) *Article 13: Proposals from the European Commission for combating discrimination*, London: CRE.

Doomernik, J. (1998) *The effectiveness of integration policies towards immigrants and their descendants in France, Germany and the Netherlands*, International Migration Papers No 27, Geneva: ILO.

EAPN (European Anti-Poverty Network) (1999a) *Racism and poverty in Europe*, Brussels: EAPN.

EAPN (1999b) *EAPN Network News No 67*, Brussels: EAPN.

ECRI (European Commission against Racism and Intolerance) (2000a) *Second report on France*, Strasbourg: Council of Europe.

ECRI (2000b) *Second report on Greece*, Strasbourg: Council of Europe.

ECRI (2000c) *Second Report on Poland*, Strasbourg: Council of Europe.

ECRI (2000e) *Second report on Norway*, Strasbourg: Council of Europe.

Fenton, S. (1999) *Ethnicity: Racism, class and culture*, Basingstoke: Macmillan.

Fekete, L. (2000) 'How the German press stoked the Lubeck fires', *Race and Class*, vol 41, no 4, pp 19-41.

Forsander, A. and Alitilppa-Niitamo, A. (2000) *Maaanmuuttajien tyollistyminen ja tyohallinto – keit, miten ja minne*, Report No 242, Helsinki: Tyoministerio.

HCI (Haute Conseil a l'Integration) (2000) *Rapport du groupe permanent charge des statistiques 1998*, Paris: HCI.

Heath, A. and McMahon, D. (2000) 'Ethnic differences in the labour market: the role of education and social class origin', Paper No 2000-01, Oxford: Nuffield College.

Heckmann, F. (1999) 'Integration policies in Europe: national differences or convergence?', paper given at European Research Conference, Obernai, France.

Helve, H. (1999) *Youth and unemployment in Finland*, Helsinki: University of Helsinki, mimeo.

Hirsch, D. (1997) *Social protection and inclusion*, York: York Publishing Services.

Holdsworth, C. and Dale, A. (1997) 'Ethnic differences in women's employment', *Work Employment and Society*, vol 11, no 3, pp 435-57.

Horndler, M. et al (1998) *The Austrian welfare state: A survey of social security systems*, Vienna: Federal Ministry of Labour, Health and Social Affairs.

Iacovou, M. (2000) 'Dropping out of school: a cross-European comparison of risk factors', paper for the Youth Research Conference, University of Keele, 3 September.

Jones, T. (1993) *Britain's ethnic minorities*, London: Policy Studies Institute.

Kertesi, G. (1995) *The changing role of race and human capital in regional unemployment rate differentials in Hungary, 1990-1994*, Budapest: ILO.

Kertesi, G. (2000) 'The decline and structural transformation of gypsy employment between 1984 and 1994', *Hungarian Economic Review*, May.

Koopmans, R. (1999) 'Germany and its immigrants: an ambivalent relationship', *Journal of Ethnic and Migration Studies*, vol 25, no 4, pp 627-47.

Macpherson, Sir W. (1999) *Official report on the inquiry into the death of Steven Lawrence*, London: The Stationery Office.

Marshall, T.H. (1963) *Sociology at the crossroads*, London: Heinemann.

Melvyn, P. (1998) *Youth unemployment – recent innovative initiatives*, UN-European Regional Follow-up to the World Summit on Social Development, Vienna: UN Office.

Modood, T., Berthoud, R., Lakey, J., Nazroo, J., Smith, P., Virdee, S. and Bershon, S. (1997) *Ethnic minorities in Britain*, London: Policy Studies Institute.

Munz, R., Seifert, W. and Ulrich, R. (1997) *Zuwanderung nach Deutschland: Strukturen, Wirkungen*, Perspektiven, Frankfurt: Campus.

NOVA (1999) *Transitions and mobility in the youth labour market*, European Network on Transitions in Youth, Oslo: NOVA.

OECD (Organisation for Economic Co-operation and Development) (2000) *From initial education to working life: Making transitions work*, Paris: OECD.

Parekh, B. (Chair) (2000) *The future of multi-ethnic Britain*, London: Runnymede Trust.

Pitkanen, M., Ylipisto, H. and Taydennyskoulutuslaitos, V. (1999) *Matkalla menestykseen?*, Report No 233, Helsinki: Tyo ministerio.

Platt, L. and Noble, M. (1999) *Race, place and low income distribution*, York: York Publishing Services.

Reiter, H. (2000) 'Young foreigners between school and work in Austria', paper prepared for COST A13 meeting, Oslo, 2 June.

Riphahn, R. (1999) 'Immigrant participation in social assistance programs', Munich: University of Munich, mimeo.

Schultz-Nielsen, M.L. (2000) 'Integrationen på arbejdsmarkedet', in G.V. Mogensen and P.C. Matthiessen (eds) *Integration I Danmark omkring årtusindskiftet*, Aarhus: Rockwool Fondens Forskningsenhed.

SCP (Social and Cultural Planning) (1998) 'Dutch prosperous but uneasy', SCP Office Press Release, The Hague: SCP.

SEU (Social Exclusion Unit) (2000) *Minority ethnic issues in social exclusion and neighbourhood renewal*, London: SEU.

Sly, F. (1994) 'Ethnic groups and the labour market', *Employment Gazette*, May, London: Department for Education and Employment.

Stille, F. (1999) 'Ethnic minorities and recent immigrants on the labour market: an introduction', European Employment Observatory, mimeo.

Threlfall, M. (2000) 'Comparing unemployment in the UK and European Union: a gender and working time analysis', *Policy & Politics*, vol 28, no 3, pp 309-29.

TUC (Trades Union Congress) (1994) *Black workers in the labour market*, London: TUC.

TUC (1995) *Black and betrayed*, London: TUC.

Valtonen, K. (1999) *The integration of refugees in Finland in the late 1990s*, Ministry of Labour Report No 224.

Valtonen, K. (2000) 'Immigrants access to employment: social citizenship approaches in Finland and Canada', Turku: University of Turku, unpblished mimeo.

van Hoof, J. (2000) 'Youth unemployment, vocational education and training policy in the Netherlands', University of Leiden, mimeo.

Varga, T.A. and Versceg, I. (1991) 'An experiment in community development in the Bakony', *Community Development Journal*, vol 27, no 2, pp 50-59.

Veenman, J. (1997a) 'Minorities in Dutch education and the labour market', Rotterdam: Erasmus University, mimeo.

Veenman, J. (1997b) 'The socio-economic position of ethnic minorities in the Netherlands', in J.-L. Rallu, Y. Corrbage and V. Piché (eds) *Old and new minorities*, London: John Libbey, pp 211-28.

Veenman, J. (1999) 'Differences in social and cultural capital: barriers in integration processes?', paper for the ESF Conference, 'European societies or European society?', Obernai, 23-28 September.

Virtanen, T. (1998) 'Racist violence from the part of skinheads: the expression of hate in Finland', in H. Helve (ed) *Unification and marginalisation of young people*, Helsinki: Finnish Youth Research Society.

Wallace, C., Spannring, R. and Haerpfer, C. (2000) 'Youth, citizenship and social capital in Europe', paper for the Youth Research Conference, University of Keele, 3 September.

Weill, P. (1997) 'The politics of immigration in France', paper for conference of Migration Dialogue, Aspen Institute, Lyon.

White, P. (1997) 'Urban management and the situation of ethnic minorities in London', in J.-L. Rallu, Y. Corrbage and V. Piché (eds) *Old and new minorities*, London: John Libbey, pp 285-307.

NINE

From externalisation to integration of older workers: institutional changes at the end of the worklife

Bert de Vroom and Anne Marie Guillemard

The central theme of this book is labour market change, its interrelationship with welfare policies, and their joint impact on citizenship. In this chapter we discuss these changes from the perspective of ageing workers. Labour market and social policies have had a major impact on the organisation of the end of the worklife for this sector of the population in the past decades. In many welfare states, social programmes have been used – as instruments for labour market strategies – to 'externalise' older workers from the labour market. This process is referred to as the 'early exit' of older workers.

Recently, this policy has been reversed. Many welfare states have tried to change the early exit culture into a late exit culture, to cope with demographic ageing, welfare state costs and new demands on the labour market. Instead of 'externalisation' of older workers, the political target nowadays is the 're-integration' of older workers.

Against the background of these developments and changes we will address two questions. Firstly, whether and how countries will be able to turn around the massive and highly institutionalised early exit into a new pattern of late exit. We assume that this change from early to late exit needs a much more complicated and fundamental change in the regulating mechanism of welfare states than is sometimes expected. At the same time, and according to the neo-institutionalist approach, dismantling a (longstanding) welfare state practice might be very difficult as a result of 'policy feedback' and 'path dependencies' (Pierson, 1994). The empirical test should be those welfare states that combine a longstanding culture of high early exit with a complex institutional structure designed to channel the process of early exit. Within the European region a number of countries seem to qualify for such a test. For empirical reference we will use France and the Netherlands to analyse the barriers and innovations required to reverse the early exit trend. Both countries are known for their high early exit cultures, but they seem to differ strongly in the success of their attempts to raise the employment activity rates of older workers. Finland is also a high exit country with a complex pathway structure. From 1995, employment activity rates among the 55-64 male age group began to increase again, in the Netherlands from 40.5% in 1993 to 48.8% in 1999 (OECD, 2000), in Finland from 36.1% in 1995 to 40.1% in 1999. The reason we have chosen to focus on France rather than Finland is that as well as being a high exit country, France also illustrates the difficulties involved in reversing the early exit trend. The activity rate for the 55-64 male group has almost stabilised at the 1995 level (38.7%). So the Dutch and French cases offer two examples of an opposite trend.

The second question concentrates on the dimension of citizenship and marginalisation. We will concentrate on whether early exit from the labour market should be interpreted as a loss of social citizenship and an increase in marginalisation. We will consider whether the reverse of the early exit trend is simply an extension of social citizenship and social inclusion or whether late exit is the result of dismantling the social right to retire early.

The two central questions are interrelated. The institutional construction of early exit pathways is at the same time embedded in a particular interpretation of social citizenship. Early exit of older workers has been defended in some countries or by some actors as an indication of higher social citizenship. Escaping from the devastated work conditions and entering the welfare state has been interpreted as a higher level of 'social citizenship'. In countries where high unemployment rates prevail, early exit has been defended as an act of 'solidarity': older workers should make room for the younger unemployed. We assume that both the reverse of the early exit culture and the increasing flexibility of the lifecourse need at the same time a new conceptualisation of social citizenship, and in particular with respect to the meaning of ageing, work and retirement. New policy concepts such as 'active ageing' and 'age discrimination' seem to reflect a new definition of a 'desirable' relation between ageing and work. At the moment the concept of 'active ageing' seems to have become the central policy paradigm in the European Union (EU). In the EU publication *Towards a Europe for all ages* (1999), active ageing was stated as the central strategic approach to ageing in the new millennium.

After a short summary of early exit patterns and the different policies and mechanisms that can explain these patterns, we will present the Dutch and French cases. We will then analyse and describe the institutional changes in both countries. This will include looking for barriers and innovations used to reverse the high early exit culture into a late exit pattern. We will then relate our findings and assessments to changes in the:

• welfare states' central paradigms
• lifecourse (in particular the increased flexibility)
• conceptualisation of social citizenship.

Early exit patterns in Europe

Most European countries have seen a substantial decrease in labour force participation by the 55-64 age group. Only Japan and some Nordic countries (Sweden, Denmark) have resisted this widespread trend. OECD and Eurostat data on variations in the employment activity rates of the male 55-64 age group from 1971 to 1999 clearly depict this trend (Eurostat 1999a, 2000; OECD, 2000).

Halfway through the 1990s only a minority of men in this age group was active within the labour market in many European countries. In France, the Netherlands, Finland and Belgium the employment activity rates are at that time below or close to 40%, which is less than half the 1971 percentage (of about 80%). In Germany, Spain, Italy and Austria, the employment activity rate of 55- to 64-year-old male workers also decreased at that time to a level of only 50% or even less. We can consider these two groups of countries as *high early exit* countries, having developed a strong early exit culture. By contrast, most Nordic countries (except Finland) and Japan may be considered as *low exit* countries where the right to work for older workers has been privileged against the right to retire early. The UK and North America are *in between* these two groups.

The massive trend towards early exit is characteristic of the 'continental' welfare state, in which work and welfare state transfer programmes have become uncoupled (for ageing workers). The Netherlands, France, Germany, but also Finland are examples of this continental early exit model. In those countries the externalisation of older workers has been channelled through a variety of institutional welfare state pathways. One pathway comprised the creative packaging of unemployment, disability, sickness, means-testing, welfare benefits, and other public and private income support programmes as transitions into the public pension system

(Kohli et al, 1991). In that sense pathways are programmatic solutions to bridge the gap between employment and the formal entry into the retirement pension system.

The concept of pathways is basically related to the social security (transfer) part of welfare states. As such, pathways can only explain one side of the logic of welfare states. Labour market policies are the other side. From the perspective of early exit it means that labour market policies might also have an effect on the 'exit choices' of both employers and workers. The question is whether labour market policies – both national and firm-level labour market policies – offer instruments and incentives to integrate older workers or not. Firm-level labour market policies are also referred to as 'human resource policies', and 'good practices' if those policies result in the integration of older workers (Walker, 1996).

Labour market integration policies and early exit pathways produce different logics: the first one stimulates entry or retaining of older workers (reduces exit), the second one stimulates exit. We have argued elsewhere that on an abstract theoretical level, it is possible to distinguish four different hypothetical outcomes (de Vroom and Naschold, 1993, p 6).

In a situation of hardly any (attractive) pathways and a relatively strong labour market integration policy the result will be '*no exit*'. The United Kingdom (UK) is sometimes interpreted as an example of this type. Since the scrapping of the Job Release Scheme in the late 1980s there is no special income scheme for older workers that could offer a welfare state pathway into early retirement. Only the general unemployment benefit (Jobseekers' Allowance) and social assistance (income support schemes) offer a marginal possibility. Labour market exit or entry in the case of the UK seems not to be determined by the 'pull effect' of welfare state pathways, but is primarily demand-side determined. At the same time there is a strong accent in the policy debate on so-called 'good practices' at a firm level. However, very little has been effectively implemented yet (Walker, 1996). The lack of welfare state pathways, economic growth and a stronger accent on labour market policies and mechanisms might explain the relatively lower level of early exit in this country. At the same time this change from welfare state programmes to labour market mechanisms has been carried through at the expense of the wage level of individual workers. It might even result in a situation of 'work without welfare'.

If an extended welfare state pathway structure goes together with a strong labour market integration policy, we probably will find '*exit and entry*' (re-integration) at the same time. In those situations we might expect that entitlements for social security pathways be strictly bound to re-integration in the labour market. This is basically the concept adopted by the 'Nordic countries' (Sweden, Norway, Denmark). Exit pathways are at the same time connected to a developed system of labour market integration policies. In these 'work-orientated societies', work and welfare are directly related, even for older workers. The result is (was) a high level of labour market participation by all groups, including older workers.

In cases where a developed pathway structure is not combined with a labour market integration policy we might expect a high level of early exit, or '*exit=exit*' that would lead to a definite position outside the labour market. This is the pattern we find in the 'continental welfare states' with their passive compensatory nature of social insurance programmes. France, Belgium, Germany and the Netherlands are extreme examples of this type. The programmatic structure of pathways does not (until recently) allow work and welfare state provisions to be combined. It is a situation of 'welfare without work' (Esping-Andersen, 1996).

A fourth, and last type, is a situation where both welfare state pathways and labour market integration policies are lacking. It is the classical model of the 'market'. Whether or not we can observe '*exit or entry*' depends on the economic situation as well as on individual circumstances and choices. Within the European region, Hungary is an example of this type. Hungary is characterised by a fragmented pathway structure with gaps between paid employment and public pension. Hungary went through serious economic problems and structural industrial changes that at the same time had a 'push effect' on the early exit of older workers. These different pressures and circumstances have created an ongoing process of early exit of older workers.

The massive trend of early exit is primarily the characteristic of what has been labelled the continental welfare state model. The lack of labour market integration policies on the one hand and the generous benefits, mainly on the basis of passive criteria for compensating risks, on the other, have set off the spiral of welfare without work.

A shared 'early exit culture' has emerged, based on a new system of rules and regulations that "police ages" (Percheron, 1991) or reorganise the lifecourse and set new thresholds and timings for passing from one phase to another. The expansion of the 'early exit culture' has changed all actors' expectations and anticipations about the end of the worklife. Depending on the dominant age of early exit, companies are treating ageing employees as redundant and definitively unemployable. Labour unions have gradually come to see exit before the official retirement age as a right (or even a duty during a period of high unemployment) for ageing wage-earners. Wage-earners have adjusted to this new age norm as well. They now think that 55 (in France) or 60 (the Netherlands) is the normal age for definitively leaving the labour market. Ageing workers are planning the end of their worklives accordingly.

The massive early exit trend has reinforced age stereotypes, as is indicated in different publications. Top management, foremen and supervisors, as well as people on the line, share the opinion that older workers are unemployable and inefficient, lack motivation, are unable to adapt to change, and cannot be retrained. As a result, older workers are experiencing age discrimination in the workplace. People in their 40s are also experiencing career problems at the end of the worklife. Firms increasingly see them as a group with no future. Some companies are reluctant to train them, because the return on investment seems too limited. They also hesitate about promoting them, since these workers are already on the way out. There is no question of recruiting from this age group, since the threshold for recruitment has been set well before 40. Once they have reached the age of 40, people in certain positions have no career prospects, and, as a consequence, have lost all motivation. At the age of 45, wage-earners may be described as 'already waiting for retirement'. This age group has become a 'risk group' that suffers from discrimination, a group that will be marginalised.

Given this strong 'early exit culture' in many welfare states we might assume that it would be difficult to reverse the early exit trend. Such a reversal would require a strong involvement of public authorities and social partners, accompanied by relevant, coherent measures to change the welfare paradigm and to implement new labour market and human resources policies that could stimulate the (re-)integration of ageing workers.

Reversal of a trend: innovations and institutional barriers

The question is whether and how countries will be able to turn around the massive trend from early to late exit. In the literature on welfare state changes, it is expected that to dismantle existing welfare state programmes needs a different policy and polity than that required to build up welfare states (Pierson, 1994, pp 1-2). There is also the issue of whether countries with a high institutionalised early exit culture will be able to turn around this process fundamentally.

We mentioned earlier that we would use France and the Netherlands as the empirical test, since they both combine a longstanding culture of high early exit with a complex institutional structure designed to channel the process of early exit.

The Dutch case

After two decades of a decreasing employment activity rate for men in the 55-64 age bracket, from 1995 this rate finally began to increase. The labour market participation rate of older women (50-64) almost doubled between 1971 and 1997, to 27%. What developments can explain this change in labour market participation of older workers? At this point we need to distinguish between a 'cultural' and an 'programmatic' explanation for the low labour market participation of older male and female workers. The early exit pattern – and the use of the described pathways – is mainly a male phenomenon. Labour market participation by females in the Netherlands has been low for decades. It has been explained as the result of the dominant 'male breadwinner/female homecarer model' (Pfau-Effinger, 1998). Due to the fragmented and short labour history, ageing women were not entitled to many of the early exit pathways.

Since the 1980s, the Conservative labour market ideology has changed in the direction of the so-called 'male breadwinner/female part-time carer model' (Pfau-Effinger, 1998). As a result, there has been an ongoing increase of labour market participation by women in the younger cohorts, in most cases in part-time work. However, the effect on the older age cohorts is still marginal.

Since early exit is a male dominated phenomenon and related to the described institutional pathways, we will concentrate on the changes in the dominant early exit pathways: the disability benefit scheme, the voluntary early retirement programme (VUT) and the unemployment benefit scheme.

Disability pathway: from rights to incentives and disincentives

Since the early 1990s, various policies have been implemented to reduce the number of people in the disability scheme. One of the first changes was the so-called 'labour-market component' in the disability determination. When a person was partly disabled, but it was expected that she or he would have serious problems in finding a (new) job within the labour market, the person was 'defined' as 100% disabled. Since the risk of unemployment was high in the 1980s, in particular for older (40-plus) (low-skilled) workers and allochthonous 40-plus workers, the disability scheme became a more attractive early exit pathway than unemployment, in particular for older workers. The disability scheme was more attractive for at least two reasons. Firstly, this scheme offers a higher and more durable transfer than the unemployment scheme.

Secondly, those who were in a disability scheme were not obliged (at that time) to look for a job.

Since the early 1990s it is no longer allowable to use the 'labour market argument' as part of the disability determination. Apart from this change, in 1993 more specified maedical criteria used to determine disability were aggravated.

In the second half of the 1990s other changes have been introduced into the system. As we have described elsewhere, these changes can be classified as a change from "a traditional emphasis on rights and duties to an increasing interest in (financial) incentives and disincentives" (van der Veen et al, 2000, p 42). Although employers can still choose to join the public disability scheme, they are confronted with premiums that rise with the number of occupational-disabled in the firm. By giving the employer more responsibility for sickness and disability the incentives for firms to develop a policy of safety and sick-leave are strengthened. Sticks and carrots were also introduced to influence the behaviour of beneficiaries. In 1995, a new legal framework was implemented that specified the financial penalties in case a beneficiary would not fulfil his duties. In the social assistance schemes both positive and negative incentives were created to stimulate active labour market behaviour. At the same time the traditional responsibility of the social partners for operating the disability system has become partly privatised.

The exclusion of the 'labour market argument' in the early 1990s seems to have had a direct effect on older workers: it has become much more difficult for them to get a (100%) disability determination. For a while, these interventions seemed to be successful. Between 1993 and 1995 the number of 55- to 64-year-old new entrees in the disability scheme decreased from 14,300 to 10,000. However, from then on the numbers increased again to 14,900 in 1997 (Ctsv, 1998; SCP, 1999, p 19). By the end of 2000, the number of participants in the disability scheme – including many older workers – had increased again.

Contextual changes might explain this increase, to a certain extent. As a result of the overall ageing of society and the dismantling of other early exit pathways (see below) the proportion of older age groups in the labour force has increased in the past decade. If we assume that ageing goes together with a higher health risk (if nothing changes in the labour conditions), than ageing of the labour force can partially explain the increase of new entrees in the disability scheme. Another explanation, which can be found in different policy documents, is related to the described increase of female labour market participation in the Netherlands. Since the risk of women becoming disabled seems to be two times higher than the risk for men (Dutch Parliamentary Documents, 2000, p 14), the increase in female labour force participation can partially explain the increase in the total number of people in the disability programme. Next to these contextual changes, the increase can also be explained by the programmatic characteristics of the disability scheme itself. The fundamental difference between the Dutch scheme and those of other countries is that no distinction (not yet) has been made between the so-called 'risque social' and the 'risque professionel'. Both types of risks are integrated in one system, which is part of a collective financial arrangement between the social partners. In most other countries both types of risk are explicitly distinguished and are related to a different system and level of financial compensation (van Ewijk, 2000, p 89). As a result, the disability schemes in the Netherlands are still much more attractive (in terms of overall level of benefit and criteria to enter) than in other countries.

These programmatic characteristics reflect some important normative principles, related to justice and discrimination. These are the classical ones in the Dutch debate and they go back to the early 1960s. It is considered unfair to have different compensation levels for the same type of health problem, just on the basis of a different origin of that problem:

> decisive is not the question how a person has become disabled, but the condition that the person is disabled and that this will have societal consequences.... Any person has the right to self-development and to equal opportunities ... sick and disabled people ought to have the same opportunities as healthy people..., so there should not be discrimination on the basis of the origin of sickness, incapacity and handicap. (Dutch Parliamentary Documents, 1963, 2001, p 133)

However, we might expect that the increase in the number of disability cases on the one side and the shift towards the incentives and disincentives on the other will put a higher pressure on these normative principles and/or on the need to improve the labour conditions (for ageing workers) and to develop new human resources strategies. So far, the second route seems to be the dominant one. Both government and national social partners stimulate a policy of active employment policies for preserving and promoting the aptness to work of people over the age of 45, even for rehabilitating them. Also, an increasing number of incidental examples of so-called 'good practices' might be interpreted as an indication of the 'second route' (de Vroom, 1996).

Early retirement: from collective arrangements to individual plans

To escape from the strong 'either/or' choice, different changes and innovations have been introduced. One new option will be a combination of VUT and part-time work. Until recently, having a paid job next to a VUT-income was not allowed.

A more fundamental change might come from the introduction of 'pre- and flexible pensions', instead of the voluntary early retirement programme. Both the social partners and national government stimulate this policy change. If policymakers succeed in replacing VUT with 'pre-pensions' than this will require a fundamental change in the basic principles of early exit.

In a pre-pension model older workers have to build up savings (from earnings) as a private plan. This is one crucial difference with the existing VUT schemes. The current working population in a sector or big company contributes (from earnings) to a fund that pays out benefits to older workers that want the use of a VUT scheme. The pre-pension scheme is an individualised scheme, whereas the VUT scheme is a collective one. The average age for entering a pre-pension scheme is (at the moment) 61; for the VUT scheme it is 60. The average level of a pre-pension benefit is 70% of the last-earned income; for the VUT scheme it is 80% of the last-earned income. Most pre-pension schemes are flexible. Workers can stop working from 55 to 65 and the level of benefit will change accordingly. It is the choice of the individual worker whether to stop earlier and/or to increase individual savings to have a higher pension wage in the end. Within the VUT system there is no financial incentive to deliberate the exit choice (by the individual worker). For that reason the state stimulates a system of flexible and pre-pensions in which a relation is established between moment of exit and the level of compensation.

Compared to the VUT schemes, pre-retirement schemes are much more individualised and flexible, but give a decreasing level of benefit to older workers who exit earlier. These new policies should break down the 'either/or' choice between work and not-work and should introduce a "choice for a more gradual cut back of work and a final retirement on a later age" (Sociale Nota, 2000, p 37). At the same time, an important incentive for applying early exit pathways will be dismantled. Until now the financing of early-retirement schemes or pre-retirement schemes is (partly) compensated through taxation. This fiscal facility will be abolished before July 2002 (Sociale Nota, 2000, p 37).

At the moment, the effect of these changes is still marginal. In a research report for the year 1995 (Inspectiedienst SZW, 1996) it is concluded that there are still many VUT schemes. Pre-pension, part-time pension and flexible retirement is only marginal: roughly 2% of all firms use these types of scheme. The general pattern is that employees, in particular those cohorts that have been 'socialised' in the expectation of early exit, still prefer to leave work before the normal retirement age. However, the new cohorts entering this phase of working life will be confronted with new individualised pathways, such as pre-retirement, flexible retirement, and a combination of early retirement and part-time work. Since these pathways will be directly related to financial incentives and disincentives that stimulate a choice for a later exit or a combination of work and exit, it can be expected that the overall employment activity rate of older workers will increase. However, this can only be expected to happen if the quality of work improves accordingly. Otherwise an increasing use of the disability pathway would be expected.

Closing the unemployment pathway: dismantling

The third early exit pathway for older workers is the '*unemployment pathway*'. In 1997, the number of older workers (aged 55 and above) in the unemployment benefit scheme was more than 100,000. That was just below the number of participants in a VUT scheme at that time. As is the case for the high number of older workers in the disability scheme, the relatively high proportion of older workers 'using' (or sent via) the unemployment scheme has a programme-based explanation. Two specific exceptions within the unemployment regulation made it possible and even attractive to use this scheme for the early exit of older workers.

The first exception was the so-called 'elderly guideline' in cases of mass dismissals. This directive legitimated the choice of older workers as the first target group for mass dismissal. In the 1970s and 1980s this rule was applied in many cases of industrial reconstruction (such as shipbuilding and within the textile industry). The second exception was the '57.5 age rule'. This rule released the older unemployed of 57.5 and older from the obligation to apply for a job.

On 1 January 1994 the 'elderly guideline' was replaced by the rule that in case of mass dismissal the group selected for dismissal should represent the overall age-profile of the company. The government is now reconsidering the 57.5 rule, and whether to reintroduce an obligation for the older unemployed to apply for a job.

Apart from these changes in the programme structure, the government is also considering introducing both negative and positive financial incentives for employers. One particular negative incentive is the introduction of a partial own risk for employers in case they dismiss older workers of 57.5 and older. In that case, the employer has to finance a proportion of the unemployment benefit for the older dismissed employee. This rule has not yet been implemented, but is a proposal. Another, positive, incentive was implemented on 1 January 2001. Employers who employ a long-term unemployed older worker aged 50 and above will receive financial compensation for doing so.

The French case

Since the early 1990s, state interventions in France have developed according to three main lines that will be described below:

- restricting early exit
- promoting measures for retaining older workers in employment
- postponing retirement through a pension reform.

Tightening early exit pathways

From 1991 onwards, public authorities decided to restrict the early exit flow out of the labour market. Measures were taken to limit early exit pathways and tighten controls over it. Three specific policies were developed.

First, public authorities tightened controls over the Special *pre-retirement Allocations* under the FNE's programme (Allocation Speciale du Fonds National de l'Emploi: ASFNE). Age-based measures in these plans were restricted by the end of 1991. Signing an ASFNE agreement with a firm provided the Employment Administration with 'leverage' to work out or diversify measures for laying off wage-earners so as to avoid, in particular, dismissing those older than 50. The government's quantitative commitment (in money) had to correspond to the firm's qualitative effort (Kershen and Nenot, 1993). Second, in 1992 it was made more expensive for firms to dismiss wage-earners older than 50. For such dismissals, a company would have to make extra payments into the Unemployment Compensation Fund (Delalande Amendment). Third, in 1992 and 1993, public measures for *gradual pre-retirement* were broadened for much the same reasons, namely in an effort to 'contain' the early exit trend and to curb its costs by partly keeping older employees in the workforce. Switching ageing employees to part-time jobs seemed like a compromise.

In a context of persistent unemployment, 'sharing work' and adjusting the time spent working seemed to provide a way to make firms start hiring, especially younger workers.

Since 1993, the Ministry of Labour administration has strongly pushed firms to use gradual rather than full pre-retirement. To its advantage, the former keeps older wage-earners in the workforce, at least partly, while also maintaining their payments into the Old Age Fund. To grant firms full pre-retirement under the ASFNE, the Ministry of Labour has made it a condition that firms implement gradual pre-retirement for their employees. This policy has strongly stimulated the growth in gradual pre-retirement. In 1995, for the first time, there were fewer admissions under the ASFNE full pre-retirement programme than under the gradual pre-retirement scheme (Baktavatsalou, 1996).

Unfortunately, the full pre-retirement programme got off to a new start in 1995 when Allocation de Remplacement pour l'Emploi (ARPE) and Allocation Chômeurs Âgés (ACA) were launched. Both were *full early exit pathways*. These new measures have totally 'cannibalised' gradual pre-retirement. They have revived the preference of both firms and wage-earners for full pre-retirement (Zaidman, 2000).

In 1995, ARPE revived the 'solidarity contracts' tradition in that it mixed up two different motivations: employment (early exit as a way to free jobs for young people, in particular) and social justice (early exit as a compensation for wage-earners who have already contributed into the Old Age Fund for too long). This arrangement enables employers to push out of the workforce those wage-earners older than 57 who have contributed for 40 years to the General Old Age Fund on condition that an equivalent number of new employees is hired. The wage-earner receives an allocation from a special fund (Fonds Paritaire d'Intervention en Faveur de l'Emploi) inside the Unemployment Fund. This undermines the radical separation of roles between public authorities and the Unemployment Fund.

In 1997, ACA came into effect. It was based on an idea of social justice, much like ARPE. Under it, older unemployed people (below the age of 60) who started working very young can receive compensation until entitlement to an old age pension. ASA (Allocation Spécifique d'Attente) was set up in 1998 to compensate older unemployed people receiving unemployment benefits or minimum income support (RMI).

Measures for keeping older wage-earners in employment or even recruiting the ageing unemployed

An active employment policy took shape in 1986-87 as part of the fight against long-term unemployment. By the early 1990s, it took the form of various measures mainly designed to modify or reduce the time spent working, resulting in the bill of law on the 35-hour working week in the late 1990s. Public authorities were aware that reform of the retirement system would not improve the ratio of total active people to inactive older people if ageing workers were not better protected and integrated in employment. Nonetheless, this awareness has not led to actions for targeting older workers to keep them in the labour market.

People over the age of 50 are not a focus for employment policy, unlike young people, women or the benficiaries of the RMI programme. The long-term jobless receive less attention form the Unemployment Fund than other age groups, even though those over 50 have a higher risk of remaining unemployed.

In France, 'affirmative action' measures in recruitment or job creation in the public sector have mainly targeted young people (for example, the 1997 Emplois Jeunes programme). A few measures open to all have aided a small fraction of ageing workers. We shall look at the three general measures: (a) aid for recruitment to lower the labour costs of 'fragile' categories in the labour force; (b) programmes for training and 'requalifying' and (c) measures for modifying or reducing the time spent working. Only a tiny proportion of public funds has been devoted to all these measures in favour of the employment of workers over 50. There is no reason, therefore, to expect substantial results. In 1992, such interventions amounted to only 7% of all measures open to job seekers aged 25 and over, whereas unemployed people over 50 made up 17% of this population (Monchois and Gelot, 1994).

Reforming the retirement system: an ongoing debate

Let us not forget that a 1983 reform lowered the retirement age to 60 in a context of worsening unemployment. The socialist government at that time did away with all measures for encouraging people to work beyond the retirement age. For instance, working a year beyond 60 does not entitle retirees to more benefits if they are already on a full pension. The French retirement system gives little room for individuals to make their own decisions (Blanchet and Pelé, 1999). Its provisions work like cut-off points.

In January 1994, Prime Minister Balladur's government reformed the General Retirement Pension devoted to all wage-earners in the private sector. The objective was to lengthen the period of contributions so as to eventually balance the books of old age funds. The main points of this reform are:

- to raise gradually the length of contribution to the General Old Age Fund required for a person to qualify for a full pension from 37 and a half to reach 40 years in 2003; people may still retire at 60 but at a lower pension rate
- to make contribution conditions to this fund stricter; the 'reference wage ' will be calculated on a gradually increasing number of years: from the best 10 years of wages before the reform up to the best 25 years for people retiring in 2008
- on drawing benefits, to index an individual's pension on prices instead of on net or gross wages – in line with what has become standard practice during the last decade, this measure will lower the relative standard of living of older pensioners; if net wages rise sharply due to high productivity growth, occasional increases beyond the consumer price index may be decided.

This reform tends to reduce future benefits for private-sector pensioners in two ways: the new reference wage is less advantageous for most people; fewer people will qualify for a full pension. It is clearly what Holzmann (2000) calls a parametric reform, or first level change according to Hall (1993).

No similar reform has yet been implemented in any of the other basic retirement schemes. The November 1995 'Juppe Plan' tried to extend this reform to other schemes; but it sparked widespread strikes, and was suspended. A new attempt made by Prime Minister Jospin from 1999 to March 2000 has not achieved a new impetus to reform.

Several reports requested by the Prime Minister have been published on retirement reform – no fewer than three by public authorities in 1999! However, none of them has come under serious discussion for implementation. The only concrete outcome of these reports has been the creation of a Retirement Council in June 2000 with the assignment to 'follow up on' the various retirement funds and write an annual report with recommendations for the government.

Conclusions

How to shift from the vicious circle of early exit to the virtuous circle of active ageing? This question condenses all the endogenous and exogenous challenges confronting European welfare states: demographic ageing with its concerns about financing old age pensions, as well as coping with labour market demands; the accelerated obsolescence of skills and knowledge along with changes in work and employment; more generally, the lifecourse reorganisation. For this reason, examining this question, illustrates possible orientations for reforming welfare states.

From the vicious circle of early exit to the virtuous circle of active ageing

How does the Netherlands manage to break the vicious circle of early exit? What is remarkable in this case is that there has not been (yet) any purposive attempt to reform fundamentally the basic rules and regulations of the existing retirement systems. Instead, we can observe institutional changes in the Dutch early exit culture. The change in the early exit culture is a result of programmatic, contextual and institutional changes. On the programmatic level we have observed the dismantling or curtailment of existing early exit pathways. The unemployment pathway has been closed, whereas the development of new 'VUT schemes' has almost come to an end. Criteria for entering the disability pathway have become much stricter. However, at the same time new early retirement pathways have been introduced, such as pre-retirement and flexible retirement. There is also now the possibility of combining part-time work and part-time VUT, representing a new opportunity. On the general level we might conclude that these new pathways have compensated the 'dismantling' of the old pathways. As such these programmatic changes do not fundamentally dismantle the general provision and entitlement of an early exit.

The fundamental change is in the basic principles that affect the claim of early exit provisions. This is what we have called the institutional change. As has been illustrated in the description of pathways, there is a clear shift from social rights and collective arrangements to incentives and individual choices. The entitlements for early exit provisions have become embedded in a system of financial incentives and disincentives. The choice for early exit has also been individualised. We have argued elsewhere that the introduction of an incentive structure reflects a break from the idiom of social rights and duties (van der Veen et al, 2000). The use of early exit programmes has changed from a collective process – a general expectation of the right of early exit, and an expectation of a public recompense – into a process of individual decisions that can be influenced by financial policy instruments. The change can be characterised as a shift from a social rights paradigm to an incentive paradigm. In other words, the Dutch have chosen to change radically the paradigm rather than just to reform rules of existing instruments, or even changes in instruments. They have undertaken a third level change, according to Hall's conceptualisation (Hall, 1993).

The change in the early exit culture is also partly the result of important contextual changes. Firstly, the change in the public opinion. There is a growing consensus in the public discourse in defining the decreasing participation of ageing workers as a negative and undesirable tendency. Within this context, age discrimination has become a rising political issue since early 1996. A variety of legal initiatives have been developed to cope with age discrimination. In 1996, a specific state-subsidised organisation was established to combat age discrimination, a further indication of the changing political context. Another important contextual change is the 'booming economy' and, as a result, an increasing demand for labour. Because older workers form an important part of the 'reserve' labour market force it is obvious that 're-integration' of older workers has become one of the policy targets.

In the French case, the pull effect of generous early exit pathways has never been seriously counterbalanced by any fundamental shift in the institutional arrangements. The timid attempts to activate the repertoire of measures for older workers were undermined by new openings of early exit pathways such as ARPE or ASA. We have observed many 'negative' public interventions – negative in that they try to restrict early exit pathways or tighten control over them. However, there have been hardly any 'positive' state interventions for improving labour market integration of ageing workers. Any that have been introduced have soon been jeopardised by the come-back of full early exit pathways opened up by social partners through the Unemployment Fund. In the case of France, we have not been able to document any deliberate shift of weight and emphasis on the various instruments and objectives of welfare policies. No paradigmatic changes can be observed.

Instead, the extreme fragmentation of French public action is obvious. The world of work and the world of social protection remain totally disconnected. The spiral of welfare without work is still prevailing. Within French public intervention there is seldom any means of regulation that crosses the lines between welfare programmes and employment policies, for example, or that allows for negotiations that could broaden the field of compromise and decompartmentalise public programmes.

As a result any attempts to work out a new contract between generations about how remunerated periods of economic activity and inactivity could be better distributed over the lifecourse have been prevented. For a country of high early exit such as France, enhancing the ability of participation in the labour market for older workers is a priority; the pension reform comes second. This main goal can only be reached by implementing a vigorous and comprehensive active employment policy targeted at workers aged 40-plus that restores and maintains their employability and therefore their individual choice in the way in which they develop their worklife at the end of their career. Instead, French public action until now has focused on reforming pension systems alone, without any attempts to reconnect older workers to the labour market via active job policies and activation of welfare entitlements. As a result welfare is further disconnected from work.

The same statement of fragmentation can be used when looking at how firms and public authorities in France interact so as to manage the end of careers. Research findings reveal strong contradictions between their conflicting rationales. Public authorities have adopted macroeconomic views in regulating the end of careers, which have no relation at all to the microeconomic point of view that prevails in firms. Companies usually handle age questions in their human resources management for reasons related to their broader objectives. As our research shows, they have their own – mainly economic or organisational – 'good' reasons, which never meet public rationale for action in labour market reform.

The diversity of situations in the world of production calls for a wide range of flexible, adaptable public measures. Instead, most of the public efforts have been concentrating on trying to reform the standards governing pension systems.

One of the main obstacles to reform has been new regulations and reorganisations relating to the lifecourse that came out from a large-scale recourse to early exit schemes. A shared 'early exit culture' has emerged that has not (yet) been counterbalanced with institutional innovations and a paradigm shift, as is the case in the Netherlands. Instead, public measures have proliferated that, subject to complex regulations, and often contradictory in goals, are administered by a diversity of actors, ranging from public authorities to social partners.

The Netherlands has more explicitly than other high early exit countries taken up the challenge confronting continental welfare states, that of trying to hook up a welfare policy with labour market integration policies and an employment policy for improving human resources. This is the price to be paid for raising the employment activity rate of people older than 50 and avoiding the end-of-career inactivity trap. Such actions call for a coordinated series of adjustments and a shift in the paradigms underlying welfare. There is no script in Europe for a 'spontaneous harmony' to emerge out of the upturn in the European labour market until 2006/2010 (Communication from the Commission, 1999). A relative shortage of labour will probably not suffice for firms to rediscover the virtues of older wage-earners and for countries on the continent to be suddenly released from the evil of high unemployment in the weakest groups.

Raising the employment activity rates of people older than 50 entails a deliberate, active policy for maintaining job qualifications and skills and for preserving the employability of people older than 40. In this respect, the strong correlation can be pointed out that exists in Europe between the employment levels of people older than 50 and efforts for training and 'requalifying/reskilling' them: the higher the employment rate of the 50-59 age group in a country, the higher the 'onsite training rate' of that age group (Eurostat, 1999a).

Most countries on the continent are not outstanding in this regard. On the whole, Scandinavia has devoted major efforts to training all age groups. In 1999, for instance, between 15% and 20% of wage-earners had received occupational training. In comparison, training efforts in countries on the continent included less than 5% of wage-earners, and an even smaller percentage of wage-earners between 50 and 59 years of age. France ranks very low in this respect. Only the Netherlands stands out on the continent in that it has devoted much more effort to training, but on a noticeably more discriminatory age basis than the Scandinavian countries (Eurostat, 1999a).

Changing exit patterns, citizenship and marginalisation

One of the dimensions of citizenship is 'participation'. The central assumption in the social citizenship debate (Dahrendorf, 1988) is that labour market participation – or in general terms 'work' – is one of the important pre-conditions of social citizenship. If so, the early exit of older workers could be interpreted as a loss of social citizenship. This is the case in countries where early exit ends up in economic marginalisation (poverty), as is the case in Hungary (Széman, 1999). Early exit in Hungary is not completely covered by (a combination) of public or private income support programmes to bridge the gap between paid employment and a public pension. Even the unemployment scheme does not cover the whole period to formal retirement. There are serious gaps for older workers. These gaps have increased as a result of the 1998 change in the age of retirement. Between 1990 and 1998 the official retirement ages were 55 for women and 60 for men; in 1998 these age limits were changed to 62 for both men and women. Because the working conditions are bad and the life expectancy is low, older workers still prefer to leave the labour market below the age of 62. Hungary went through serious economic problems and structural industrial changes that at the same time had a 'push effect' on the early exit of older workers. This resulted in an ongoing process of early exit of older workers. The main pathway is unemployment. The number of registered (older) unemployed is increasing and these people are no longer covered by the pension and healthcare systems. Early exit in this case looks like a clear case for the loss of social citizenship as well as increased social marginalisation.

However, what if early exit is embedded and integrated in the overall welfare system, based on a solid transfer system without financial gaps between income from work and old age pension? In that case early exit might be interpreted as an early entrance to a new social status and an earlier escape from the devastated work conditions. The Dutch early exit scheme VUT is an example of such a model.

At this point the question of participation is directly linked to the question of 'rights', the other dimension in the concept of citizenship. Work can be interpreted as a right, but the same can be said for early exit and/or early retirement. This is exactly where we can observe social and political conflicts in countries that try to reverse the early exit trend. The massive early exit trend has institutionalised in many 'exit countries' a so-called exit culture and social expectations of the right to have an early exit. In such a case the 'right to early exit' has replaced the right, or even the duty, to work. The spheres of work and non-work have been uncoupled.

However, the dilemma between work and non-work has become much more complicated. Until recently the questions of rights, duties and participation could be directly related to the traditional lifecourse model. In the first phase, young people are educated and prepared for the world of work (second phase). In the third phase senior citizens are entitled to retire and will receive a payment for not working. The erosion of the Fordist system of production has put an end to the relationship between successive, orderly, foreseeable phases in the lifecourse, and leads to the 'deinstitutionalisation' of the threefold organisation of the lifecourse (Guillemard, 1991). The massive trend of early exit can be interpreted as one of several trends that have contributed to the deinstitutionalisation of the traditional model. The normative standard of a uniform period of work has been broken into pieces. As a result, many provisions and entitlements that are directly related to the traditional uniform period of work are increasingly coming under pressure.

Instead of the traditional lifecourse a new, flexible organisation of the lifecourse is emerging in many modern welfare states. The various socially defined phases of time overlap in complex, diverse ways. This new flexibility results in uncertain, destandardised and mixed trajectories, as education, work and inactivity alternate in complex, variable ways that are difficult to define and to manage.

The 'old' welfare state models and their assumptions with respect to the relation between work, welfare and age seem to become increasingly out of joint and out of time with the new needs for security that more flexible lifecourse trajectories have bred. They are incapable of covering the new risks related to an accelerated obsolescence of skills and know-how, the numerous interruptions people experience during their career, and the periods of inactivity throughout the lifecourse.

If we are increasingly moving in the direction of a flexible lifecourse the whole question of work-related rights, duties and participation will change fundamentally, also for ageing workers. We assume that this flexible lifecourse will not only have an effect on the policies to re-integrate older workers, but it might as well affect the concept of social citizenship.

Reforming continental welfare state in phase with the new flexible lifecourses: 'social drawing rights'

The new, flexible, diversified phases in the lifecourse and the new needs for security related to them are increasingly out of joint with the rigid instruments used by welfare policies inherited from the Fordist model, based on a strict tripartition of the lifecourse. The gap between rigid welfare arrangements and the new needs arising out of a more flexible organisation of the lifecourse is widening. These include the need for protection against the rapid obsolescence of know-how and skills, the need to change occupations several times, and the need to spread periods of 'inactivity' out over the lifecourse. In reaction to this, the trend towards a new 'flexisecurity' model, which can be observed in many European welfare states, and which was illustrated in this chapter for the Netherlands, might give a boost to a new paradigm of flexible welfare.

New measures such as the 'social drawing rights' proposed by Supiot (1999) can be interpreted as well as a new conception of welfare. 'Social drawing rights' represent a means for 'resynchronising' welfare with work in the information era. These measures represent a new type of social entitlement, one that does not have a risk as a counterpart but, instead, a previously accumulated 'credit' that the beneficiary may use when he or she wants to. This credit will enable individuals to manage time. They will be able to benefit, as they choose, from paid periods of economic inactivity interspersed, as a function of their needs, throughout the lifecourse. This would result in new ways for individually choosing how to spread out education, work, family obligations and leisure during life.

This social drawing rights instrument can provide a way out of the system of homogenous, standard norms (the fixed retirement age, lifelong employment with a single employer and so on) and a way toward, taking into account the wide diversification of career and trajectories in existence today. These rights are aimed at providing security for individual trajectories instead of guaranteeing job security. In this sense, they 'resynchronise' welfare during the information era in phase with changes in jobs and the resulting changes in lifecourse trajectories. This social drawing rights instrument must lie at the centre of any reform of continental welfare states aimed at providing a new flexisecurity. It is the essential means for converting the labour market flexibility of time, imposed by the world of production, and the individualisation of lifecourse trajectories, into a collectively managed freedom.

Nonetheless, converting continental welfare states toward this new – more flexible but also more individually chosen – form of entitlement, or of 'social rights', supposes complex and interrelated programmatic, contextual and institutional changes, as was illustrated for the Dutch case. One crucial factor seems to be the relevant actor system of employers, labour unions and public authorities. These actors have to work out a new logic for negotiations and regulations. This 'logic' must differ from the 'neo-corporatist' forms that, having prevailed until now under the continental welfare state model, have led to a segmented, fragmented welfare system. Comparing the Dutch and French case at this point we might conclude that in the Dutch case a more fundamental change in the actor system has occurred than is the case for the French situation. The French case seems to be captured in the existing actor constellation and its logic, and as a result in the 'right of early exit'.

Acknowledgements

This chapter is partially based on the results of the COST A13 working group 'Ageing and Work'. We wish to express our appreciation for the work of all the participants in this working group that has helped us to write this chapter.

References

Baktavatsalou R. (1996) 'Les dispositifs publics de Préretraite en 1995', *Premières Synthèses*, no 35-2, Paris: DARES.

Blanchet, D. and Pelé, L.P. (1999) 'Social Security and retirement in France', in J. Gruber and J. Wise (eds) *Social security and retirement around the world*, Chicago, IL: University of Chicago Press.

Ctsv (1998) *Augustusrapportage arbeidsongeschiktheidsverzekeringen 1998*, September, Zoetermeer: Ctsv.

Dahrendorf, R. (1988) *The modern social conflict*, London: Weidenfeld and Nicolson.

de Vroom, B. and Naschold, F. (1993) 'The dialectics of work and welfare', in F. Naschold and B. de Vroom (eds) *Regulating employment and welfare: Company and national policies of labour force participation at the end of worklife in industrial countries*, Berlin/New York, NY: Walter de Gruyter.

de Vroom, B. (1996) *Combating age barriers in job recruitment and training: The National Report of the Netherlands*, Dublin: European Foundation for the Improvement of Living and Working Conditions.

Dutch Parliamentary Documents (1963) Document 27171/3, (Parliamentary year 1962-1963), 'sGravenhage: SDU.

Dutch Parliamentary Documents (2000) Document 27402/2, (Parliamentary year 2000-2001), 'sGravenhage: SDU.

Esping-Andersen, G. (ed) (1996) *Welfare states in transition*, London: Sage Publications.

European Commission (1999) *Towards a Europe for all ages* (Commission 1999, 221) Brussels.

Eurostat (1999a) *Labour force survey*, Luxemburg: Office for Official Publications of the European Communities.

Eurostat (1999b) *Demographic statistics*, Luxemburg: Office for Official Publications of the European Communities.

Eurostat (2000) *Yearbook 2000*, Luxemburg: Office for Official Publications of the European Communities.

Guillemard, A.M. (1991) 'Pathways and their prospects: a comparative interpretation of the meaning of early exit', in Kohli et al (eds) *Time for retirement: Comparative studies of early exit from the labor force*, Cambridge: Cambridge University Press, pp 362-87.

Hall, P.A. (1993) 'Policy paradigms, social learning and the state: the case of economic policy making in Britain', *Comparative Politics*, vol 25, no 3, pp 275-96.

Holzmann, R. (2000) 'The World Bank approach to pension reform', *International Social Security Review*, vol 53, no 1, pp 11-34.

Inspectiedienst SZW (1996) *Ouderenbeleid in Cao's en arbeidsorganisaties*, The Hague: Ministerie van Sociale Zaken en Werkgelegenheid.

Kershen, N. and Nenot, A. (1993) 'La fin des préretraites ou l'éternel recommencement?', *Droit social*, no 5, May, pp 470-82.

Kohli, M., Rein, M., Guillemard, A.M. and van Gunsterden, H. (eds) (1991) *Time for retirement: Comparative studies of early exit from the labor force*, Cambridge: Cambridge University Press.

Monchois, X. and Gelot, D. (1994) 'Les bénéficiaires de la politique active de l'emploi de 50 et plus', in A.M. Guillemard and L. Salzberg (eds) *Emploi et vieillissement*, Paris: La Documentation Française.

OECD (Organisation for Economic Cooperation and Development) (2000) *Employment outlook 2000*, Paris: OECD.

Percheron, A. (1991) 'Police et gestion des ages', in A. Percheron and R. Rémond (eds) *Age et politique*, Paris: Economica.

Pfau-Effinger, B. (1998) 'Gender cultures and the gender arrangement – a theoretical framework for cross-national gender', *Innovations*, vol 11, no 2, p 147.

Pierson, P. (1994) *Dismantling the welfare state*, Cambridge: Cambridge University Press.

SCP (Social and Cultural Planning Agency) (1999) *Rapportage Ouderen 1998*, 'sGravenhage: SCP.

Supiot, A. (1999) *Transformation of labour and future of labour law in Europe*, Report for the European Commission, Paris: Flammarion.

Széman, Z. (1999) 'National profile Hungary', in B. de Vroom (ed) *Working Group Ageing and Work: National profiles*, Enschede: University of Twente.

van der Veen, R., Trommel, W. and de Vroom, B. (2000) 'Institutional change of welfare states: empirical reality, theoretical obstacles', in H. Wagenaar (ed) *Government institutions: Effects, changes and normative foundations*, Amsterdam: Kluwer Academic Publishers, pp 33-53.

van Ewijk, C. (2000) *Ageing in the Netherlands*, The Hague: CPB, Netherlands Bureau for Economic Policy Analysis.

Walker, A. (ed) (1996) *Combating age barriers in job recruitment and training*, Dublin: European Foundation for the Improvement of Living and Working Conditions.

Zaidman, C. (2000) 'Les dispositifs de cessation d'activité: etat des lieux et évolutions souhaitables', in D. Taddei, *Retraites choisies et progressives*, Paris: La Documentation Française, pp 95-121.

TEN

Movements by the unemployed in France and social protection: the *Fonds d'urgence sociale* experience

Denis Bouget

With more than 10,000 demonstrations each year, including 1,000 in Paris alone, social protest continues to play a fundamental role in French political life. Since the mid-1980s, some have been organised by 'new social movements' (Waters, 1998, p 183), involving anti-racist movements, solidarity movements, AIDS advocatory movements and so on. This chapter will analyse a short period of social evolution in France: the protest actions by the unemployed in 1997-98, the immediate reaction of the French government, which distributed one billion French francs (FF) to claimants through a social relief fund called the *Fonds d'urgence sociale* (FUS), and its consequences for the social welfare system. It is difficult to analyse this short episode and avoid two stumbling blocks on which understanding comes to grief. One mistake would be to underestimate the exact social role of the opinion voiced because the movement appears to be more or less hidden or confined to the outer limits of society and because it seems to exert little influence. The FUS was a temporary scheme that had no significant impact on the basic social protection systems in France. However, this interpretation neglects the close reciprocal interrelationship between the existence of the protests and the social protection system that inspired them. Another error is to overestimate the action of the movements by the unemployed: tough militant demonstrations tend to be violent and the media exaggerates the situation at a point in time that does not represent long-term reality.

This chapter will analyse the relation between the movement by the unemployed and the French social protection system, since this episode of the FUS reveals its many weaknesses. The first section explains the reasons for potential conflict between the French social welfare system and the unemployed. It highlights the confused relationship between solidarity and social citizenship. The second section describes the history of the movements by the unemployed in France, their demonstrations, their links with other new social movements, and the dissatisfaction that fuelled their specific claims partly as a result of the Juppé plan and the strikes in 1995. The third section analyses the social policy responses and government decisions concerning the demonstrations in 1998, especially the creation and the management of the FUS, which confirms a shift towards a residualised model of citizenship. We will conclude by offering general lessons on the long-term changes and consequences of these protests.

Unemployment and social protection in France

Description of the system and its principles

The unemployment benefit system is based on social insurance financed by wage-based contributions and on social assistance, a 'solidarity' fund financed by national taxation.

After the Second World War, France created a social protection system based on social insurance. Social security was created in 1945 to cover social risks and focused on pensions, family benefits and health services (Dupeyroux, 1995). A general scheme to cover unemployment in the private sector was set up in 1958 and was called *Union interprofessionnelle pour l'emploi dans l'industrie et le commerce* (UNEDIC). Today, UNEDIC still remains, operating on the same principles and independent of social security and its reforms. National policy is implemented by local branches, called the *Associations interprofessionnelles pour l'emploi dans l'industrie et le commerce* (ASSEDIC). They collect all the social contributions from the firms and they pay unemployment benefits to claimants.

As a model of social insurance, UNEDIC obeys several rules and principles. It is not a state body, but a private non-profit organisation managed according to the 'paritarian' principle. This means that UNEDIC is managed by representatives of employers from professional associations and representatives of employees from trade unions. Insurance premiums are paid by employers and employees in accordance with the 'paritarian' principle. Wages and professional incomes form the basis of contribution. All private firms obey the same schedule of contribution rates for each employee. This schedule is based on the principle of progressivity: the rates slightly increase as the individual wage goes up.

The only contributors are the socially insured. Individuals' social rights, especially the eligibility for unemployment benefits, are based on a 'socially insured' status, defined by payment of social contributions before an individual becomes unemployed. Eligibility criteria for unemployment benefits are also similar in all sectors: a minimum period of work (four months), age (16-60), and waiting period (a minimum of one week).

Another basic principle of the French social protection system is equality for everybody confronted by risk and non-discrimination between risk classes within each group of insured persons (Lattès, 1996, p 15; Blanchet, 1996, p 33). The social insurance system produces horizontal solidarity among employees and their families, which justifies and organises redistribution of income from the employed to the unemployed.

Unemployment benefit is wage-related. Its duration is related to age and the period in work (MISSOC, 2000). The amount varies in accordance with the individual's previous contribution record. The proportionality between benefits and earnings refers to the compensatory principle of the social welfare system within groups of employees or workers. Unemployment benefit cover is neither founded on basic need or on any principle of basic income, for example.

As with other social risks, unemployment insurance is compulsory for every employee. This removes adverse selection effects and reduces the social division of society. Hence, many economists understand social contributions as earmarked taxes.

Since 1992-93, a new rule stipulated that individual benefit be reduced as the period of unemployment lengthened. Consequently, the benefit is called *allocation unique dégressive*. After 30 months in unemployment, entitlement to UNEDIC-ASSEDIC benefit runs out. The unemployed can then demand 'solidarity' benefit. In a perfect model of social insurance, people who are not socially insured or who are family members of the claimant receive all their social allowances from the assistance sector. A Bismarckian model cannot work without sustaining public assistance for poor and vulnerable groups (children, disabled, or elderly people in a non-contributory sector (Eardley et al, 1996a, 1996b). This distinction between social insurance and social assistance (sometimes called '*solidarité*' today) is very marked in French social welfare (Esping-Andersen, 1990; Ploug and Kvist, 1996), especially as regards protection for the unemployed. In 1984 an important reform distinguished the solidarity scheme – financed by and under the responsibility of the state – from the social insurance scheme which remained managed by UNEDIC. Today, this solidarity scheme means that unemployed people who have exhausted their social insurance-based benefit receive public assistance from the state. The most well known is the *allocation de solidarité spécifique* (ASS), which is a categorical minimum income for the unemployed, situated within the assistance sector. The allowance varies following a marginal rate of 100%, amounting to FF2,552, equivalent to €389, (the same as RMI) in 2000.

However, policies for combating poverty are today becoming increasingly complex because of the growing embeddedness of social institutions (de Gaulle Anthonioz, 1995). Intervention by the public bodies may be seen as a set of social policies designed to offset the failure of the contributory system.

The principles of social protection for the unemployed are similar to other schemes in the French social protection system (sickness, family and pensions): paritarism, socially insured status, compulsion, wage based, wage-related allowance, the compensatory principle and a dual system. However, several features of unemployment benefit differ from other insurance schemes. Historically, socially insured status focused on the welfare of the worker and his or her family. Entitlements were mainly derived from employment, and family member benefits depended on the entitlements of the breadwinner. Within the UNEDIC, unemployment benefit was and still is totally independent of any family criteria (arrangement, size). Reforms of unemployment benefits in 1984 and 1992 retained the Bismarckian model, while the reforms of the other social insurance schemes experienced several contradictory trends throughout the 1980s and 1990s, sometimes tending towards a privatisation of the system and sometimes towards a state system of social protection.

In short, the French system is based on professional solidarity, sometimes on work-based citizenship.

Unemployment, social exclusion and social protection

After the Second World War, the creation of the social security scheme failed to gather all the previous funds into a single administrative body. The idea then was to extend social security to achieve universal social protection, because the French system was originally based on full-time paid work contributions during the Fordist era of full employment (Esping-Andersen, 1996). This extension occurred in the 1970s. Until the oil crisis, economic growth guaranteed full employment. People could be either socially insured, or claim as a breadwinner's dependent. This extension logically entailed a decrease in the intervention of social assistance under the responsibility of public agencies. Several benefits hitherto managed under social assistance by the state or local government were turned into social security benefits (housing benefits, disability allowances) managed by the social security institutions. Until the 1970s,

France had sustained the futuristic ideology of a non-poverty society. The conjunction of full employment and social insurance was able to fulfil the dream of universal social protection. This universal breadwinner model represented social citizenship in a Keynesian welfare state, a system largely based on work and social contributions.

In the early 1980s, new factors cropped up called *nouvelle pauvreté* (new poverty) or social exclusion (Bourdieu, 1993; Robbins, 1994; de Gaulle Anthonioz, 1995; Paugam, 1996; Room, 1999). Most of the roots of growing poverty in this decade originated in the economic field: unemployment, long-term unemployment and precarious working conditions (such as temporary work and low pay for young employees). Poverty and social exclusion were and still are a temporal process that affects several vulnerable groups including the unemployed, young people, wives, single parents and immigrants. However, at the same time, there are several differences compared with past poverty:

• in France, senior citizens are no longer considered to be vulnerable; elderly and retirement policies since the 1960s have been successful
• social exclusion is more an urban problem than a rural one
• the temporal process of social exclusion has created a generational distortion: young people seem to be more vulnerable
• poverty mostly affects isolated people.

The creation in 1988 of the minimum income scheme, called the *Revenu minimum d'insertion* (RMI), for people older than 25, was implemented to fight poverty and social exclusion. It was also based on a social citizenship doctrine and combined an allowance and a programme of integration. Simultaneously, it gradually developed as an unemployment solidarity scheme (Belorgey, 2000). Today, 90% of the recipients of RMI who are unemployed do not receive any form of unemployment benefit. This means that RMI has become the third component of the unemployment benefit system in France, besides the ASSEDIC (social insurance) and the ASS (specific unemployment assistance).

The gradual impoverishment of young people and adults since the 1980s has highlighted several failures in the French social protection system (Rosanvallon, 1981, 1995; Castel, 1995). The objective of universality was supposed to derive from the contributory system; elements of universalism and citizenship-based rights were coupled with the dominant social insurance model (Clasen, 1997). However, over time an inconsistent situation developed between the small financial contribution of the state and its great juridical involvement. Government intervention gradually became commonplace (specifying allowance amounts, eligibility criteria and so on), without any change in financial contribution. This continued until the creation of a new earmarked tax, the *contribution sociale généralisée* (CSG) in 1990.

Despite the wishes of policymakers, it has always been impossible to bring all categories of contributors together into a single body, a problem that all governments have had to face. Since its creation in 1945, social security has continued to be differentiated by occupational groups (Baldwin, 1990; Clasen, 1997; Palier, 1997; Bouget, 1998). Each social institution has tried to protect its managerial autonomy based on parity between employees and employers that 'excluded' the state. Throughout the 1990s, this autonomy was well illustrated by an underlying conflict between the government and UNEDIC, mainly concerning financing problems such as the balance on the deficit of the UNEDIC budget.

Since the creation of the French social protection system, the paritarian rule (employers/employees) of management of the social welfare system has never been an appropriate response to extensive social rights for all the citizens or residents in the country. In the same way, the paritarian rule failed to manage the social welfare system when society suffered from a high chronic unemployment rate, a huge change in working conditions and from precariousness. Consequently, an increasing section of the population lost access to a social welfare system dominated by contributions. They were entitled to benefits as citizens, but received only 'solidarity' benefits via public assistance. The problem of non-contributory benefits became more and more acute in an economy with high unemployment. The emphasis on equity and the extension of means-testing, even in the contributory sector, had simultaneously shifted the idea of solidarity based on horizontal income redistribution towards vertical income redistribution. A contributory system could not cope with this shift from horizontal to vertical solidarity. As we can see, '*solidarité*' had at least three meanings in the 1980s and the 1990s. Historically, it represents a major feature of the work-based system of social protection (Baldwin, 1990). In the 1980s, the reference to 'solidarity' is used by new social movements that seek to develop a participatory culture involving the marginalised elements of society. It is explicitly used by governments to justify and to implement new schemes of social assistance. The concept of social citizenship has more or less followed the same trajectory. In the name of equity, and to target those most in need, social citizenship becomes an ideological reference to justify new social policies for the socially excluded.

Since the creation of the French social security system in 1945, financial problems have constantly been on the agenda (Dupuis, 1995). Since the late 1980s, social insurance funds have been threatened with bankruptcy because they have experienced chronic deficit. The financial burden has fallen on the programmes of unemployment, healthcare, retirement pensions and also on family policy.

Social contributions have also been blamed for increasing labour costs, thereby having a negative employment effect. The basis of the social contribution, being attached to wages, triggered a high tax on labour that has produced a more severe effect on unskilled labour costs.

In the early 1990s, the French system seemed unable to provide solutions to several problems:

- the rise in healthcare expenditure
- the future of pensions on a 'pay as you go' basis in an ageing society
- the increasing poverty or social exclusion which mainly derived from unemployment and job insecurity
- the chronic and increasing deficit in social protection
- the European and international dimensions of social policies (Beck et al, 1997).

While the French social protection system was not the main cause of unemployment and social exclusion, it was able to influence its duration by implementing new eligibility criteria for unemployment benefits. In 1984, the reform of social protection for the unemployed created a clear dividing line between the contributory sector (UNEDIC) and the non-contributory sector (state). The aim of this reform was to improve the respective institutional role of each participant and to clarify the process for claiming unemployment benefits. Paradoxically, this rational improvement in management has reinforced social dualism and the hierarchy between contribution-based social entitlements and assistance-based social rights. This social dualism was highlighted by the action of the movements by the unemployed.

Movement by the unemployed in France

The permanent drawbacks in French social protection, exposed in the previous section, forged a background from which two other significant events evolved and which sparked the movement by the unemployed: the increase in long-term unemployment on the one hand and the strategy of the French trade unions on the other.

Since the early 1980s, permanent and occasionally deep economic recessions caused massive unemployment that was both extensive and intensive. Long-term unemployment had gradually been identified as the main cause of job insecurity and social exclusion (Paugam, 1992, 1996, 2000), because the long-term unemployed lost social entitlement to any contributory unemployment benefit. During the last two decades, the increase in long-term unemployment (see Figure 10.1) helped to construct a new social group. This creation of an autonomous social group was also reinforced by several targeted employment policies in favour of the long-term unemployed, identifying them as a group. When socially insured employees became unemployed, the contributory system (ASSEDIC) provided unemployment benefit for a limited period. After that, they became a *fin de droit* (without any social right to benefits) because they had exhausted their social entitlements and gradually shifted towards public assistance. As explained in the previous section, they gradually 'sank' into public assistance for the poor.

Faced with this trend, the trade unions were obliged to reflect the political interest of both the employees at work and the unemployed. In France, trade unions are still characterised by low levels of membership among the employees, the lowest among developed countries (less than 10%). There are several trade unions, including the *Confédération générale du travail* (CGT), *Confédération française démocratique des travailleurs* (CFDT), *Force ouvrière* (FO) and *Confédération française des travailleurs catholiques* (CFTC). For several decades, they have been gradually losing their influence among the employees; membership fell from 20% in 1970 to less than 10% in the late 1990s. However, they continue to utilise representative positions in various official institutions, especially within the social security organisation (family, sickness and pensions) and unemployment insurance (UNEDIC, ASSEDIC), which are based on representative parity between employer associations and trade unions. Officially, all workers' interests, both those of the employed and unemployed, are represented by trade unions.

Since the early 1980s, this conventional view of the role of trade unions had become fractured. A significant number of employees and unemployed people considered that their interests (unemployment benefit and so on) were insufficiently supported by the traditional trade unions. Strikes in firms started without the agreement of the trade unions and more frequently turned into spontaneous workers' movements, often called '*coordinations*', that is, under direct representation of those in the strike (nurses, farmers, and so on). Strikes gradually gave birth to these new spontaneous organisations that rejected the bureaucratic style of traditional trade unions and their inability to resist employers who were cutting

Figure 10.1: Unemployment rate and long-term unemployment in France (1970-98)

Source: INSEE

their labour force during periods of economic recession. The unemployed argued that trade unions either focused their actions on defending insider interests (civil servants and so on) or collaborated with different governments in reducing labour market rigidities to develop greater flexibility within personnel management in the firm.

The unemployed did not gradually identify themselves with trade union action. In fact, sporadic demonstrations by the unemployed against the trade unions emerged and their movements articulated specific claims.

Small associations of unemployed workers sprang up all over France. According to several indicators, by the mid-1990s there were about 8,000 such associations. These were often very small, isolated and scattered and were partly organised by various national associations: *association pour l'emploi, l'information et la solidarité des chômeurs et des travailleurs précaires* (APEIS), *Agir ensemble contre le chômage* (AC), *Mouvement national des chômeurs et des précaires* (MNCP).

Throughout the 1980s and the 1990s, the unemployed also launched sporadic demonstrations, especially against the local branches of the ASSEDICs, the funding body in charge of contributory unemployment benefits. There was a convergence with other protest movements that sprang up within the voluntary sector and charitable institutions undertaking voluntary work for poor and excluded people. Besides a renewal of voluntary work for the poor (for instance, restaurants for the poor), these new movements protested against public bodies in the name of fundamental social rights in favour of the 'have-nots' (people without a job, education, a flat or a house, an identity card, and so on). For instance, the movement *Droit au logement* (Right to housing) organised militant action such as occupying empty flats, in favour of housing for the poor. Other popular movements helped immigrants to obtain French identity cards via extensive demonstrations against the government. New worker organisations, '*coordinations*' – spontaneous protest groups born out of local demonstrations in firms, movements by the unemployed and new charitable and protest institutions – gradually created a part of the 'new social movement' in France that often broke away from the other traditional social institutions and trade unions (Pendariès, 1995; Demazière, 1996; Combesque, 1998; Dethyre, 1998; Salmon, 1998).

This trend was not confined to France: the organisation of and action by the unemployed extended to Europe. The groups built a European network for the unemployed. They held several European demonstrations or marches (Brussels 1994, Amsterdam 1995, Luxembourg 1997) and received support from European deputies in the 'European Convention for full employment'.

Claims from the movement by the unemployed were divided into two parts, claims for the long-term unemployed, and those for the short-term unemployed. The main long-term claim was for full employment. They requested a reduction in the working week (to 32-35 hours per week), reflecting the popular idea in France that a reduction in the supply of work causes a decrease in unemployment. They also demanded legal representation within the paritarian branches (ASSEDIC) that manage unemployment benefits. Certain associations also called for a basic income scheme.

In the short term, the claims focused more on insecurity in daily life: an active opposition to the eviction of tenants, the requisitioning of empty houses in favour of poor people, demonstrations against ASSEDICs in favour of the *prime de Noël* (a yearly ASSEDIC unemployment benefit distributed in December), free public transport, and the increase in and standardisation of the various minimum incomes in the French social protection.

They refused the traditional pattern of assistance for the poor, and defended the idea of universal general social protection that entailed equal social rights. However, the originality of their claims was that they combined two types of social culture. On the one hand, they reflected the culture of the workers' movement in France, the trade unions' culture of claim and demonstration and, on the other hand, they claimed social rights that historically belonged more to the social assistance sphere.

Contradictions within French social protection, especially in the organisation of the unemployment benefits gradually became acute (as was seen in the previous section). Since the reforms of 1984 and 1992, stricter criteria of eligibility to unemployment benefit over a reduced period of time and a decreasing allowance over time had gradually been introduced to balance the UNEDIC budget. This reform and these permanent financial adjustments decreased the percentage of the unemployed who received the ASSEDIC benefit (Table 10.1) and entailed a further shift from the insurance sphere to the assistance sphere. The more socially fragile were increasingly diverted towards assistance schemes. In 1997, UNEDIC management produced a budget surplus but, simultaneously, reduced its social fund. This fund was reserved for the *fin de droits*, or the have-nots, thereby forcing more poor unemployed people on to means-tested social assistance.

Table 10.1: Statistics on unemployment benefits and recipients

	1980	1993	1998
% of unemployed who receive an ASSEDIC benefit	75.0	62.0	42.0
% of unemployed who receive an ASS		10.0	10.0
Replacement rate* of the ASSEDIC benefit (%)		61.0	70.0
Replacement rate* of the ASS (%)		40.0	41.0

*Amount of the benefit divided by the previous wage (%)

Source: UNEDIC, INSEE

The immediate consequences of these contradictory events were several demonstrations by the unemployed before and after the Christmas of 1998, which compelled the French government to intervene in their social conflict with the ASSEDICs:

• the occupation of public buildings became longer and longer, sometimes coming close to violence
• small scattered groups of unemployed people became coordinated nationally, more or less on the same pattern as other previous protest movements (nurses, farmers and so on)
• the strength of movement by the unemployed grew, thanks to the support of some French trade unions (CGT), which overall were divided towards this movement
• embryonic Europeanisation extended the action of the unemployment movements (marches to Brussels in 1997 before the Amsterdam Treaty, the Renault-Vilvorde events in 1998 when Renault closed down their factory in Belgium)
• a close coverage of the movement in the media (on French TV and in newspapers) provided all French people with more information
• the increasingly inconsistent management of unemployment benefits by the UNEDIC and the ASSEDICs gave this movement strong popular legitimacy.

The movement by the unemployed also demanded government action to raise minimum incomes by:

• lowering the age criterion for the RMI to 18 instead of 25
• providing a relief fund to replace the *Prime de Noël*
• raising minimum income up to FF3,500 per month instead of FF2,500, especially the RMI and the ASS
• a standardisation of minimum incomes.

Despite this activity, for several reasons, the voice of the unemployed, in the long term, was probably weak. The action of the movement by the unemployed was often caught between trade union action on the one hand, and social assistance on the other. These unemployed groups failed to obtain any political representation within different official institutions in France. They were not recognised by the trade unions who viewed them as illegitimate competitors, and they did not gain any representation on the administration of social assistance.

In the wake of the transitory and sporadic government policy, the attitudes and the role of the movement by the unemployed was also ambivalent. On the one hand, because of their role as claimants, several local groups refused to participate in the management of the FUS. On the other, they operated as a pressure group and used their influence to create significant publicity to swell the demand for benefit.

Local studies indicate the range of social action achieved by the movement by the unemployed. Close media coverage focusing on some tough local events (Marseille, Seine Saint Denis) concealed a significant weakness in the movements in many other French *départments*.

Finally, the unemployed movement reflected many features of the new social movements: independence from the major political parties and trade unions, new forms of action involving the socially excluded, and the short-term and ad hoc nature of their organisation (an informal network of local associations) (Waters, 1998; Appleton, 1998). The social structure of the unemployed remained very heterogeneous. The movement was the product of growing long-term unemployment and had little socioeconomic identity. High long-term unemployment in France, since the middle of the 1980s, was a structural feature that was the main cause and component of social exclusion. However, its recent dramatic drop has weakened this structural interpretation, linking social exclusion to long-term unemployment. As the unemployment rate fell, the strength and the voice of this group declined, as national economic performance reduced any potential social identity among the unemployed.

Government reactions: *Fonds d'urgence sociale*

Throughout 1998, the French government attempted to introduce several social policies to stop the daily demonstrations by the unemployed. In fact, the government was not prepared to manage this conflict. As a result, its attitude was hesitant and changeable: its decisions were largely an improvised response to social pressure. Several decisions or proposals were announced. Before the Christmas holidays of 1998, the government expected the actions by the unemployed movement to weaken but, faced with the continuing strength of the movement, it proposed accepting its claim for specific representation of the unemployed on ASSEDIC; almost all the trade unions rejected this proposal. The French government adopted a step-by-step policy. On 12 January 1998 it decided to distribute urgently FF1 billion to 'very poor people'; this fund was the FUS. The government also commissioned a statistical analysis of the FUS at the national level (SESI, 1998), a report to analyse the problem of minimum incomes in

France (Join Lambert, 1998) and studies to analyse the implementation of the FUS at the local level.

Analysing the short history of the limited FUS reveals several characteristics of the fragmented French social protection system for the unemployed and the shift towards restricted social citizenship inspired by the residual model of social protection.

The fund was distributed among the *départements* according to two criteria: the local unemployment rate and the proportion of RMI recipients among the inhabitants. Within each *département*, the *Préfet* – the local representative of the central government – organised the distribution through a *Mission d'urgence sociale* (MUS), which gathered voluntary representatives from social institutions including:

- social services of the *département*, which manage local social assistance
- the *Direction départementale d'action sanitaire et sociale* (DDASS), which is the local government office for various social policies
- the *Caisses d'allocations familiales* (CAF), which are the local branches that distribute family benefits
- the ASSEDIC, which is the local branch that distributes contributory unemployment benefits
- the *Centres communaux d'action sociale* (CCAS), which are the local council social centres
- the *Agence nationale pour l'emploi* (ANPE), which registers the unemployed.

In each *département*, a local form of benefit was swiftly set up and distributed to potential claimants. Locally, the MUS had to decide on the criteria of eligibility and the amount of benefit to allocate to each person.

This episode came to a close once the fund was exhausted (around July–August 1998). It is instructive to analyse some lessons from this exercise.

Demand for FUS benefit: poverty

In January and February 1998, a high flow of demands arrived at the offices of the *Préfet* in each *département*. This flow was influenced by local social 'mobilisation' in favour of the unemployed. After February, the influence and the action of the movements by the unemployed waned and the flow of demand also dropped. The information contained in these demands has been analysed in several studies to identify the claimant population. The results often contradict popular ideas about them.

In 1998, the demonstrations by the unemployed were interpreted as the emergence of a new social group, excluded from French social protection. However, contrary to expectations, the FUS did not cast light on a new type of poverty. All the surveys show that the social 'profile' of the applicants for FUS was largely similar to those observed in other surveys of poor people (isolation, single parenthood, very low resources and chronic poverty, unemployment, debts, and so on) or to the social profile of recipients of other social assistance programmes. Common distinctions between applicants coming from the social insurance side (ASSEDIC) and applicants coming from the assistance side were difficult to perceive.

According to popular opinion, claimants were supposed to live in urban more than rural areas, mainly because demonstrations by the unemployed in urban areas were more widespread than in rural areas. However, statistical and local studies do not characterise them as an urban phenomenon because in rural areas, several agencies were also able to promote FUS (town councils, local social insurance agencies in rural areas, social workers).

Another paradox is that few RMI recipients (10-20%) demanded the FUS benefit (Fassin et al, 2000). Only the RMI recipients who were in debt (especially housing debts) felt it was legitimate to demand the FUS. This reveals a huge gap between the principles underpinning the FUS and its actual application. It had officially been launched to help people who had suffered an accident, an exceptionally bad event, whereas the real expression of the demand was the revelation of chronic poverty, insufficiently ameliorated by minimum income guarantees or other specific benefits designed to combat poverty.

There is also a sizeable gap between the action by the unemployed and the government initiative, which did not refer to unemployment but to poverty.

Distribution of FUS benefits: urgency versus equity

Eligibility criteria for the FUS were quickly established, but in some confusion. At the national level and according to the government, the main criterion was to be in extreme poverty, combined with exceptional events (such as sudden indebtedness, high unforeseen expenses). The national reference was the existence of distress but without any other precise guidelines. At the local level, each *Préfet* had to implement this general, vague rule in the *département* and sometimes specified more detailed criteria. These ranged from no supplementary criteria at all to a precise schedule defining the amount of benefit according to existing income, household size, debt level and so on. Within the assessment committee (MUS), the members distributing the individual allowances often had to build a doctrine of eligibility and rules guiding eligibility criteria and amount of benefit. Local studies of the implementation of the FUS in France stress the improvisation of local rules on a daily basis, called '*doctrine empirique*'.

Equity principles used to manage the FUS combined the following sources: vague recommendations by the government (extreme poverty, exceptional events), sometimes a more detailed list of criteria decided by the *Préfet* (the income schedule, for example), and the '*doctrine empirique*' of the MUS. Sometimes, in a *département*, the final rules for decision-making were based on explicit means-tests, sometimes on internal rules of the MUS hardly known by the claimants.

Faced with the vagueness of eligibility criteria and the priority of the urgency, the decision process in the distribution of the benefit requires interrogation. Non take-up (van Oorshot, 1991, 1996; Atkinson, 1995; Math, 1996) has been studied as an important cause of social policy inefficiency. Within the FUS experiment, it could happen frequently and for several reasons:

- mobilisation of the unemployed varied widely according to the *départements*; it was very weak in many local areas
- the uncertainty of eligibility criteria resulted in hesitant behaviour by the unemployed regarding applications
- a section of people who felt themselves unable to fill in the request form gave up applying
- the tasks and the behaviour of social workers were uncertain and ambiguous; sometimes they helped the claimants, sometimes they refused to help them
- certain unemployed people refused to apply for the allowance because they considered that they were entitled to unemployment benefit from the UNEDIC-ASSEDIC and not from the public assistance for the poor
- sometimes local decisions explicitly excluded certain social groups from the FUS (immigrants, Gypsies, and so on).

The vagueness of eligibility criteria explains why the decisions of the MUS were hardly sensitive to poverty among applicants. Sometimes, the recipients of RMI were officially refused because they had a permanent income. The issue of debt was a commonly applied criterion but only for small debts because another institution was in charge of the management of deeply indebted households.

There were several effects from the supply side. One of the most important factors that influenced eligibility for benefit was previous contacts with social workers. The probability of receiving benefit was higher in these cases. This occurrence reflected a common phenomenon concerning other benefits (Gilles-Simon and Legros, 1996, p 54). In general, social workers often appear as a key element in aiding access to social benefits in France. For instance, among poor people who apply for RMI, the percentage of recipients of social benefits is higher when they are in contact with social workers.

Much of the poor quality administration found in the FUS stemmed from an impossible balance between urgency and equity. According to local studies (Bouget, 2000), the average period for administering FUS benefit, that is the duration between the date of application and the date of the decision by the MUS, was three weeks. This result demonstrates the complexity of all the decision processes in social action. In general, urgent intervention in social policies (Maurel, 1993; Dourlens, 1998) is justified by specific personal circumstances, mainly chronic and extreme poverty or/and exceptional events that are liable to cause social catastrophe. The indebtedness of poor households commonly illustrated this phenomenon in the FUS episode.

This focus on urgency highlights the inefficiency of several social protection schemes in France, which demonstrate the length of time taken to assess claims and deliver benefits, even for poor people. For instance, the time taken to assess a claim for RMI can be more than six months. This illustrates the contradiction between the prolonged administrative process required by bureaucratic organisation and the accumulation of criteria of eligibility on the one hand, and the needs of poor people, which justify urgent action, on the other.

Urgent intervention in FUS provision was enacted with certain opacity or with an indetermination that facilitated local adjustments and local strategies. This shift from social rights to discretionary intervention could also reinforce moral distinctions between the deserving and the undeserving poor (Fassin et al, 2000; Retière, 2000).

All these phenomena show the impossible balance in the FUS episode between urgent intervention and the rules of equity, because the compilation of information took too long, especially the verification of household income, and common principles of equity were too vague to determine the amounts of social benefits. This time dimension seems self-evident and dominates other criteria, especially social rights and equity of decisions.

Pragmatism in organisation under a priority of urgency

Today, within the fragmented French system of social protection, any emergency social policy needs the cooperation of other social institutions. Many social programmes to combat poverty in France are based on this principle, because no single social agency has enough authority to combat social exclusion alone. In the case of the FUS, local state administration (*Préfet*) was unable to implement the whole programme. Therefore, its administration in each *département* was based on a voluntary, pragmatic and local partnership comprising a range of social institutions (as outlined above), united in the MUS. This partnership was a skilled one and was able to start very quickly because a large number of institutions were already involved in other similar social policies that stimulated an institutional learning in practice.

The partnership came under the supervision of the *Préfet* and several partners agreed to contribute to the management of the FUS. However, this participation was more or less a 'constrained voluntary participation' and consequently, the partnership was unstable and short lived. The state sought financial participation by other social institutions to broaden the funding but, except for the ASSEDICs, most social institutions refused to supplement the state fund because they feared being drawn into a 'catch-22' situation.

During the last two decades, within a fragmented system, each social institution has sought to protect itself from externalities produced by decisions by others. This institutional protectionism in a very fragmented and corporatist system has automatically created 'gaps' in social protection because no single institution can guarantee social rights for all. The accumulation of specific benefits, for the sake of efficiency, did not guarantee real social cover for poor people because non-take-up could be large and unknown. Gaps in support have been complemented with excess support, because pragmatism has generated a multiplicity of benefits and a piling up of urgent interventions that have not been particularly well coordinated.

The discretionary rules of FUS management were also interpreted as a political response to cope with the daily demonstrations by the unemployed movement in December 1997 to January 1998. Local strategies varied from one *département* to another. Some decided to apply severe criteria from the outset (January and February 1998). In this way, they could stretch the budget over a longer period; taking the opposite route, other *départements* decided to apply generous criteria to give immediate satisfaction to poor people and to the unemployed, ignoring the long-term future. Nothing was planned as regards continuing the FUS, which appeared to be a central political decision within the social sphere. Local political representatives feared a 'come-back' by the state against the decentralisation process of social policies in France. Social workers were also scandalised by this discretionary and short-term policy of the government (Autes, 1992).

This episode also reflects the reluctance of local authorities and social insurance institutions to be over-involved in national social policies. Since the 1980s, there has been a gradual accumulation of benefits in favour of the poor, but with no clear hierarchy or priority or subsidiarity rules. One hypothesis is that, faced with extreme poverty, social insurance has largely become inefficient. However, we also need to question the role of decentralisation and local strategies in assistance policies. An implicit subsidiarity rule tended to compel the state to relieve extreme poverty, which seems largely to contradict the supposed efficiency of action by local public bodies to combat social exclusion at a local level.

Social assistance and minimum incomes

The knowledge of the limits to minimum incomes in France is not new (Vanlerenberghe, 1992; CERC-Association, 1995). Since the start of the RMI, they have been thoroughly described, especially their two drawbacks: the insufficiency of the amount and the complexity of eight different minimum incomes. Two demands remain over time: to increase the amount of minimum incomes and to standardise them. Rather than increase the minimum income in January 1998 (a claim by the unemployed), the French government preferred to create a new scheme, the FUS. In March 1998, the report by M.T. Join Lambert revived the same claims. However, contrary to the claims of the unemployed and also the recommendation of M.T. Join Lambert, the Fight Against Social Exclusion Act (29 July 1998), did not improve minimum incomes, or introduce standardisation. It only included a specific and permanent scheme for relief intervention (CASU), which today looks quite as frail as the FUS.

In December 1998, further demonstrations by the unemployed emerged. The government immediately decided on a retrospective hike in minimum income for 1998 and another increase in 2000. Standardisation continues to be disregarded, despite the publication of a report (Belorgey, 2000) that again insists on reform. Since the FUS episode, the standardisation of minimum incomes has remained untouched.

Compared with the minimum incomes in France, the FUS episode can be considered as a new progression of pure economic assistance (Gough, 1999):

- the absence of clear criteria of eligibility raised the discretionary dimension of the benefit
- the benefit clearly imposed no obligations; it was a long way off activation policies
- the benefit was totally external to the remit of social work, of any personal restoration, and of any increase in employability; it was totally divorced from *accompagnement sociale*, that is integration policies for individuals.

The FUS simultaneously showed the limits of individual support and was a break with this trend. This break or opposition was largely legitimated by the unemployed movement, which considered that people needed cash benefits to boost their income without any personal social services, which were perceived as a tutelage.

Conclusions

In France, many reforms in social protection have been justified by budget deficits. However, all the polls demonstrate that the system was and is largely supported by the population. One of the consequences of the FUS episode is to show publicly several shortcomings of the system. This reduced its strong popular legitimacy and changed the nature and the content of social citizenship, which become a 'slippery term' (see Chapter Three of this book). The extension of the notion of citizenship has become so wide as to render it indistinct.

The short history of the FUS reveals some of this trend. Within the French organisation, in covering the risk of unemployment, the contributory sector can be described as the full social rights sector, whereas the solidarity sector is part of the assistance sphere. This forges a hierarchy between social rights for the socially insured, whose rights derive from the contributions they pay to the socially assisted, who receive benefits in the name of national solidarity. However, both can refer to social citizenship. The contributory sector is an element of the Bismarckian model in France that can be justified by the idea of social democracy (paritarian management of the social security in a Fordist era). The social assistance sector, through the increasing reference to fundamental rights, also refers to social citizenship.

The FUS showed a new and original type of social movement combining the classical strategies of labour demands, albeit external to trade unions, to obtain social benefits marked by assistance characteristics. The unemployed movement has also been analysed as a 'new citizenship' because it has worked as a pressure group, demonstrating in favour of a marginalised section of the population and claiming employment as a fundamental right.

However, the detailed presentation of the management of the FUS also showed the limits to the reference to social citizenship in the French social protection system. The increase in unemployment meant the contributory sector of social insurance failed to become a universal scheme. The fragmentation of the French system and its complexity has also reduced the quality of the reference to social citizenship. Despite all reforms of the French social welfare system since its creation, UNEDIC really has remained a 'perfect' Bismarckian model. This 'autonomy' has remained until now, even in the new paritarian scheme of unemployment insurance, within the framework called *Refondation sociale*, which is a new liberal reform of the unemployment insurance scheme largely imposed by the employers associations (CNPF) in 2000-01.

The following features characterise the FUS episode:

• contrary to expectations, the distribution of the FUS allowance did not reveal a new social group of poor people
• the implementation of the FUS alternated between the political aim of social harmony and economic aid
• the distribution of the allowance was a pure public assistance scheme without any strict control of the income, or any obligation by recipients to integrate or become actively involved in the labour market
• the necessary partnership revealed permanent tensions between the fragmented institutions and the procedures they followed
• the partnership also revealed a tension between social policies designed to serve fundamental rights (food, housing, education and so on), and the pressing need to unify these initiatives in the fight against poverty in France.

The categorisation of social citizenship has become fragmented. The term social citizenship has been used by all the institutions and social groups to justify their actions.

Acknowledgements

This chapter is largely inspired from a synthesis report, *Mieux connaître les problèmes et les pratiques révélés par la mise en place des Fonds d'urgence sociale en France*, of seven local studies to the Ministry of Social Affairs. I wish to thank the authors of the local reports, the anonymous referees and also Noel Whiteside who scrutinised my paper.

References

Appleton, A. (1998) 'The new social movement phenomenon: placing France in comparative perspective', *West European Politics*, vol 21, no 3, pp 57-75.

Atkinson, B.A. (1995) 'On targeting social security: theory and western experience with family benefits', in D. van de Walle and K. Nead (eds) *Public spending and the poor, theory and evidence*, Washington, DC: World Bank/Johns Hopkins University Press, pp 11-24.

Autes, M. (1992) *Travail social et pauvreté*, Paris: Syros Alternatives.

Baldwin, P. (1990) *The politics of social solidarity, class bases of the European welfare state 1875-1975*, Cambridge: Cambridge University Press.

Beck, W., van der Maesen, L. and Walker, A. (1997) *The social quality of Europe*, The Hague/Bristol: Kluwer Law International/The Policy Press.

Belorgey, J.M. (chair) (2000) *Minima sociaux, revenus d'activité, précarité*, Paris: Commissariat Général du Plan.

Blanchet, D. (1996) 'La référence assurantielle en matière de protection sociale: apports et limites', *Economie et Statistique*, nos 291-2, Paris: INSEE, pp 33-48.

Bouget, D. (1998) 'The Juppé Plan and the future of the French social welfare system', *Journal of European Social Policy*, vol 8, no 2, pp 156-72.

Bouget, D. (2000) 'Mouvements des chômeurs, institutions sociales et pouvoirs publics: l'episode du Fonds d'Urgence Sociale', *Revue Française des Affaires Sociales*, vol 55, no 1, pp 51-75.

Bourdieu, P. (1993) *La misère du monde*, Paris: Éditions du Seuil.

Castel, R. (1995) *Les métamorphoses de la question sociale, chronique du salariat*, Paris: Fayard.

CERC-Association (1997) *Les minima sociaux: 25 ans de transformations*, Les Dossiers de CERC-Association No 2, Paris: CERC-Association.

Clasen, J. (ed) (1997) *Social insurance in Europe*, Bristol: The Policy Press.

Combesque, M.A. (1998) *Ca suffit!*, Paris: Plon.

de Gaulle Anthonioz, G. (1995) *Evaluation des politiques publiques de lutte contre la grande pauvreté*, Paris: Journal Officiel, Avis et Rapports du Conseil Economique et Social No 3.

Demazière, D. (1996) 'Des chômeurs sans représentation collective: une fatalité?', *Esprit*, no 11, November, pp 12-32.

Dethyre, R. (1998) *Chômeurs, la révolte ira loin*, Paris: La Dispute.

Dourlens, C. (1998) *Dans les labyrinthes de l'urgence, le cas de l'Adiministration Sanitaire et Sociale*, Rapport au Ministère de l'Emploi et de la Solidarité, Paris: Cerpe.

Dupeyroux, J.J. (1995) *Droit de la sécurité sociale*, Paris: Dalloz.

Dupuis, J.M. (1995) *Le financement de la protection sociale*, Paris: Presses Universitaires de France.

Eardley, T., Bradshaw, J., Ditch, J., Gough, I. and Whiteford, P. (1996a) *Social assistance in OECD countries: Synthesis report*, Department of Social Security Research Report No 46, London/Paris: HMSO/OECD.

Eardley, T., Bradshaw, J., Ditch, J., Gough, I. and Whiteford, P. (1996b) *Social assistance in OECD countries: Countries reports*, Department of Social Security Research Report No 47, London/Paris: HMSO/OECD.

Esping-Andersen, G. (1990) *The three worlds of welfare capitalism*, Cambridge: Polity Press.

Fassin, D., Defossez, A.C. and Thomas, V. (2000) 'Les inégalités de chances dans l'accès aux secours d'urgence', *Revue Française des Affaires Sociales*, vol 55, no 1, pp 121-38.

Gilles-Simon, M.O. and Legros, M. (1996) 'Le Non-Recours chez les Pauvres: une Approche Empirique', *CNAF, Recherches et Prévisions*, no 43, March, pp 51-8.

Gough, I. (1999) 'Social assistance in OECD countries', Conference Reforming Social Assistance and Social Services, International Experiences and Perspectives, European University Institute, December.

Join Lambert, M.T. (1998) *Chômage: Mesures d'urgence et minima sociau; problèmes soulevés par les mouvements de chômeurs en France, Fin 1997-Début 1998*, Paris: La Documentation Française.

Lattès, G. (1996) 'La protection sociale: entre partage des risques et partage des revenus', *Economie et Statistique*, nos 291-2, Paris: INSEE, pp 13-32.

Math, A. (1996) 'Le non-recours en France: un vrai problème, un intérêt limité', Cnaf, *Recherches et Prévisions*, no 43, March, pp 23-32.

Maurel, E. (1993) 'L'urgence sociale: tabou?', *LIR*, no 70, June, pp 4-8.

MISSOC (2000) *Social protection in the member states of the European Union, 1999*, Luxemburg: Office for Official Publication of the European Communities.

Palier, B. (1997) 'A liberal dynamic in the transformation of the French social welfare system', in J. Clasen (ed) *Social insurance in Europe*, Bristol: The Policy Press, pp 84-106.

Paugam, S. (ed) (1996) *L'exclusion: L'Etat des savoirs*, Paris: La Découverte.

Paugam, S. (1992) *La disqualification*, Paris: Presses Universitaires de France.

Paugam, S. (2000) *Le salarié de la précarité*, Paris: Presses Universitaires de France.

Pendariès, J.R. (1995) 'Les mouvements de chômeurs et de précaires: contradictions et enjeux', *M*, no 78, August-September.

Ploug, N. and Kvist, J. (1996) *Social security in Europe, development or dismantlement?*, Kluwer Socac Series on Social Security, vol 3, The Hague: Kluwer Law International.

Retiere, J.N. (2000) 'En retard pour l'aide d'urgence: analyse des courriers des demandeurs', *Revue Française des Affaires Sociales*, vol 55, no 1, pp 139-56.

Robbins, D. (1994) *National policies to combat social exclusion, Third Annual Report*, Brussels: Observatory on National Policies to Combat Social Exclusion, CCE-DGV.

Room, D. (1999) 'Social exclusion, solidarity and the challenge of globalization', *International Journal of Social Welfare*, vol 8, no 3, pp 166-74.

Rosanvallon, P. (1981) *La crise de l'Etat-providence*, Paris: Le Seuil.

Rosanvallon, P. (1995) *La nouvelle question sociale; repenser l'Etat-providence*, Paris: Le Seuil.

Salmon, J.M. (1998) *Le désir de société, des restaurants du cœur au mouvement des chômeurs*, Paris: La Découverte.

SESI (Servicer des Statistiques des Etudes et des Systèmes d'Information) (1998) *Eléments d'etudes pour un bilan du Fonds d'Urgence Sociale*, Paris: Ministère de l'Emploi et de la Solidarité.

van Oorschot, W. (1991) 'Non take-up of social security benefits in Europe', *Journal of European Social Policy*, vol 1, no 1, pp 15-30.

van Oorschot, W. (1996) 'La question du non-recours aux prestations sociales', Cnaf, *Recherches et Prévisions*, no 43, March, pp 5-18.

Vanlerenberghe, P. (1992) *RMI, le pari de l'insertion: Evaluer pour proposer*, Paris: La Documentation Française.

Waters, S. (1998) 'New social movement politics in France: the rise of civic forms of mobilisation', *West European Politics*, vol 21, no 3, pp 170-86.

ELEVEN

Changing welfare states and labour markets in the context of European gender arrangements

Birgit Pfau-Effinger

Concepts of citizenship and gender

In the last decades of the millennium, women have increasingly been integrated into Western European labour markets. However, there were considerable differences in the development paths of European labour markets concerning the structures of labour market integration and labour market exclusion, indicated by the development of labour force participation rates of women. The differences also concern the forms in which women were integrated into waged work. In most countries, it is mainly the part-time employment of women that has increased[1]. The proportion of women working part time today varies to a high degree in the European Union, from 11% of all employed women in Finland to 67% of all employed women in the Netherlands (OECD, 2000). How can such differences be explained?[2]

Social integration and social exclusion of women within labour markets was in the last years often discussed in the framework of a broader debate on welfare state policies, social inequality and social citizenship[3]. This debate was inspired by T.H. Marshall's work on social citizenship, conceptualised as a means to measure the degree to which welfare states promote social integration of all citizens on the basis of equality (Marshall, 1950, pp 5-6). Feminists have criticised this approach for it was based on a male norm: on waged work being the implicit basis of citizenship (Pateman, 1988). It was argued that women were for a long time excluded from paid work and are still not yet fully included; instead, they are seen as being responsible for unpaid domestic care work (Orloff, 1993; Lewis and Ostner, 1995). According to this argument, citizenship rights based on domestic care work in Western societies are of minor quality – women are seen as 'second class' social citizens (Orloff, 1993; Sainsbury, 1994). The question of which type of social citizenship can contribute to comprehensive and full social integration of women into society, to the improvement of gender equality and the gaining of "equal social worth" of women and men according to Marshall's ideas (1950), is crucial for the analyses and interpretation of cross-national differences in the labour force participation of women in European countries, particularly also in relation to part-time work of mothers. In a majority of approaches to social citizenship in feminist discussion (see Orloff, 1993; Sainsbury, 1994; Lewis, 1997, 1998), the full integration of women into waged work, and a full provision of public childcare, are seen as an avenue to full citizenship of women and gender equality. Cross-national differences in the labour force participation of women, and with respect to full-time versus part-time integration, are accordingly most often seen as indicating a differing quality of social rights of women, of their right to be 'recommodified' (Ostner, 1994).

This approach has been criticised by Knijn and Kremer (1997): they argue for a concept of 'including' citizenship, by which they mean that social citizenship should include the right to care, as well as the right to be cared for, guaranteed and promoted by the welfare state. This has far-reaching consequences concerning the interrelations of labour market, gender and citizenship: it would mean that women (and men) could also gain full citizenship if they take the responsibility in the field of domestic care work.

In general, there are substantial problems connected to the way concepts of social citizenship, labour market and gender are discussed:

• the way social citizenship is conceptualised is in part more a normative than an analytical approach
• it is implicitly based on the assumption of coherence between welfare state policies and labour market behaviour of women
• the dimension of 'culture' is not systematically integrated into analyses
• social change is often not conceptualised.

Citizenship as normative approach

In the current debate, often abstract concepts of social citizenship are, from a theoretical feminist perspective, discussed without reflecting that different concepts may match different societal contexts. Ruth Lister (see Chapter Three), in a more elaborated approach to the relationship of gender and social citizenship, points to the interrelation between citizenship and social agency. According to her argument, social citizenship rights can be subject to processes of renegotiation and are in principle open to re-interpretation and renegotiation of social actors. If we conceptualise citizenship in that way, we should also consider that in different societies the question of which concept of social citizenship is adequate for promoting full social integration and gender equality might be answered in different ways by women and their representatives, mainly the feminist movement, because of differing cultural and institutional traditions in these countries[4]. The theoretical concept of social citizenship should not be used in a normative, essentialist way (see also Bang et al, 2001) but in the first line as an analytical concept, to analyse and compare welfare state policies.

Citizenship as coherent unity of welfare state policies and labour market behaviour

A shortcoming of these approaches is that they often conceptualise citizenship as a coherent unity of the way in which welfare states shape and construct social citizenship rights on one hand, and the patterns of labour market behaviour of women on the other. They often do not adequately take into account the ways in which welfare state policies – and the ways they define social citizenship rights – are embedded into society. In particular, this means that they do not respect adequately the complex interplay of welfare state policies, labour markets, culture and social agency, which might be connected with tensions, contradictions and asynchronies between the way welfare states define social citizenship on one hand, and the way individuals use social rights on the other. Individuals do not simply react in their behaviour to state policies.

Lack of culture dimension as explanation for cross-national differences

The role of cultural values and ideals for the construction of social rights by the welfare state is usually neglected in these approaches. We must examine the idea that the social practice of individuals is heavily influenced by predominant ideals and values concerning the 'correct' division of labour between both genders. Individuals act within a complex framework of different types of institutions, cultural values and ideals and social structures. This is not in principle coherent, but can be characterised by contradictions and asynchronies. The underlying cultural ideals and values for the construction of social citizenship by the state and the social practices of individuals are crucial to explain why social citizenship is defined in different ways in differing welfare states, and why also social practices of citizenship vary. It is also necessary systematically to include culture – the dimension of societal ideas, meanings and values – into any theoretical framework for the explanation of cross-national differences in the employment patterns of women and their links to social citizenship rights.

Missing conceptualisation of social change

These approaches are static and do not really conceptualise change within welfare state policies, the way welfare states construct social citizenship, and the way this interrelates with social and cultural change.

The theoretical framework for cross-national analyses should take into account the way welfare state policies define social citizenship of workers and carers, and are embedded into the respective societal context (see also Bang et al, 2001).

Cross-national analysis of gender policies of welfare states in the framework of gender arrangements

This section will outline a way to analyse welfare state policies and their impact on the labour market integration in a gender perspective in the framework of the theoretical approach of the 'gender arrangement' (Pfau-Effinger, 1996, 1998a, 2000).

How can the 'societal context' of welfare state policies be conceptualised? In a very general understanding, it is on the one hand formed by the interplay of welfare state policies with other institutions such as the labour market or the family. These interrelations are the main subject of the '*effet sociétal*' approach (Maurice et al, 1986; Maurice, 1995). Maurice et al argue that these interrelations form a particular profile in each society. This profile is substantially influenced by the cultural basis to which they refer. The societal context is therefore on the other hand also formed by 'culture' – constructions of sense such as knowledge, ideals and values to which individuals and institutions refer, including ideas about what is 'good' and 'bad' (Neidhard, 1986). Welfare state policies and culture are mutually interrelated in complex and also perhaps in contradictory ways. They form a complex framework for social agency and social structures. Social actors contribute to the reproduction or, under certain conditions, change of elements within this framework, by conflicts, negotiation processes and compromises. These theoretical assumptions refer to the theories of David Lockwood (1964) and Margaret Archer (1995) (see also Pfau-Effinger, 2000).

Theoretical approach of the 'gender arrangement'

The approach of the 'gender arrangement' which I have introduced in earlier publications (Pfau-Effinger, 1988a, 2000) refers to a certain part of this societal context, namely the interplay of culture, institutions, social structures and agency in relation to gender (Pfau-Effinger, 1996, 1998a, 2000). It is based on the assumption that within the general cultural framework, in every modern society certain uniform ideas exist about the desirable, 'correct' form of gender relations and of the division of labour between women and men. These are institutionalised as norms and therefore remain relatively constant. There is in principle a '*longue durée*' of these cultural values and ideals. These values and ideals are defined here as the 'gender cultural system'. At different social levels the dominant values and norms form a main reference point for the gender discourses and gender practices of each new generation of actors – both at the level of institutions (such as the welfare state and firms) and at the level of everyday life. Cultural change may be caused by contradictions within the gender culture and/or by the development of new cultural ideals within particular social groups. The development of the gender culture is interrelated but is also relatively autonomous in relation to the *gender system* (or gender order). This comprises the pertinent structures of gender relationships, as well as the relations between different societal institutions with reference to gender structures. Connell (1987) distinguishes three gender structures, which are interrelated, but in part are also relatively autonomous from each other: divisions of labour, power and 'carthexis' (the emotional and sexual relationships between genders). Three societal institutions are of most importance for the gendered division of labour in modern industrial societies: the labour market; family/ households, and the state; the education system is also influential. The role of collective actors is important, particularly that of the feminist movement (Mósesdóttir, 1995).

The respective *gender arrangement* forms the framework produced by the gender cultural system and the gender system (or gender order). Such an arrangement stresses the overall binding contents of gender culture and the gender structures. In turn, these are the result of social negotiations and struggles within the binding contents of the gender culture and on the gender structures.

The question of which ideals and values are dominant within the gender cultural system is the result of conflicts, negotiation processes and compromises of social actors with differing power levels at an earlier stage of historical development. The gender cultural system has a strong impact on the gender discourses and practices of each new generation of actors. The gender cultural system also forms a main reference point for social action and policy formulation at the level of the welfare state, where it is implemented as norms and expectations of what is normal, and as a central basis for the institutional construction of social citizenship. It also has this influence in other institutions, such as the labour market and the family, and on collective actors and individuals themselves.

However, under certain circumstances individuals or groups of social actors develop new ideas, or adopt ideas from different contexts, and may try to negotiate a new dominant gender arrangement. This is particularly the case if tensions and contradictions inside the cultural or the social system, or between both systems, have developed. A good example for such contradiction at the cultural level was the development in West Germany in the 1960s. During general processes of democratisation after the end of the Second World War, the idea of autonomous and equal citizens that are integrated into society by the labour market gained cultural importance, whereas the cultural foundation of social integration of married women was still based on the idea of personal dependency within marriage. This was the central cultural contradiction to which the new developing feminist movement in the 1960s and 1970s referred and which they took as a starting point for their policies, which were mainly directed at implementing cultural change (Pfau-Effinger, 2000).

Change at the level of gender culture can thereby contribute to change in welfare state policies. The outcome is influenced by the power relations between these actors, for instance between the feminist movement as a new social movement on the one hand, and the Conservative political parties on the other. The cultural foundations of welfare state policies are mutually interrelated with the dominant cultural ideals about family and gender relations in the population and form a cultural reference point for other institutions such as the labour market and the family (Pfau-Effinger, 2000).

The theoretical differentiation between gender cultural system and gender system is particularly important when analysing a change of gender arrangements. Change at the cultural and the institutional level can take place at differing speeds and create various tensions, breaks and asynchronies between both levels. It can also contribute to the emergence of contradictions and asynchronies in the relationship between gender policies of welfare states, cultural orientations, and labour market behaviour of women, which we would not understand without analyses of the complex interplay of cultural and institutional change.

Classification of gender arrangements by the dominant gender cultural models

The 'profile' of gender arrangements can be described by the dominant gender cultural models. I have earlier suggested (Pfau-Effinger, 1998a, 1999a) a classification of gender cultural models, based on the following criteria:

- cultural ideals about the gender division of labour, the main spheres of work for women and men, the social valuation of these spheres, and the way in which dependencies between women and men are constructed
- the cultural construction of the relationship between generations, that is the construction of childhood, motherhood and fatherhood.

Using this classification model it is possible to distinguish between at least six gender cultural models in Western Europe, which include more traditional and new cultural models. These are the:

- family economic gender model
- male breadwinner/female homecarer model
- male breadwinner/female part-time carer model
- dual breadwinner/state carer model
- dual breadwinner/dual carer model
- dual earner/marketised female carer.

There also exist mixes between these models. One example is in Sweden, where a dual breadwinner/dual carer model is combined with elements of private care for children, and mothers in the phase of active motherhood tend to work part time (although mostly with long hours not much below the level of full-time employment). In some countries different gender cultural models are dominant at the same time, as in Germany where in former West Germany the male breadwinner/female part-time carer model is dominant, while in the former German Democratic Republic the dual breadwinner/dual carer model is the central model. A co-existence of two dominant models can also occur when the gender arrangement is in the transformation process from one dominant family model to another. This is the case in the Netherlands, where at the cultural level the dual breadwinner/dual carer model is dominant, whereas in practice most couples still live in correspondence with the male breadwinner/female part-time carer model (Pfau-Effinger, 2000).

The explanation of welfare state policies is not restricted to the influence of cultural values and ideals alone. Welfare state policies are also the result of differing interests of social groups and some social groups have more power than others. Welfare state policies therefore contribute substantially to the development of social inequality, including gender inequality. In this view, gender culture, institutions, gender structures and social actors are mutually interrelated within the gender arrangement, and the concept forms an appropriate framework for cross-national analyses of differing welfare state policies and their dynamics of change (Pfau-Effinger, 1998a, 1999a).

Interrelations of welfare state policies and social practices of individuals within the gender arrangement

The interrelations between welfare state policies and social practices of individuals are a complex matter. The social action of individuals is not a simple outcome and not determined by state policies, although this is often assumed when data on behaviour (such as the labour force participation rates of women) are used as an indicator for welfare state policies. Such an assumption does not reflect the fact that the social behaviour of individuals is a process that takes place in a complex field of influences, where cultural ideals and values also play an important role. Duncan and Edwards (1997, 1999) have criticised the assumption of 'rational economic man' on which analyses of the impact of welfare state policies on behaviour are often based. According to their argument, individuals do not simply act according to principles of 'economic rationality' but also with respect to principles of 'moral rationality'. In turn, these principles are related to cultural ideals and values. Similarly, Pfau-Effinger (1998a, 2000) found that cross-national differences in the development of female labour force participation rates and part-time working in Finland, the Netherlands and West Germany cannot be explained by simply referring to welfare state policies. Instead, the complex interplay of culture, institutions, structures and social actors within the respective gender arrangements must be considered.

So long as the respective gender arrangement is coherent, the labour force participation rate of women may to a large degree conform with the aims of welfare state policies. This is because in such cases welfare state policies and behaviour refer to the same set of cultural values and ideals on gender relations, as for example in West Germany and the Netherlands in the 1950s and 1960s. However, in times of social and cultural change in the respective gender arrangement, things can be different. Women may act according to new cultural orientations in spite of welfare state policies that are traditionally orientated and sanction their new behaviour negatively so that this even seems to be 'irrational'[5]. For example, in the Netherlands and West Germany in the 1970s it was possible that, according to cultural change, women became more orientated towards waged work and increasingly participated in the labour force, whereas welfare state policies were still Conservative and promoted the housewife model of the family. Change may take place at the level of culture and in the behaviour of individuals while welfare state policies still promote more traditional gender cultural models, particularly in those cases in which the power relations still favour traditional (usually male) elites (Pfau-Effinger, 2000)[6]. Cross-national differences in the gender policies of welfare states, and in the ways in which they construct social citizenship, can be substantially explained by differences in the gender cultural foundations to which welfare state policies refer, and by the interests of those social groups that are influential in reconstructing old compromises, or in the struggle for new compromises. The gender policies of welfare states overlap in a specific way with those policies of welfare states that refer more closely to the differing class interests of capital and labour, the varying outcome of which has been conceptualised by Esping-Andersen (1990) as 'welfare regimes'. The respective combination of gender culture with the class-based welfare regime contributes substantially to cross-national differences of social policy between societies with similar gender cultures (Pfau-Effinger, 1999b, 1999d, 2001)[7].

Analyses of changes in welfare state policies within European gender arrangements

To understand changes of welfare state policies, the differentiation between both dimensions of welfare state policies – policies that are directed towards the capital-labour arrangement, and policies that are directed to the gender arrangement – is important. Both can develop in different ways. In the Netherlands, for example, in the 1950s and 1960s the welfare state was organised on the basis of more or less social democratic ideas about the capital-labour arrangement, in combination with a gender policy that was based on the gender cultural model of a male breadwinner–female home carer family. As a consequence of a modernisation of the gender arrangement, labour force participation rates of women have been – and are – increasing with a strong dynamic since the 1970s.

Labour force participation rates of women in countries that have been classified by Esping-Andersen as 'conservative' welfare regimes, for example, are changing with such a dynamic that they soon might adapt to the level of social democratic welfare states. However, the development of these welfare regimes took a different direction with respect to other central features that are related to the capital-labour arrangement and distinguish them from each other. Already today, the labour force participation rates of women in Finland, a social democratic welfare regime, and Germany, a Conservative welfare regime, are similar. So it does not make much sense to discuss the issue of 'path dependency' of welfare state policies without distinguishing between both dimensions.

Modernisation paths of gender arrangements

It is possible to distinguish at least three different modernisation paths of gender arrangements in western European countries in which the form and degree of women's labour force participation developed in different ways (Pfau-Effinger, 1998a, 1999b, 2000). These modernisation paths can be characterised by the change in the dominant gender cultural model. They started with distinctly different gender cultural models and ended (for now) with different models. Changes in welfare state policies did not always correspond to cultural change, but there were substantial time lags and discrepancies between the two.

The first modernisation path characterises development in West Germany and in the Netherlands. It started with the traditional male breadwinner/female carer model and developed towards a modernised version in West Germany of the male breadwinner/female part-time carer model and a dual breadwinner/dual carer model in the Netherlands. The traditional male breadwinner/female carer model is a cultural model that represents the 'Parsonian' model of the gendered division of labour and reflects the cultural traditions of the urban bourgeoisie (Pfau-Effinger, 1998c). This conforms to the idea of the basic differentiation of society into public and private spheres. Men are regarded as breadwinners who earn the income for the family in the public sphere with waged work, whereas women are primarily regarded as being responsible for the work in the private household including childcare, and thus become dependent on the income of 'their' breadwinner. This is also based on a social construction of childhood according to which children need special care by their mother at home to be supported comprehensively as an individual being. The male breadwinner/female part-time carer model is a modernised version of the male breadwinner model. Here, the cultural construction of motherhood is in principle based on the idea of a parallel combination of unpaid caring and part-time paid employment as well as on the financial dependency of the caring mother on the male breadwinner during the phases of active motherhood. In contrast, the dual breadwinner/dual carer model reflects the notion of a symmetrical and equitable integration of both genders into society. Childrearing is to a large extent the responsibility of both parents. The basic idea is that the family economy consists of an equal distribution of domestic work – in particular childcare – and waged labour between a female and male household member where there is mutual dependency of both spouses.

While the gender arrangements of these countries were characterised by a relatively high degree of coherence in the 1950s and 1960s, change since the 1970s took place at different speeds and at different levels. It led to manifold discrepancies, contradictions and asynchronies between (and inside) the cultural and the institutional level and at the level of social agency of women. Cultural change often preceded change of welfare state policies and was a main cause for change of the labour market behaviour of women, whereas welfare state policies took a considerable time to react to cultural change and change in the employment behaviour of women.

The second modernisation path of gender arrangements is a certain variant of the first one in that it equally started with a male breadwinner/ female carer model and was modernised in the direction of a male breadwinner/female part-time carer model. However, it ended with a male breadwinner/female marketised carer model. This model is based on the idea of full integration of women and men into full-time waged work. The family is seen as responsible for organising and paying for marketised childcare, by using commercial childcare facilities or by employing childminders in the household. This is a new model that has gained increasing importance in countries such as Britain (and the US), where welfare state interventions are much less seen as a solution to problems of labour market exclusion than in other welfare regimes (Crompton, 1998; Yeandle, 1999). The welfare states of these countries in the 1990s started an 'activation' policy to integrate the whole population into the labour market, but without also providing a comprehensive social citizenship right to care or to be cared for or a comprehensive infrastructure for childcare. As a consequence, manifold tensions and contradictions emerged at the cultural level, between the cultural recognition of the need of children to be cared for on the one hand, and the cultural ideas about the working mother and the liberal, non-interventionist welfare state on the other. The market solutions for childcare provision, which are culturally seen as the main alternative, are mainly available for middle-class families. The chances to combine waged work and care differ considerably for women of different social classes. The situation is particularly difficult for single-parent families (Daly and Lewis, 1998).

The third modernisation path of gender arrangements started with a family economic gender model and ended with a dual breadwinner/ state carer model, as in Finland. The family economic model is in principle based on the cooperation of women and men in their own family business (farm or craft work), in which both genders contribute substantially, and in mutual dependence, to the survival of the family economy. Children were treated as members of the family economic unit, that is, as workers, as soon as they are physically able to contribute. The dual breadwinner/ state carer model was then adapted to the modern industrial society with employment usually taking place outside the home. What changed was the main mode of social integration: now the main sphere for social integration for everyone was the labour market (Anttonen, 1997). This model is based on the idea of the full-time integration of both sexes into the employment system. Women and men are seen as individuals, who in marriage are both breadwinners who earn income for their own living and for that of their children. The task of caring for children is substantially seen as the task of the welfare state, not only of the family.

The welfare state played a crucial role in the modernisation processes that occurred within this development path. Following a substantial expansion of the social care services sector after the Second World War, welfare state policies started to implement a comprehensive public infrastructure for childcare and, at the same time, create a large sector of jobs for women in the public sector. As a result of a considerable increase in the quality of public childcare and the introduction of a university education for professionals in this sector since the 1980s, the quality of public childcare as well as the quality of the jobs for women in this sector is comparably high (Julkunen and Rantalaiho, 1991; Kröger, 1996; Anttonen, 1997). Because of the individualisation in terms of social security and income, and because of the comprehensive integration of the adult population into the labour market, single mothers are not particularly discriminated against in terms of income and social security. When Finland experienced a deep recession, mainly caused by the loss of Eastern European markets in the 1990s, this resulted in a higher financial burden for private households. However, this did not result in the comprehensive public provision of social care services being questioned (Anttonen, 1997).

Welfare state policies to promote gender equality

As described above, within European countries different cultural ideas about the interrelationship of labour market integration and social inclusion of women (and men) prevail, which are not all based on full labour market integration of women. There is not one unique conception of social citizenship that would be the 'best', 'most women friendly' one and would create 'equal social worth' (according to Marshall, 1950) for women and men.

Welfare states promote the aim of gender equality best if they refer to the innovative, egalitarian elements within the respective gender cultural models shared by the majority of women. The Netherlands gives a good example of the importance of analysing the interrelations between welfare state policies and the cultural ideals of women. Part-time work by women (and also by men) has been substantially promoted by the state, in a relatively protected form and with similar quality to full-time jobs (Plantenga, 1996). We could conclude that this promotion of part-time work for women was a more traditional gender policy, based on the exclusion of women from full-time employment. However, this would be a misleading interpretation. An analysis of change in cultural orientations in the attitudes and behaviour of women (and men) towards waged work helps to understand and interpret this development more adequately. The modernisation path of the gender arrangement was based on cultural change, as described in path one above. It ended up in the cultural dominance of a new and more egalitarian model that can be classified as the dual breadwinner/dual carer model. It is based on the idea that fathers as well as mothers work temporarily part time, which is also indicated by the results of the ISSP (see Haller and Höllinger, 1994). The promotion of part-time work by the state can be seen as an element of an equalising gender policy. It is also supported by the feminist movement as a contribution to greater gender equality (Plantenga, 1996). In social practice, by the millennium this model had been realised only to a limited degree. Even though the rate of men working part time was the highest in Europe by 1998 (at 19%) (OECD, 1998, p 192), it is still mainly women who work part time. This means that they are dependent on the income of their male breadwinner so long as they are partnered. To empower women adequately, with respect to the dominant cultural model of gender equality, a stronger promotion of part-time work for men would be needed. Some type of substitute for the loss of full-time income would also be necessary to free part-time working individuals from dependency on a breadwinner. However, there is a strong pressure for change towards more equal family and employment patterns. Post-divorce social protection for carers is relatively high. In the case of single-parent families, the state acts as a substitute for the male breadwinner and pays a type of income to the heads of these families, which is considerably above the subsistence level (Bussemaker and van Kersbergen, 1994). Also, a universal retirement scheme with a minimum retirement pension that is above the subsistence level minimises the risk of poverty for workers who previously combined employment and care by working part time (Bussemaker and van Kersbergen, 1994; Knijn, 1994; Plantenga, 1996). This is different for instance to Germany where no minimum pension exists (Veil, 1996; Ginn and Arber, 1998).

In other words, the promotion of part-time work in this particular context of time and space was an important step towards greater gender equality (Plantenga, 1996; Pfau-Effinger, 1998b). In contrast in Finland, a cultural model of full-time employment for all adults and comprehensive public childcare is dominant (Anttonen, 1997). Here, during the transition to an industrial and service society, the traditional gender cultural model of both partners contributing to agricultural work was transformed into a dual breadwinner/state carer model. The tradition of full participation of all women in employment was maintained during this process, but adapted to the new situation of work outside the home by a strong expansion of the public social services sector and of comprehensive public childcare provision. The gender cultural tradition of the housewife family, and the idea of private, individualised childhood in the family, was never dominant in Finnish history. Therefore part-time work by mothers does not have any cultural basis, and does not match the employment orientations of women. Instead, women in Finland are usually orientated to continuous full-time employment (Pfau-Effinger, 1994, 1998a, 1999a). This is why the share of women working part time was always only about 10%-11% since the beginning of the 1970s (OECD, 1996, p 192, 1998, p 192). In this societal context, any promotion of part-time work by the state would not contribute substantially to the empowerment of women. The introduction of relatively generous parental leave legislation was unsuccessful partly because of the lack of cultural tradition for a longer family break. Only a limited proportion of all mothers take it, and if they do, most of them only take it for about half a year instead of the three years possible (Nikander, 1992; Haataja, 2000).

Dynamics of change

The role of social actors is crucial to explain the changes in welfare state policies and labour markets in the framework of changes of gender arrangements. Gender arrangements can change because of contradictions that have developed in the gender cultural system or within the gender system (or the gender order). However, change only takes place if some groups of social actors refer to these contradictions and struggle for changes at the cultural or institutional level. In that case, the existing gender arrangement can be subject to discourses, conflicts and negotiation processes that aim to implement an innovative type of gender arrangement. Mósesdóttir (1995, 1999) has analysed how the social powers that influence the nature of the welfare state as a regulator of gender relations can be identified. According to her argument, the role of the feminist movement in history was particularly important to the way in which the welfare state refers to gender relations. This was also one main finding of a cross-national study that I undertook on the change of gender arrangements in the Netherlands, Finland and West Germany from the middle to the end of the 20th century. It turned out that the role of the feminist movement is an important explanatory factor for the way in which welfare state policies reacted to the development of new cultural models of the family (Pfau-Effinger, 2000).

However, we cannot expect that feminists in different countries always have the same political aims. Differences can be explained by the differing gender cultural contexts, or else by the social class of the activists and the way in which they refer to the cultural orientations and interests of the majority of women. Because of this it is important to analyse how the feminist movement in the context of time and space refers to cultural change at the level of the majority of women, and how it mediates these changes into the political arena. A feminist movement whose policy is based more or less on a consensus among feminists and whose aim is to integrate women into the decision-making process of welfare state institutions, as in the Netherlands and Finland, seems to be more successful in promoting the realisation of new cultural models of motherhood than a feminist movement that is split by conflict and remains a social movement instead of integrating women into welfare state institutions, as is the case in West Germany. According to the findings, the way in which the feminist movement is related to the cultural orientations of the social groups it represents also plays a major role (Pfau-Effinger, 2000). In Finland and the Netherlands, feminists stressed the societal importance of maternity and used it as a cultural resource to improve the situation of women. In the Netherlands, feminists used maternity to promote a state policy favouring the dual breadwinner/dual childcare provider model, whereas Finnish feminists used it as a central value for promoting the dual breadwinner/state childcare provider model with its principle of 'public motherhood' and significant state responsibility for children. West German feminists, by contrast, did without this concept; they even contributed substantially to the cultural devaluation of motherhood. They were less successful than their European neighbours (Pfau-Effinger, 1998a, 2000).

Conclusions

Cross-national analyses of welfare state policies, the way in which these construct social citizenship, and the patterns of change in labour market integration of women should be based on a theoretical approach that takes into account that in each society these processes are embedded in a specific context and that they should be analysed in relation to this context. The issue of which conception of social citizenship is the best way to gender equality and can contribute to realising 'equal social worth' (according to T.H. Marshall's ideas) among women and men cannot be answered in a general, abstract way; but the answers can be different in different societies. Full labour market integration of women does in a certain context, but not per se, lead to full citizenship for women, and the other way round: in some countries, a dual integration into waged work and care responsibilities at home of women and men is seen as the 'best' combination of social integration with the idea of gender equality.

Notes

[1] I would like to thank the editors who with their comments have supported me to clarify my arguments.

[2] Part-time work has often been characterised as some type of marginalised employment, although the findings of recent empirical research have outlined that this can only be said for some European countries and for certain fields of part-time employment (see the contributions to Fagan and O'Reilly, 1998).

[3] For an overview on concepts of citizenship see Lister (1997), Chapter Three in this book and Siim (1998, 2000).

[4] There may even be discrepancies between innovative cultural ideals of the majority of women and the cultural ideas to which women active in the feminist movement refer, as in West Germany in the 1970s and 1980s (Pfau-Effinger, 2000).

[5] For a critical look at the idea about economic rationality of labour market behaviour of women see Edwards and Duncan (1996). Women may also use the political and institutional framework of the welfare state in new ways that deviate from the original aims of these policies.

[6] However, welfare states can also act as pioneers, as is the case in Sweden and Norway, where the states tried to motivate fathers to 'active fatherhood' and introduced a father's quota into the parental leave legislation (Siim, 2000).

[7] Simon Duncan and Ros Edwards (1999) have introduced a framework for classifying social policy which uses such a combination, and which they call the 'genderfare' model. This is based on the assumption that policy variations reflect variations both in the capital-labour contract and the gender contract (or gender culture), and that these are mutually interrelated. According to this model, welfare states vary according to the specific way in which both types of contract are shaped.

References

Anttonen, A. (1997) 'The welfare state and social citizenship', in I. Kauppinen and T. Gordon (eds) *Unresolved dilemmas: Women, work and the family in the United States, Europe and the former Soviet Union*, Aldershot: Ashgate, pp 9-32.

Archer, M.S. (1995) *Realist social theory: The morphogenetic approach*, Cambridge: Cambridge University Press.

Bang, H., Jensen, P. and Pfau-Effinger, B. (2001) 'Contextualization of gender policies of European welfare states', in S. Duncan and B. Pfau-Effinger (eds) *Gender, work and culture in the European Union*, London: Routledge.

Bussemaker, J. and van Kersbergen, K. (1994) 'Gender and welfare states: some theoretical reflections' in D. Sainsbury (ed) *Gendering welfare states*, London/Thousand Oaks, CA/New Delhi: Sage Publications, pp 8-25.

Connell, R. (1987) *Gender and power: Society, the person and sexual politics*, Cambridge: Polity Press.

Crompton, R. (1998) 'The equality agenda, employment, and welfare', in B. Geissler, F. Maier and B. Pfau-Effinger (eds) *Der Beitrag der Frauenforschung zur sozioökonomischen Theorieentwicklung*, Berlin: Sigma, pp 154-76.

Daly, M. and Lewis, J.A. (1998) 'Introduction: conceptualising social care in the context of welfare state restructuring', in J.A. Lewis (ed) *Gender, social care and welfare state restructuring in Europe*, Aldershot: Ashgate.

Duncan, S.S. and Edwards, R. (1997) 'Lone mothers and paid work: rational economic man or gendered moral rationalities', *Feminist Economics*, vol 3, no 2, pp 29-61.

Duncan, S.S. and Edwards, R. (1999) *Lone mothers and paid work, and gendered moral rationalities*, London: Macmillan.

Edwards, R. and Duncan, S.S. (1996) '"Rational economic man" or lone mothers in context? Lone mothers, paid work and social policy', in E. Bartolala-Silva (ed) *Good enough mothering: Feminist perspectives on lone motherhood*, London: Macmillan, pp 149-73.

Esping-Andersen, G. (1990) *The three worlds of welfare capitalism*, Cambridge: Polity Press.

Fagan, C. and O'Reilly, J. (eds) (1998) *Part-time prospects*, London: Routledge.

Ginn, J. and Arber, S. (1998) 'How does part-time work lead to low pension income?', in J. O'Reilly and C. Fagan (eds) *Part-time prospects*, London: Routledge, pp 156-74.

Haataja, A. (2000) 'Caring mothers as part of the labour force? Problems with the statistics', Paper presented to the workshop of the COST A13 working group on 'Gender', Berlin, November.

Haller, M. and Höllinger, F. (1994) 'Female employment and the change of gender roles: the confluctual relationship between participation and attitudes in international comparison', *International Sociology: Journal of the International Sociological Association*, vol 9, no 1, pp 87-112.

Julkunen, R. and Rantalaiho, L. (1991) 'Crisis of caring: towards new solutions of welfare services', in A. Kasvio, C. Mako, M. McDaid (eds) *Work and social innovations in Europe. Proceedings of a Finnish-Hungarian seminar in Helsinki*, 11-13 September 1990, Tampere: Tampereen yliopisto, pp 293-320.

Knijn, T. (1994) 'Fish without bikes: revision of the Dutch welfare state and its consequences for the (in)dependence of single mothers', *Social Politics*, vol 2, no 1, pp 83-105.

Knijn, T. and Kremer, M. (1997) 'Gender and the caring dimension of welfare states: toward inclusive ctizenship', *Social Politics*, vol 5, no 3, pp 328-61.

Kröger, T. (1996) 'Policy-makers in social services in Finland: the municipality and the state', *Scandinavian Journal of Social Welfare*, vol 5, pp 62-8.

Lewis, J. (1997) 'Gender and welfare regimes: further thoughts', *Social Politics: International Studies in Gender, State and Society*, vol 4, no 2, pp 160-77.

Lewis, J. (1988) *Gender, social care and welfare state restructuring in Europe*, Aldershot: Ashgate.

Lewis, J. and Ostner, I. (1995) 'Gender and the evolution of European social policy', in S. Leibfried and P. Pierson (eds) *European social policy: Between fragmentation and integration*, Washington, DC: Brookings Institute, pp 159-94.

Lister, R. (1997) *Citizenship: Feminist perspectives*, London: Macmillan.

Lockwood, D. (1964) 'Social integration and system integration', in G.K. Zollschan and W. Hirsch (eds) *Explorations in social change*, Boston, MA: Mifflin.

Marshall, T.H. (1950) 'Citizenship and social class', Reprinted in T.H. Marshall and T. Bottomore (eds) (1992) *Citizenship and social class*, London: Pluto Press.

Maurice, M. (1995) 'Convergence and/or societal effect for the Europe of the future?', in P. Cressey and B. Jones (eds) *Work and employment in Europe: A new convergence?*, London/New York, NY, pp 137-58.

Maurice, M., Sellier, F. and Silvestre, J.J. (1986) *The social foundations of industrial power*, Cambridge, MA: MIT Press.

Mósesdóttir, L. (1995) 'The state and the egalitzarian, ecclestiastiacal and liberal regimes of gender relations', *British Journal of Sociology*, vol 46, no 4, pp 623-42.

Mósesdóttir, L. (1999) 'Breaking the boundaries', in J. Christiansen, P. Koistinen and A. Kovalainen (eds), *Working Europe: Reshaping European employment systems*, Aldershot: Ashgate, pp 97-136.

Neidhard, F. (1986) '"Kultur und Gesellschaft". Einige Anmerkungen zum Sonderheft', in F. Neidhard, R.M. Lepsuis and J. Weiss (eds) *Kultur und Gesellschaft, Kölner Zeitschrift für Soziologie und Sozialpsychologie*, vol 27, Opladen: Westdeutscher Verlag, pp 10-19.

Neidhard, F., Lepsius, R.M. and Weiss, J. (eds) (1986) *Kultur und Gesellschaft, Kölner Zeitschrift für Soziologie und Sozialpsychologie*, vol 27, Opladen: Westdeutscher Verlag.

Nikander, T. (1992) *The woman's life course and the family formation*, Helsinki: Statistics Finland.

OECD (Organisation for Economic Cooperation and Development) (2000) *Employment outlook*, Paris: OECD.

OECD (1998) *Employment outlook*, Paris: OECD.

OECD (1996) *Employment outlook*, Paris: OECD.

Orloff, A.S. (1993) 'Gender and the social rights of citizenship', *American Sociological Review*, vol 58, pp 303-28.

Ostner, I. (1994) 'Independence and dependence – options and constraints for women over a life course', *Women's International Studies Forum*, nos 2-3, pp 129-39.

Pateman, C. (1988) *The sexual contract*, Stanford, CA: Stanford University Press.

Pfau-Effinger, B. (1996) 'Analyse internationaler Differenzen in der Erwerbsbeteiligung von Frauen – theoretischer Rahmen und empirische Ergebnisse', *Kölner Zeitschrift für Soziologie und Sozialpsychologie*, vol 48, no 3, pp 462-92.

Pfau-Effinger, B. (1998a) 'Gender cultures and the gender arrangement – a theoretical framework for cross-national comparisons on gender', *Innovation: The European Journal of Social Sciences*, Special issue on 'The Spatiality of Gender' edited by S. Duncan, vol 11, no 2, pp 147-66.

Pfau-Effinger, B. (1998b) 'Culture or structure as explanations for differences in part-time work in Germany, Finland and the Netherlands?', in C. Fagan and J. O'Reilly (eds), *Part-time perspectives*, London: Routledge, pp 177-98.

Pfau-Effinger, B. (1998c) 'Der Mythos von der Hausfrauenehe. Entwicklungspfade der Familie in Europa', *Soziale Welt*, vol 49, no 2, pp 167-82.

Pfau-Effinger, B. (1999a) 'Defizite der Theoriebildung zu den Grenzen wohlfahrtsstaatlicher Geschlechterpolitik', in S. Hradil (ed) *Verhandlungen des 29. Kongresses der Deutschen Gesellschaft für Soziologie, des 16. Österreichischen Kongresses für Soziologie und des 11. Schweizerischen Kongresses für Soziologie 'Grenzenlose Gesellschaft?'*, vol 1, Plenumsveranstaltungen, Freiburg: Centaurus, pp 203-18.

Pfau-Effinger, B. (1999b) 'Welfare regimes and the gender: Division of labour in cross-national perspective – theoretical framework and empirical results', in J. Christiansen, A. Kovalainen and P. Koistinen (eds) *Working Europe – Reshaping European employment systems*, Aldershot: Ashgate, pp 128-56.

Pfau-Effinger, B. (1999d) 'Change of family policies in the socio-cultural context of European Societies', in A. Leira (ed) *Family policies:Yearbook of comparative social research*, Stamford, CA: JAI Press, pp 135-59.

Pfau-Effinger, B. (2000) *Kultur, Wohlfahrtsstaat und Frauenerwerbstätigkeit im europäischen Vergleich*, Opladen: Leske und Budrich.

Pfau-Effinger, B. (2001) 'Soziokulturelle Bedingungen staatlicher Geschlechterpolitik', *Kölner Zeitschrift für Soziologie und Sozialpsychologie, Sonderband, Geschlechtersoziologie*, vol 53, no 4.

Plantenga, J. (1996) 'For women only? The rise of part-time work in the Netherlands', *Social Politics*, vol 4, no 3, pp 57-71.

Sainsbury, D. (1994) *Gender equality and welfare states*, Cambridge: Cambridge University Press.

Siim, B. (1998) 'Towards a gender sensitive framework for citizenship', in J. Bussemaker (ed) *Citizenship and transition of European welfare states*, London/New York, NY: Routledge, pp 85-118.

Siim, B. (2000) *Gender and citizenship: Politics and agency in France, Britain and Denmark*, Cambridge: Cambridge University Press.

Veil, M. (1996) 'Zwischen Wunsch und Wirklichkeit: Frauen im Sozialstaat. Ein Ländervergleich zwischen Frankreich, Schweden und Deutschland', *Aus Politik und Zeitgeschichte. Beilage zur Wochenzeitung Das Parlament*, pp 29-38.

Yeandle, S. (1999) 'Gender contracts, welfare systems and "non-standard working": diversity and change in Denmark, France, Germany, Italy and the UK' in A. Felstead and N. Jewson (eds) *Global trends in flexible labour*, Basingstoke: Macmillan, pp 95-118.

TWELVE

A second order reflection on the concepts of inclusion and exclusion

Asmund Born and Per H. Jensen

Citizenship is a multidimensional concept. It refers to (a) rights and duties, (b) the individual's ability to participate in various spheres of society, such as social, economic and political life, and (c) citizenship which helps to construct identities. Citizenship leads to inclusion in society, while loss of citizenship leads to exclusion or marginalisation. Within this frame of reference, the foregoing chapters have elaborated on theories, concepts and knowledge. They have contributed to the political and scientific debate concerning the relationship between changes in labour market, welfare policies, citizenship and marginalisation. The discussion frames a space rich with overlapping, conflicting scientific theories and political implications. However, so far the basic line of argument has never really been questioned. Thus, a common feature has been that these arguments proceeds from problems (labour market), then to deficits in remedies (welfare state) designed to rectify diminishing rights/participation (citizenship) and finally to marginalisation. Differences certainly exist – this has been shown by the way in which the authors contributing to this book have disagreed over the exact nature of the relationship between the labour market (problem or solution) and the welfare state (solution or problem). However, as a political project the authors unanimously agree that citizenship is good and marginalisation is bad.

   Most probably, this is due to the fact that most research into the causes and effects of marginalisation and exclusion predominantly communicates with the political system. Researchers who actually use the concepts of marginalisation and exclusion usually have the objective of developing new empirical insights that may pave the way for the formulation of new strategies and new policies for re-integrating marginalised and excluded groups back into the societal fabric. Hence, researchers who use the concepts of marginalisation and exclusion use, as a starting point for their analysis, observations of marginalised positions, such as long-term unemployment, social vulnerability and poverty. Questions such as 'from what and by whom are vulnerable groups excluded?', 'why is integration desirable?' and 'into what are they being integrated?' are seldom thematised. Much research into marginalisation and exclusion rests on an implicit notion of normality and deviance, on the basis of which observations are made, interpretations promulgated and distinctions theorised into models. As a consequence, research into marginalisation and exclusion is first and foremost descriptive and normative, leaving the relationship between the phenomena in focus and the changes in their societal perception in the shade as 'objective' staging.

Such research practices certainly lead to a proliferation of new insights, but they also leave us with a certain unease concerning our position as scientists. This unease arises from the fact that the implicit notion of normality and deviance helps to structure the questions we ask, the observations we make, and the solutions we propose. The implicit notion of normality and deviance functions as a 'blind spot' (Luhmann, 1995a) that influences political intentions, overall perceptions of society, embedded valuations of citizenship, views about work and life, about centre and margin, and about inclusion and exclusion. To unravel the reasons for our unease and contribute to the ongoing discussion about concepts, we will take a step back from the level of first order observations (of marginalisation and citizenship) and operate on the level of second order observations (or in our case self-observation), as Luhmann (1984) calls it.

We will not attempt to question the political preferences of scientists, or question the conclusions of specific studies. Instead, we shall discuss the hidden 'logics' that operate whenever observers use dichotomic concepts, here focusing on the concepts of 'inclusion' and 'exclusion', which seem to be the archetypal concepts behind many of the chapters in this book.

We will first establish the landscape that has been used by scholars to describe the forms, causes and effects of marginalisation and exclusion, scholars who explicitly reflect on the very use of the concepts of inclusion and exclusion. This will lead us to a discussion of the political implications of the use of the concepts in terms of social integrative ambitions, means and instruments accompanying the concepts. We next turn to the concepts themselves and their performative effects on the researcher's analytical horizon. We shall argue that due to their dichotomous structure, 'inclusion' and 'exclusion' tend to have profound effects on the possible insights and theoretical positions of the researcher. We are so to speak trying to catch 'the logical mechanisms' of the dichotomic observation and 'the blind spot', the spot from where observations take place. We also contrast a

Durkheimian paradigm with at Mertonian one, since we believe that the modern use of the concepts of inclusion and exclusion is associated with a Mertonian rather than a Durkheimian approach. As such, we believe that the modern use of the two concepts reflects a theoretical move away from the Durkheimian notion of an immanent, co-variating, relationship between parts and wholes of societies. Instead, the relationship between parts (inclusion and exclusion) and whole (society) is conceived instrumentally and varies according to political and individual intentionality. When we question the blind spot and the dichotomous observation, it becomes obvious that we as scientists are not describing and suggesting, but creating, whenever we observe marginalisation. This is important to bear in mind, as our addressees, the politicians, are not only facilitating participation, but are also struggling to maintain control over participation, aided by research.

To provide other ways to conceptualise and deal with marginalisation and citizenship, we introduce the German sociologist Niklas Luhmann. Luhmann offers another perspective on 'inclusion' and 'exclusion', reconnecting these concepts with conceptions of society. His starting point is that the concepts of inclusion and exclusion are epistemic tools in societal self-observation. Society is not an evident frame of reference for the observer, but emerges for the observer as the unique outcome of discourses (systems), and their specific way of discursivating the very concepts of inclusion and exclusion. This suggests that the social sciences might contribute to social critique only as far as they study the internal relations between societal discourses and their use of inclusion/exclusion as observation tools, instead of leaving this in the 'Mertonian' shade.

We suggest that late modern society is no longer a unity providing citizenship with a self-evident frame of reference. Instead, society has dissolved into separate and largely non-hierarchical systems of communication (law, economy, art and so on) from which we might be excluded according to the conditions of the very system. This has several effects, which will be discussed in the final section of this chapter. The more important of these effects are that:

- the 'natural' referentiality between citizenship and society disappears and is replaced by ad hoc and partial membership of floating communities emerging through actualised memberships
- rights no longer have the same effects that they had within the high modern society, since the legal and constitutional system is but one among several systems struggling for hegemony over the narrative about society

- there is no longer any reason to believe that identity derives its meaning from an overarching society or an overarching labour market, since identity has turned into a variable figure in time as well as in space.

To grasp these new conditions, we must substitute our sociological dichotomies and their silent a priori with concepts that are sensitive to the proliferating differentiations of society, labour markets, *and positions of observation*. Yet even if we provide some hints as to the direction of these concepts, the task still looms on the horizon.

Concepts in use

In an attempt to define and operationalise the concept of 'marginalisation' in a systematic way, Johannessen (1997) states that, broadly speaking, the concept refers to unfavourable material living conditions and a lack of social integration. Marginalisation signifies a deviation or distance from accepted norms and standards for life in modern society. It is possible to talk about degrees of marginalisation, since marginalised persons occupy different positions on the continuum between integration and exclusion, while the concept of exclusion refers to a permanent state of deprivation of resources and permanent expulsion from the social structures of society (Johannessen, 1997).

Marginalisation and exclusion are multidimensional phenomena. In accordance with the classic division between market, state, and civil society, or Marshall's (1950) famous distinction between civil, political and social citizenship, three arenas are designated for the study of marginalisation: economic, cultural, and collective (see, for example, Strobel, 1996; Johannessen, 1997). From an economic perspective, the degree of marginalisation is measured in terms of whether the individual has access to basic material resources and a means of making a living. In the cultural perspective, marginalisation is experienced as a lack of identity in the multicultural society; while from the collective perspective, the core feature of marginalisation is participation in economic, social, and political life. This perspective couples marginalisation with the societal norms and rules for participation. When these perspectives are combined, the concept of marginalisation signifies positions on a scale of better or worse life conditions, more or less cultural affiliation, and more or less participation. Simultaneously, all the intermediate positions contain a latent risk of exclusion.

According to Johannessen (1997), the phenomenon of marginalisation also has a subjective side, since it seems unreasonable to classify persons as marginalised or excluded, inasmuch as individuals themselves prefer not to participate in or to break the dominant and accepted norms of living. Thus, the concept of marginalisation refers solely to those aspects of deprivation and lack of control that are experienced involuntarily. Following this line of argument, marginalisation is possible only insofar as other citizens or observers expect participation, cultural identity, or a certain living standard.

The concept of marginalisation contains a profusion of possible meanings. Marginalisation will thus depend on the:

- position of the individual on the continuum integration-exclusion with respect to resources and identity
- amount and type of arenas to which one has access
- inclination of the individual to deviate from the norms.

With different combinations of these dimensions, the amount of different infusions of meaning increases considerably. Depending on 'personal' preferences, the researcher may register on formal or informal norms, and compromise between collective norms and individual preferences.

Silent content of inclusion

The literature on marginalisation exhibits a certain degree of agreement on the probability of different types of trade-offs between political, economic, and social marginalisation (Berghman, 1995; Andersen, 1996). It is understood that a person can be economically excluded and culturally included at the same time (Strobel, 1995). Persons living in a ghetto under difficult economic conditions can be very active in the organisation of social and cultural activities (Jordan and Redley, 1994). In the same way, we can see that the practices of different poverty-stricken cultures (rap music, punk fashions, hip slang or other forms of interaction) may be adopted by other strata in society. In this perspective, marginalisation as a collective phenomenon is not only a negative sum of single individuals; it signifies the very borderline between cultures.

Inclusion in one sphere and exclusion in another is quite possible. This might, however, be subdued by the overwhelming tendency to see inclusion as being exclusively synonymous with inclusion in the labour market. The position within the labour market or the distance from the labour market (for example, part-time work, short-term or long-term unemployment) is normally seen as a central criterion for assessing the proportion and degree of marginalisation (Berghman, 1995; Johannessen,

1997). Marginalisation from the labour market is seen as the most devastating form, since it leads to further social and political marginalisation (as in the title:'Society is polarised: it starts in the labour market, continues in the social policies and ends in the civil society' [Møller, 1989; our translation]). The labour market thus becomes the central point underlying the conceptual distinctions between centre and periphery (Møller, 1989; Andersen, 1999).

For most scholars studying marginalisation, their underlying project is the re-integration of the marginalised individuals. Integration into the labour market defines the space of possible actions against exclusion. From this line of reasoning, waged labour and achieving some degree of self-sufficiency comprise the silent content of inclusion, whenever marginalisation is the category of observation. On this basis, it is possible to speak about 'the labour market' and the 'labour market policy' as if these phenomena were not an effect of the researcher's delimitation of spheres and choice of categories – delimitations and choices that would be less self-evident if the 'marginalised' were to describe society. However, our point is that a centre-based conceptualisation and definition of marginalised positions – 'the marginal' – prevents us from observing society from the point of view of the marginalised. In constructing the concepts of marginalisation and exclusion, we exclude the perspectives of the excluded and marginalised.

Implications

A common feature of the concepts of exclusion and poverty is that they contain notions of objective and identifiable borderlines, such as between being poor or not, being inside or outside mainstream society and so on. Such categorical boundaries tend to impede our knowledge about the relationship between exclusion and the constitution of society. Instead, our attention tends to be focused on the creation of distinctions and their operationalisation (Goodin, 1996). We expend our energies trying to construct categories that can divide groups and in deciding which (groups of) people are on the 'right' or 'wrong' side of the line. As such, 'differences' in terms of economic, social and political conditions are presuppositions behind the concept of poverty as well as of exclusion. No direct parallel can be drawn between the two concepts, since it makes a difference whether you use the one or the other to signify a field of problems (Meyers, 1993). Each of the concepts has its own internal logic and dynamic, determining which aspects of a phenomenon are highlighted. Using different concepts privileges different views and possible insights, in the same way that different concepts prepare different discourses, excluding some topics while highlighting others (Levitas, 1996).

The concept of poverty, with its distinction between relative and absolute poverty, has traditionally been orientated towards the question of inequality and has been sustained by indignation about the unequal distribution of life conditions and life chances. By contrast, the concepts of inclusion and exclusion express a positional perspective, that is, to be on one or the other side of the borderline, epitomised as being in or outside the labour market (Levitas, 1996). The concept of exclusion becomes part of a new hegemonic discourse, undermining the poverty discourse with its focus on material inequality. The concept of exclusion discards the discourse on inequality, as it is possible to be on the 'right side' of the inclusion/ exclusion line and still be far from the 'centre' and without adequate resources: it is possible to be 'included' and 'poor'.

Meyers (1993), Strobel (1996), and Thompson and Hoggett (1996) have tried to go beyond some of the dilemmas of the concepts of marginalisation and exclusion in discussing social-integrative instruments. They suggest a combination of universalism and selectivism, in which abstract and universal rights are designed in such a way that they are able to meet the situation and capacity of the single being. The isolation of means from ends gives rise to several problems:

- Integration is reduced to a question of how to design the most effective instruments of integration. In this way, issues of social integration and social change are turned into technical questions that can be handled through prudence, reason, insight, and declarations of intent. This argument presupposes that we have forgotten the sociological axiom that social conditions are not changed through acts of will; rather, there are structures of society that 'direct' our will (Durkheim, 1982).
- With the reduction of integration into technicalities, the concept of integration tends towards a totalitarian logic. Social integration as a matter of technicality contains the idea that all individuals could be integrated into society and normalised. Behaviour that deviates from the norm and manifests itself on a scale of 'more' or 'less integrated' could be interpreted as a discrepancy between our expectations and our present technical abilities (Luhmann, 1997, p 630).
- The totalitarian logic of integration is sustained through simple and banal observations, such as you cannot imagine society without deviants, such that inclusion exists only where exclusion is possible. Durkheim has described this complementarity in a precise way, when he writes about crime saying that crime "is an aspect of the public health, an

integrating part of any sound society" (Durkheim, 1982). Disintegration is a mode of adaptation divergent from the forms valued by the majority (Durkheim, 1982). This argument indicates that disintegration functions as mechanisms of integration among the non-integrated.

- Prejudices, classifications, distinctions ('us/them') and practices in society *actively* exclude by defining certain individuals and groups as undesirable, as Goodin (1996) and others have shown. In this perspective, attempts of the welfare state to take into account the different needs and positions of social groups and individuals by means of generative politics (Giddens, 1994) serve only as a symbolic reproduction of the existing differences; they are simply putting a new face on oppression. This is especially the case insofar as 'differentiated integration' presupposes a downgrading of rights in favour of the use of social therapeutic instruments of integration.

The literature on exclusion and marginalisation has great difficulties in isolating, both descriptively and analytically, those processes leading to exclusion. The included as well as the excluded are usually described as homogenous groups at variance with the needs and perspective of the researcher. Often, 'the socially excluded' are referred to without precise characterisation of who is included in this category and without precise reference to how, from what, and by whom, they are excluded. Our gaze is averted from the circumstances that create exclusion in the first place. Focusing their attention on the political system, researchers on marginalisation often seem to mistake the critique of the efficiency of the political system for a critical sociological position.

Mechanisms privileging an asymmetric view

The concepts of inclusion, exclusion, integration, and marginalisation can be interpreted in a multitude of ways. This is due to their 'multi-semic' and 'euphemistic' nature (Silver, 1994). Simultaneously, the concepts have been freed from their fixation to basic ideas about society, so that any trace of a compulsive logic between concepts and meaning disappears. The concepts are open to any type of combination or contrast according to the needs and intentions of the user.

Nevertheless, there are indications of a certain regularity in the array of possible meanings. This regularity derives from a privileging inherent in the combination of concepts. This inherent privileging seems to create a space of subsequent privileging or a barrier at the discursive level. To substantiate this hypothesis, we will try to locate and elucidate the mechanisms of privileging at the micro level of concepts. We will demonstrate that the conceptual pairs of inclusion/exclusion and integration/marginalisation are affected by four mechanisms:

- the dichotomous organisation of the concepts
- the asymmetric nature of the dichotomies
- their capacity to conceal their own conceptual context
- the asymmetry hiding itself.

First mechanism

The first mechanism is related to the dichotomous organisation of the concepts, constituting the world as either in or out, before or after, good or bad. This dichotomous view organises the basic assumptions accordingly and has several effects. First, the gaze is orientated towards presence or absence, that is the objective existence of the research target. We seek out what is measurable, to register a position on one side or the other of a boundary. This orientation towards categorisation occurs whether the point is to observe according to an objective criterion (such as older or younger than 60 years of age), or to disregard an 'objective' criterion (man or woman). Second, emergence can only be registered as something on a scale of more or less, while the very quality of the movement and the development is precluded as a theme. The main effect is that concepts orientated towards an established process turn static. They are sensitive only to the position in the process, and cannot grasp the volatile and moving creation of meaning in the process. The dichotomy impels us towards a positional registration and the drawing of boundaries, while the underlying processes remain black boxes.

The dichotomous approach nevertheless has obvious advantages. It permits a separation between the political intention and the scientific observation. The scientific task is to register and deliver knowledge about marginalisation/exclusion as objective/given phenomena, while intention is a political domain, irrespective of the fact that the researcher's choice of concepts and approach is normatively and politically motivated. The dichotomous approach permits that the relationship between ends (to bring some person or group from one side of the borderline to the other) and choice of means (the political tools) is objectified as registration of effects, irrespective of the infusion of specific meaning by the involved parties (such as the marginalised).

Second mechanism

The second mechanism is related to the asymmetry of the concepts. Observation always contains a 'positive' and a 'negative' value, in the philosophical sense of value. The negative side is always defined from the positive side as an inevitable logical implication. The effect of this asymmetry is that it exacerbates the technical aspects of the conceptualisation and its use. Observers are compelled to constitute the other side as the absence of certain qualities, to which they themselves grant importance as individuals, groups or classes. This is the most important aspect of the privileging process. The very 'slide' from pure difference (/) to privileging (+/–) is in the construction of difference as 'other' (ie othering) (to be discussed as a value problem in the fourth mechanism).

The second aspect of the asymmetry is situated in the field between language and cognition. Whenever the inclusion/exclusion dichotomy is applied in an observation, the inclusion pole is collective, either directly or indirectly. As an operation bound to the semantic and communicative level, it incorporates a social unit in which the observer is inscribed. In contrast, the exclusion pole is not necessarily collective. Instead, it is individualising by nature in as much as the exclusion pole is conceptualised as difference and deviation from the other side, that is, not by markers of its own, signifying collectivity. Even when a concept such as 'group' is applied, it generally signifies an amount of individuals and not a group in the sense of a collective. The point here is that policies will also tend towards individual re-establishment of the individual's ability to become a member of that collective understood as being 'the included'. Obviously, concepts can be created so that they contain collectivity (as in many cultural concepts), but the idea of collectivised exclusion will threaten the logic embedded in the asymmetry of the inclusion/exclusion dichotomy.

Third mechanism

The third mechanism is the conceptual dependency on other concepts and discourses that are concealed due to the natural self-evidence of the dichotomous form. Distinctions such as good/bad and in/out are by necessity embedded in concepts, ideas, presuppositions and discursive practices about society, individual, social relations and so on, what Deleuze calls 'indirect discourses' (Deleuze and Guattari, 1998). These elements remain unarticulated as floating signifiers (Laclau and Mouffe, 1985). In

Luhmannian terms, the point is that every positive/negative dichotomous distinction is always embedded in an overarching unity hidden from observation by the observer, who sees society in terms of dichotomies (Luhmann, 1984). The concepts are autonomised, and no conceptual element points towards the criteria behind the choice of criteria.

To the degree that basic assumptions about individual and society form part of the observation and reflection, they are treated as external points of reference, that is, as axiomatic or meta-theoretical positions substantiating a researcher's choice of topic and object. In effect, the concepts exclude the discussion of the unlimited variety of social life, and the specific dichotomous structure of the concepts does not allow for empirical variable elements. If we allowed 'those out there' to formulate their own horizon of meaning and image of society, it would require reformulation of 'the other's out-position' as something 'different', requiring totally different categories. To construct a horizon of meaning from the position of the observed would be a direct challenge to the researcher's dichotomous worldview. The categories 'included'/'excluded' remain coarse analytical categories. Even though they may be disguised as empirically sensitive, they obstruct a reading of the world from the ongoing creation of meaning by the marginalised and excluded themselves.

Fourth mechanism

The fourth mechanism is the way in which the asymmetry hides itself. This is one of the Baconian epistemic problems connected to the almost invincible condition that any observer regards him or herself as a representative of the desirable. It has the nature of self-evidence, and it is difficult to escape the tendency to observe the lives of 'the others' in the light of our own life. Once more the basis of the observation is made inaccessible. Those categorised as 'different' are subsumed under the idea of being dysfunctional, as technical problems of regulation, instead of being seen as the creation of our own observations.

This hidden valorisation is also connected to the fact that the researcher has to conceptualise the qualities considered to be of crucial importance for the collective life under study. Concepts that mirror society and self are an unsuitable basis for a critique of the very society that made the conceptual construction possible in the first place. Hence, no critique is implied by the registration of 'others', since the construction of 'other' follows the hidden ideas of researchers regarding what is 'attractive'. The conceptualisations and the knowledge will never contribute to a discussion of basic societal problems of solidarity and values.

The hidden valorisation automatically directs the discourse towards evaluation of more or less suitable and effective agents and institutions for integration. Social integration turns out to be a question of technicalities within subsystems. Within this logic, we can – in the sociological or political systemic perspective – sustain the idea of a society even when the only integration lies in our signification of 'the others' as needing to be integrated and included. Included only signifies the feeling of being part of a self-righteous, yet hidden, collectivity of observers.

Losing sight of basic assumptions about society

The privileging mechanisms described above are not necessarily unknown to the researcher who uses the concepts of inclusion/exclusion and integration/marginalisation. However, without continuously reflecting on the mechanisms during the research process, even the most critical intentions will end up as social therapy; the outcome of the research process may be cascades of new or alternative remedies for social integration, and hardly ever new and alternative insights. Hence, it is no surprise that these concepts are so attractive to the political discourse.

Nor is it difficult to understand why these concepts undermine critical reflections. The debate about inclusion and exclusion is legitimated as a scientific discourse through references to sociology, while aspects of the same sociology have tended to become non-critical and instrumental. Let us illustrate this tendency by referring to the paradigmatic shift from Durkheim to Merton. Using the concept of 'anomie' as our point of departure, we will briefly demonstrate how the development from Durkheim to Merton has disconnected the concepts from basic assumptions about society. It is not our intention to canonise the conservative and consensus-orientated sociology. It is not entirely unjust to label Durkheim a 'state ideologist', and in several of his writings he argues in an instrumental fashion (see, for example, Durkheim, 1986). Also, Merton's more conflict-orientated reflections contain much more than instrumental rationality.

The concepts of inclusion/exclusion and integration/marginalisation inscribe themselves in a landscape constituted by Durkheim (Österberg, 1988, Chapter 4). In Durkheimian thinking, integration and differentiation are mutually constituted phenomena. In modern society and its division of labour, social differentiation manifests itself as highly divergent normative structures, that is, highly varying patterns of behaviour, obligations, and expectations in the different subsystems of society. However, from a Durkheimian perspective we cannot imagine a society without a minimum of interconnectedness between the different parts; that is, we cannot imagine a society without a collective set of morals and a system of shared values (values being self-substantiating, and not means for other goals). In modern society, organic solidarity is the moral element of collective life that keeps the different parts of society together (Durkheim, 1964). Organic solidarity is a consequence as well as a precondition for the functioning of highly differentiated societies.

Durkheim saw individuals as epochal representatives rather than as prime movers of society. The individual is constituted in the nexus between norms and values (Parsons, 1968, p 388), between the collective moral and the normative structures in the subsystem to which the individual belongs. Following this line of argument, integration depends on whether the nexus between values and norms is capable of creating humans with the capacity to act within society. As such, disintegration (anomie) manifests itself in the individual as a feeling of isolation, confusion, and the inability to orientate oneself (Durkheim, 1952).

While Durkheim sees expectations and aspirations of individuals as a function of their position in the social structure, Merton (1968) starts with universalising expectations and the goals that individuals desire to achieve; he tends to universalise the goals of individuals as a priori and culturally predefined. Such goals might be interpreted, for instance, as integration in the labour market. As the goals of individuals are predefined, disintegration becomes a question of discrepancies between goals and means (instruments) at hand. Such discrepancies manifest themselves in so far as the means or instruments do not allow the actor to reach the goal. In case of such discrepancies between goals and means, the actor may choose to renounce the predefined images of 'the good life', leading to resignation, or the individual may choose illegitimate means to obtain the goal, creating deviant behaviour and cultural chaos.

According to Merton, disintegration (anomie) emerges when the social structures, which he defines as the interlinkage between the goals and means, are 'unbalanced' or 'poorly regulated' (1968). Merton articulates a moral dichotomisation of social structures into 'good/bad' and 'desirable/ undesirable' (Elias and Scotson, 1994). This is possible only because he disconnects reflections on goals and means from basic assumptions about society – one can hardly speak of a society as good or bad. Merton disregards the fact that anomie and disintegration are an integrated part of social life itself (following the thoughts of Durkheim). Merton's morally based dichotomies generate ideas about the possibility of and need for correcting the non-desired social structures through rational intervention. The overall message is that adequate policies and institutions must be developed so that the greatest number of people may achieve the predefined goals (for example integration within the labour market). The task of sociology is to provide the knowledge around which social actors may generate interests and actions.

The turn from a Durkheimian to a Mertonian position of observation represents a distinctive shift in the gaze of the sociological observation. Durkheim raises the problem of order and integration in relation to social solidarity, that is, as a question of a shared value system that keeps society together. Merton (1968) focuses on the problem of order and integration as a question of rationality and technicalities. Here, sociology becomes part of a project for providing knowledge about how to reproduce order and the predominant values in society (such as integration into the labour market).

The Mertonian line of thinking has infused the concepts with instrumental meaning, which distances them from basic theory as well as any critical intention of the observer. Merton's perspective is seductive, because he enables us to observe partial phenomena in society without having to confront more fundamental problems of theory and observation. Simultaneously, the political perspective, that is, the need for adequate political action, is a natural offspring of our observations. Institutionally, a whole political structure has been constructed around our dichotomies, but intellectually we have been imprisoned by instrumental thinking, even though it appears as a development of capacity.

Reconstructing the gaze

We will now reconstruct the relationship between the concepts and the societal reflection. The concepts of inclusion/exclusion should not be seen as representations of objective phenomena. Rather, they should be seen as a way of organising the gaze, as epistemic tools through which a societal self-observation is organised. Hence, when second order observers question the concepts and their relation to society, they actually ask which topics are being focused on, how and under which condition inclusion/ exclusion is used.

A communicative perspective

Throughout our argument, the German sociologist Niklas Luhmann has loomed in the background, helping us to orientate our gaze towards dichotomies in operation. Luhmann has enabled us to pose the questions and search for the implications of the conceptual constructions. So we shall briefly present Luhmann's reflections around inclusion and exclusion as tools of observation. As Luhmann defines the social (the object of sociology) as communication, we will take as our point of departure a short description of the dichotomous nature of communication. From there we will explore some of the communicative consequences implied when the concepts of inclusion and exclusion are activated as dichotomies in communication. Our next step shifts the level of analysis from communicative operations to societal communicative systems (law, economy and so on). Here we outline some consequences for the relation between inclusion/exclusion and the overall conditions for the reproduction of the actual society. During our presentation, we will try to maintain the general presentation of Luhmann's theory at a minimum, but some of the unfamiliar notions have to be presented along the road for the reader to appreciate our arguments.

Communicating about society through the concepts of inclusion and exclusion

Luhmann's point of departure is a critique of Parsons. He accepts the Parsonian ambition to connect inclusion and overall societal reproduction, but he criticises the unilateral focus on the side of inclusion, as it prevents any type of systematic theorising of exclusion. Instead, Luhmann argues that theory must reflect on the very distinction between inclusion and exclusion in communication, and the conditioning of the distinction when actualised.

Communication is seen as a process proceeding through selections in which any next step adheres to a previous dichotomic possibility. You can either adhere to the topic (+) or shift (−), and whenever the communication runs along the marked side, we know what is the topic. The negative side remains the domain of contingent possibilities (unmarked space). For the observer of communication, this means that you can observe a unity, which lies above the selections, something that the communication cannot observe in action (as such a shift would open another communication). This overarching unity is called 'the system'. The system is immanent in the distinctions in use, and different distinctions trigger different systems or subsystems (Luhmann, 1984). An example might be the economic communication system, which employs distinctions between wage/non-wage, profit/non-profit. The topic of the communication as well as the points of adherence to the communication thus depend on the coding (the +/−). The first question is: What is the topic when the concepts of inclusion and exclusion are activated as the coding of a communication?

When the concepts of inclusion/exclusion are used in communication and observation, the crucial issue, according to Luhmann, concerns how a person or group in question can be understood as related to a given social structure. In this perspective, the question is not whether a person is or is not included, but the very conditions for participation. The topic of the communication is how 'persons' are signified and made relevant in a given society (Luhmann, 1995b, p 241). Whenever we use the terms 'included' or 'inclusion' we are referring to the more or less specified conditions for inclusion. Since inclusion is one side of a distinction, it always refers to its opposite, exclusion, while exclusion will remain the unmarked side of the dichotomy. This does not mean that we cannot specify the counter-conditions to inclusion, only that exclusion will always occur through the conditions for inclusion, and in that a conditioning of the overarching communicative social system will emerge. It is therefore through the communicative construction of persons and groups not fit for integration that the social 'solidarity' and its conditions, the social differentiation, emerge in communication (Luhmann 1997, p 621). The effect is that whenever we raise the topic of inclusion and exclusion, the underlying topic is societal integration and its form.

To make the conceptual relations between inclusion/exclusion and integration more precise, we might ask how the social forms of integration have developed. This question must be answered at the system level if we are to escape circularity. In the tradition of Durkheim, Luhmann describes society through the concept of differentiation, and his '*Leitfrage*' is therefore: how does the relationship between the inclusion/exclusion distinction and the forms of social integration and social differentiation evolve?

Integration is defined as mutual delimitation of the degrees of freedom as to adherence in communication (Luhmann, 1995b, p 238). This definition refers to communicative expectations, the point being that the more you are integrated, the narrower the array of communicative expectations. Imagine the closure of the communicative expectations of the villager, compared to the expectations of the newly landed Martian, the first being rather predictable and hence, integrated.

Integration entails the delimitation of communicative possibilities through mutual expectations. In different historical and cultural contexts, expectations are institutionalised in different ways and in each system they will appear as normality. At the societal level, the question about inclusion/exclusion becomes one of how a given society signifies persons and what rules operate to assign positions making it possible to manage mutual expectations.

Inclusion/exclusion and the functionally differentiated society

As we have concentrated on the current discussions of inclusion and exclusion, we will here present those aspects of Luhmann's thought that concern late modernity, or what he calls the 'functionally differentiated society'. As Luhmann has defined the social as communication, the difference between societies lies in how they organise communication. In the segmented and stratified society, the capacity to communicate is organised around the social aspect of communication, that is, the subject-position (to use a Foucauldian term [Foucault, 1972]). In the segmented and stratified society, observations that rely on the concepts of inclusion and exclusion tend to focus on the social conditions for participation in communication (Luhmann, 1997).

In modern and late modern society, differentiation follows other paths. Society has developed into functionally differentiated communicative systems with their own codes, symbolic structures, institutions and practices (for example, law, economy, love). These systems are by nature open to everybody; that is, the condition for participation is not established from outside through social inheritance or the like. In principle, the individual can step into any systemic communication, and the subject-position is specifically regulated not on the basis of any overarching societal structural feature, but by the individual communicative system itself.

The evolution into functional differentiation builds on the already established differentiation of 'included' and 'excluded' as it has developed in the stratified society, and at the same time the concepts are freed from the yoke of the stratified society. In principle, the individual may step in or out of communicative systems according to what provides meaning ad hoc. At the level of communicative systems, this means that the system grants the access, and as inclusion depends on the highly differentiated possibilities of communication, the political implication is that access is not open for long-term coordination from outside. The other side of this condition is that the person who cannot exploit his or her participatory chances is individually responsible (recall how the actor is defined within legal or liberal economic systems). In this way, exclusion is simply hidden as a socio-cultural form (Luhmann, 1997, p 625).

Through the functional differentiation of society, the regulation of inclusion and exclusion is left to the functional systems themselves, and, as mentioned, there is no central overarching instance (what is inclusion

273

in law is defined by the legal system, just as the definition of art is defined within the art system). From here it is possible to maintain the image (in the media system) that society has never before demonstrated a higher degree of access to inclusion. Accordingly, we have developed a totalitarian logic in which everyone is alike and equal, and included in society and inequality as to life conditions is at best seen as a question of time. Within this totalitarian logic, exclusion is described as a residual problem, and is not a threat to the totalitarian logic itself (Luhmann, 1997, p 26). At the semantic level, exclusion is thematised as dire warnings, and not as a part of the societal reality (Luhmann, 1997, p 626). As a consequence of functional differentiation, late modern society is able to contain extremely large differences in the distribution of goods, and at the same time repeat a stable semantic framing, where inequalities are always characterised as temporary (not as destiny) and each system is firmly secluded from the others (Luhmann, 1995b, p 249).

However, the reality seems to be the opposite, as exclusion from one system may imply exclusion from other systems according to Luhmann (Luhmann, 1997, p 630). This is due to the fact that the isolation and autopoiesis (the internalised reproduction of the systems and their access codes) of the different systems produce deviation amplification and positive feedback loops. Seen from the perspective of integration, it could be said that inclusion in one system does not automatically lead to inclusion in other systems, while exclusion from one system probably involves exclusion from other systems. At the societal level, inclusion in one or several systems does not result in societal integration, since precise communicative expectations in one system do not account for expectations in the other systems. On the other hand, those excluded from all systems are highly integrated, since we have precise expectations about their systemic performance: they are unable to perform communicatively (Luhmann, 1997, p 631).

Inclusion/exclusion and systemically differentiated communication

Inclusion is totally dependent on the singular communicative system. The conditions for semantic actualisation of the problem of inclusion and exclusion are also conditioned by the single system. Viewed from an action-orientated perspective, the problem is that the problems of exclusion and inclusion cannot find their solutions in the single communicative system, since every system closes around its own codes. Even though all the systems semantically use universal terms, they have no universal meaning or effect.

Inclusion is only imaginable vis-à-vis exclusion, while the problem of amplification does not depend on the functional system. Semantically, the problem is almost inaccessible, as the same notion of 'individual freedom' is historically repeated from system to system (Luhmann, 1995b, p 246), simultaneously combining exclusion with individuality and separating individual situations from sociocultural structure. On this basis, we observe the emergence of new 'secondary' systems orientated towards the problems of exclusion (Luhmann, 1997, p 633). However, as with all other communicative systems, they are bound to their own selectivity and instrumental worldview. Labour market or welfare politics could be cited as examples, since each of these close around their own codes, work or not or poor or not. In late modern society, inclusion means inclusion in different closed communicative systems, the effect of which is that inclusion is always partial and fluctuating.

No communicative system can handle the domain of exclusion. Even if communicative systems are universally applicable, they construct the environment from inside (think about law) and are capable of seeing only a segment of the domain of exclusion. This limitation also applies to the political system when it attempts to create policies for the excluded (Luhmann, 1995b, p 260). On this basis, Luhmann reflects on the relationship between functional systems and inclusion/exclusion, pondering whether the relationship has been reversed, so that the inclusion/exclusion precedes the specific systemic participation. Observing through the dichotomy of inclusion/exclusion is a way of grasping the overarching mechanism of late modernity (Luhmann, 1997, p 632). Within this framework, the conceptual prism of inclusion/exclusion is never an instrumental observation of different groups and people, but a tool for observing the very society through its basic communicative dichotomy.

Conclusions

In this chapter we have argued that the concepts of inclusion and exclusion are not to be discussed as conceptual representations of existing objective phenomena, but as epistemic tools for facilitating societal observations and discourses. We have argued that the occurrence of the concepts is not to be scrutinised with reference to ongoing changes in life conditions and some arbitrary and idiosyncratic essentialism on behalf of the researcher. Rather, we have suggested that integration is defined as the capacity to participate in communication, so that the appearance of the concepts of inclusion and exclusion are to be valued from their ability to highlight the evolution and forms of communicative integration.

We have demonstrated some of the current positions and how they 'load' the concepts with more or less arbitrary content. We have discussed the consequences of the dichotomic nature of the concepts, these being the four mechanisms masking the 'political' nature of the research. We then argued that the very archive from which research draws its concepts has fortified the anti-critique as social science turned from societal-critical to societal-instrumental. Finally, we have accepted the dichotomic nature of the concepts and the embedded mechanisms, inquiring as to how it might be possible to reconstruct the relationship between the concepts and their societal conditions. Our solution is to view inclusion and exclusion as communicative concepts, conceptualising the conditions for communicative participation.

The most important consequence for research questions based on the distinction between inclusion and exclusion is that any scientific matrix is an internal creation of the scientific system, thus never mirroring any outside real development in inclusion and exclusion. This internal coding shares the conditions of the other communicative systems. Inclusion/exclusion is a dichotomy with an internal relationship between the two sides. Using the distinction in a scientific observation invariably entails performing a selection and never an operation on a scale of more or less (Luhmann, 1995b, p 240). The communicative selection is bound to mask its own overarching specificity. Whenever inclusion/exclusion is applied as a concept, it refers to a communicative system. The question is which system? We have endeavoured to show that those scholars scrutinised here refer primarily to the political system of the welfare state than to the subsystem of social science.

Seen as operation, observing through inclusion/exclusion is internally related to the societal context in a constitutive way. This means that any study of inclusion and exclusion must study the relationship between the distinction in use and the conditions for use, what in the Luhmannian vocabulary is called 'the differentiation of society'. The point is that there is no overarching system from where to argue that inclusion/exclusion refers to anything but the observing system itself. Hence, when the concept is used in the political system, it is always part of the coding of this system – power/no power, government/opposition – and when it is used in the legal system it refers to specified rules (legal or not) no matter how the alleged excluded feels about it. Accordingly, the economic or any other systems have their own ways of defining inclusion, exclusion and integration. When the scientific system bases its concept of inclusion and exclusion on the distinction between labour/or not, cultural participation/or not, we are talking about highly political choices. However, being installed on the deepest level of scientific observation, the conceptual level, they are immune to basic critique. The scientific community differentiates into various schools of scientists, each using the concept of inclusion and exclusion according to their divergent political affinities. The conceptual critique is set aside, to be replaced with policy proposals better left to the political system.

In as much as society is constituted by a variety of closed systems, it is impossibe to talk about one citizenship delivering fundamental inclusion and the right to participate. Instead, it is more natural to talk about a plurality of relationships and how they set free the capacity of lifelong normalism.

References

Andersen, J. (1999) 'Social and system integration and the underclass', in I. Gough and G. Olofsson (eds) *Capitalism and social cohesion*, London: Macmillan, pp 127-48.

Andersen, J.G. (1996) 'Marginalisation, citizenship and the economy: the capacities of the universalist welfare state in Denmark', in E.O. Eriksen and J. Loftager (eds) *The rationality of the welfare state*, Oslo: Scandinavian University Press.

Berghman, J. (1995) 'Social exclusion in Europe: policy context and analytical framework', in G. Room (ed) *Beyond the threshold: The measurement and analysis of social exclusion*, Bristol: The Policy Press, pp 10-28.

Deleuze, G. and Guattari, F. (1998) *A thousand plateaux: Capitalism and schizophrenia*, 8th edn, Minneapolis, MN: University of Minnesota Press.

Durkheim, E. (1952) *Suicide*, London: Routledge.

Durkheim, E. (1964) *The division of labor in society*, New York, NY: The Free Press.

Durkheim, E. (1982) *The rules of sociological method; and selected texts on sociology and its method*, London: Macmillan.

Durkheim, E. (1986) 'The concept of the state', in A. Giddens (ed) *Durkheim on politics and the state*, Cambridge: Polity Press, pp 32-72.

Elias, N. and Scotson, J.L. (1994) *The established and the outsiders*, London: Sage Publications.

Foucault, M. (1972) *The archaeology of knowledge*, London: Routledge.

Giddens, A. (1994) *Beyond left and right*, Cambridge: Polity Press.

Goodin, R.L. (1996) 'Inclusion and exclusion', *Archives Européennes de Sociologie*, vol 37, no 2, pp 343-71.

Johannessen, A. (1997) *Marginalisering og ekskludering – samme eller forskjellige fenomener?*, Oslo College: HiO Notat, p 6.

Jordan, B. and Redley, M. (1994) 'Polarization, underclass and the welfare state', *Work, Employment & Society*, vol 8, no 2, pp 153-76.

Laclau, E. and Mouffe, C. (1985) *Hegemony and socialist strategy: Towards a radical democratic politics*, London: Verso.

Levitas, R. (1996) 'The concept of social exclusion and the new Durkheimian hegemony', *Critical Social Policy*, vol 16, no 1, pp 5-20.

Luhmann, N. (1984) *Soziale Systeme, Grundriss einer allgemeinen Theorie*, Frankfurt: Suhrkamp.

Luhmann, N. (1995a) 'Why "systems theory"?', *Cybernetics & Human Knowing*, vol 3, no 2, pp 3-10.

Luhmann, N. (1995b) 'Inklusion und Exklusion', *Soziologissche Aufklärung 6. Die Soziologie und der Mensch*, pp 237-64.

Luhmann, N. (1997) *Die Gesellschaft der Gesellschaft*, Frankfurt: Suhrkamp.

Marshall, T.H. (1950) *Class, citizenship and social development*, Cambridge: Cambridge University Press.

Merton, R.K. (1968) *Social theory and social structure*, New York, NY: The Free Press.

Meyers, D.T. (1993) 'Social exclusion, moral reflection and rights', *Law and Philosophy*, vol 12, no 2, pp 217-32.

Møller, I.H. (1989) *Samfundet polariseres – Det begynder på arbejdsmarkedet, fortsætter i socialpolitikken og slutter i det civile samfund*, Ålborg: ATA-forlaget.

Österberg, D. (1988) *Metasociology – an inquiry into the origins and validity of social thought*, Oslo: Norwegian University Press.

Parsons, T. (1968) *The structure of social action*, New York: The Free Press.

Silver, H. (1994) 'Social exclusion and social solidarity: three paradigms', *International Labour Review*, vol 133, pp 531-78.

Strobel, P. (1996) 'From poverty to exclusion: a wage-earning society or a society of human rights?', *International Social Science Journal*, vol 48, no 2, pp 173-89.

Thompson, S. and Hoggett, P. (1996) 'Universalism, selectivism and particularism: towards a post-modern social policy', *Critical Social Policy*, vol 16, no 1, pp 21-43.

THIRTEEN

Concluding remarks

Jørgen Goul Andersen and Per H. Jensen

The two overall aims of this book have been to contribute to the understanding of the interrelationship between changing labour markets, welfare policies, and citizenship, and to present a citizenship approach to this type of analysis. As to the first point, exogenous changes, in particular globalisation and technological change, increase pressures towards achieving higher inequality and labour market marginalisation. Such tendencies are not all that new, but there is little doubt that they are reinforced. What perhaps counts even more is that globalisation at the same time weakens the traditional remedies of the nation state against such inequalities and labour market marginalisation. However, the question remains: to what extent are they weakened?, or, what is the strength of such changes, and are traditional policies entirely unsustainable? Next, there is the question about alternatives: is it inevitable to deregulate and develop policies that function in conformity with the market, as suggested by OECD and others, or is it possible to develop new types of welfare policies that to a larger extent combine flexibility and security (or 'flexicurity') as has been suggested by the International Labour Office? Beyond this partly normative discussion, there is the question of what actually determines policies and policy change.

Addressing these questions from a citizenship perspective does not dictate a completely different type of analysis. However, it does direct more attention to other policy effects than just employment as a goal in itself. Formulating such side-effects in terms of citizenship rather than just 'equality', 'distributional effects', or 'poverty' gives them a clearer focus.

Turning to the dependent variables, a citizenship approach challenges the tendency to conflate labour market integration with social integration. A citizenship approach distinguishes between labour market marginalisation and marginalisation in other areas of social action. It also specifies social participation (in the broadest sense), political participation, and orientations or identities as the core dependent variables. These variables together cover the individual's status and possibilities to act as an equal (and responsible) citizen in society. This throws up the question: is employment a necessary precondition for 'full' citizenship, and if so, why? Is it the membership of a community at the workplace (as communitarians would have it), is it the identity that follows from having the capacity to provide for yourself (as liberals would have it), or is it rather a question of insufficient economic resources (as traditional social democrats would have it)? What can be done by the welfare state, and what role do civil society institutions such as the family play in maintaining citizenship for those who are marginalised or excluded from the labour market? Are such associations the same for men and women, for young people and the old, for ethnic minorities and the majority population, and so on?

However important these questions are as guidance for creating policies (and for our knowledge about economics, politics and society), our knowledge about most of these questions is rudimentary. Many of these questions can also be addressed from other perspectives; for example, there are big overlaps with a poverty approach and with a social exclusion approach. The main advantage of a citizenship approach is that it provides a comprehensive framework that can address all these questions, both about independent and dependent variables, and it can bring together different research traditions. The contributions to this book have provided a first impression of what we can expect to find by digging around in the archaeological site.

Following the logic above, the first major theme addressed in this book was the issue of changing labour markets in a globalised economy. In Chapter Two, Peter Plougmann argued that profound changes are taking place – changes that tend to lead to widespread marginalisation in the labour market, and to considerable polarisation between different regions and different segments of the population in Europe. This argument about redistribution of employment opportunities and life chances is based on a scenario where:

- trade unions will disappear or lose influence
- the demand for skills anchored in the industrial society will decrease
- economic growth will be concentrated on relatively few urban regions in Europe
- a new large reserve army will emerge originating from Eastern Europe and North Africa
- the demand for flexibility among workers will increase.

This scenario calls for new types of welfare policies. As there is increasing evidence to support the proposition that there is an interrelationship between trust and economic growth (as in Catalonia, Denmark, Ireland and Bavaria), it becomes a new and important task for the welfare state to help create trust between firms, employees, local authorities, and civil society at the regional level. Second, as individuals who do not adapt to the 'knowledge intensive' economy run an ever stronger risk of being marginalised, it is increasingly important that the welfare state improves the opportunities for lifelong learning among all segments of the population.

However, even if this is followed, Peter Plougmann conceives individualisation, segmentation, and polarisation to be inevitable outcomes of changing labour markets in a global economy. Somewhat more optimistic suggestions are put forward in Chapter Six (by Jørgen Goul Andersen and Knut Halvorsen). This chapter addresses the question of the relationship between changing labour markets and welfare policies, in particular mainstream arguments about the pressures on European welfare states to make more market-orientated changes achieve higher flexibility as suggested, for example, in the OECD Jobs Strategy. It is argued that quite a few such recommendations rest more on theoretical considerations than on hard empirical evidence. On the basis of the most recent developments in unemployment in Europe it is claimed that the arguments about the superiority of the American labour market/ welfare policy in terms of reducing unemployment and increasing employment are not that convincing. It is argued that most of the smaller European countries are doing increasingly well, and that there may be several routes to increasing employment, including market-orientated strategies as well as others. It is also argued that while traditional Keynesian policies are not sustainable, traditional policies designed to improve competitiveness such as wage moderation seem quite efficient.

The second major theme addressed in this book is the relationship between welfare policies, citizenship and agency. Ruth Lister in Chapter Three, apart from elaborating and clarifying the concept of citizenship, focuses on the impact of globalisation on the relationship between citizenship and changing welfare states. According to Lister, the most general tendency is to undermine citizenship at all levels, from the local to the global. At the global level, a European citizenship is surely emerging. Nonetheless, large parts of the population such as immigrants and asylum-seekers are even formally exempted from fundamental rights in the European societies. At the local and national level, pressures on welfare states have generally led to loss of citizenship and recommodification.

First, welfare states are facing a process of residualisation, that is, welfare states increasingly provide inadequate social protection, most significantly in the UK but also observable on the continent. Second, welfare states are increasingly achievement orientated, since they promote work obligations in exchange for social provisions. All these processes are gendered. The increasing emphasis on paid employment helps to devaluate unpaid domestic care work, and consequently the status of women and mothers in contemporary societies. From a gender perspective, such tendencies may be counteracted by the development of a decent public infrastructure of social support, especially one like the Scandinavian model which has relatively cheap, high quality childcare institutions, allowing women to participate fully in all aspects of social and political life. However, as indicated above, Lister does not see much hope for such welfare state developments, because she observes a general tendency towards a more conditional and exclusive interpretation of social citizenship in the European region.

As argued by Ruth Lister, citizenship is a dynamic concept in which processes and outcomes are dialectically related. This calls for analysis of the processes of restructuring of the welfare states and their implications for citizenship. It is a widespread argument that the welfare state is resistant to change because of existing institutions, policies, and interests.

In Chapter Four, Jørgen Goul Andersen analyses the changing Danish labour market and welfare policies, and their underlying philosophies of unemployment. He argues that quite far-reaching changes have taken place, not dictated by economic pressures but rather facilitated by institutional and political learning, including a more or less paradigmatic shift in ideas. He points to the fact that there are very few veto points in the Danish political system, since the social partners, by and large, have not participated much in designing these changes. This leaves considerable room for agency, in particular for negotiations between political parties. Finally, he argues that in spite of a significant tightening of the rules, a rather generous system remains.

Then in Chapter Five, Willem Trommel and Bert de Vroom analyse equivalent changes in the Dutch welfare state. They make a distinction between changes of social policy programmes, and changes in policy implementation and organisation. They observe that even though cutbacks have been made in social policy programmes, this has largely been compensated for by the emergence of new types of welfare mix programmes. But 'deep-core' changes have occurred in policy implementation and organisation. New steering mechanisms such as incentives and disincentives have been introduced, and decentralisation and privatisation in policy implementation have been stimulated. These changes reflect a change in the images of people and organisations, which could be perceived to be a mirror of the 'third way' strategy argued by Anthony Giddens. As such, profound and fundamental changes in the Dutch welfare state have taken place, but these are not visible if the gaze is only orientated towards the structuration of social policy programmes.

As argued by Denis Bouget in Chapter Ten, the French labour movement has been weakened during the last decade, and this weakening of pro-welfare state interest groups has tended to undermine social protection of the marginalised segments within the labour market. However, on the other hand, and in line with the arguments of Pierson (1994), welfare state programmes have helped to structure the emergence of new interest groups, that is, the unemployed movement, which has succeeded in putting back together (parts of) the French welfare state. The French case shows that policy choices made in the past tend to generate the formation of new interest groups to defend existing social policy programmes, as old interests groups fade away.

From the experience of these three countries, it hardly seems possible to make any strong generalisations about the change-resistant character of welfare states. On the one hand, evidence from the three studies indicates that even though these welfare states underwent considerable change, it does not amount to a strong and unambiguous residualisation as Ruth Lister finds for Britain in Chapter Three. However, the choice of countries may be quite decisive for the result when we analyse the relationship between citizenship and welfare state changes. Also, more needs to be known about the actual impact of such reforms in terms of citizenship.

A third major theme of this book is the relationship between changing welfare states and marginalisation. We approach the theme through three different 'windows': youth, ethnicity and older workers. Each of these 'windows' focuses on different dimensions of marginalisation, that is, economic, social and political marginalisation. Beginning with youth, it is well known that most (but not all) EU countries are marked by high levels of youth unemployment, which may lead to political marginalisation and political alienation. It has been shown that young unemployed people across Europe show more distrust towards the political system compared to young people in employment. Taking this observation as her point of departure, Torild Hammer in Chapter Seven analyses how different welfare state regimes (Scotland and five Nordic countries) and different types of entitlements within each regime condition political participation among unemployed youth. In general, she finds no significant differences in the level of political activity across countries: there is little evidence to substantiate the classical assumption that economic marginalisation leads to political marginalisation. On the contrary, the data appear to indicate that unemployment as such is a cause of reduced participation, supporting arguments about the crucial importance of employment being a condition of citizenship. However, within the group of social beneficiaries, Hammer finds tendencies of political polarisation. On the one hand, compared to other unemployed young people, social beneficiaries tend to be more left-wing in political orientation, and more negative to regular channels of politics by performing irregular political activity. However, on the other hand, substantial groups of social assistance recipients are not interested in politics. Both observations are seen as an indication of distrust in the formal political system among young social assistance claimants. It does seem that the most vulnerable segments among economically marginalised youth are exposed to political marginalisation and polarisation.

In Chapter Eight, Gary Craig pioneers cross-national research on ethnicity. At present, there are no easily accessible comparative data on this, which makes cross-national research on ethnicity a very difficult task. However, what is found of more or less commensurable data indicates that the issue of ethnicity poses an important problem from a citizenship perspective, a problem that is most typically not addressed very seriously. Not only are members of minority ethnic groups formally excluded from political citizenship in some countries (and many are informally excluded from it in all countries); they also suffer from cumulative disadvantage within the labour market. Although some minorities have begun to match host country nationals in terms of education achievement and good quality employment, many fall behind at school, on moving into further education and on entry into the labour market. Discrimination and structural racism deny effective social citizenship to large groups among ethnic minorities across the European Union. Against this background Craig proposes a long range of anti-discriminatory measures, from the local to the global, which may widen the opportunities for ethnic minorities in society at large and within the labour market in particular.

Like immigrants, older workers have been functioning as a reserve army for the last decades. During times of high and enduring unemployment most European countries have experienced an externalisation of older workers from the labour market. However, due to ageing populations and the fear of high dependency ratios in the future, older workers have recently been subject to re-integration measures in most European welfare states. In Chapter Nine, Anne Marie Guillemard and Bert de Vroom discuss whether and how countries will be able to turn around the massive and highly institutionalised early exit into a new pattern of late exit, using France and the Netherlands as their test cases. They observe that massive measures have been used in both France and the Netherlands to reverse the early exit trend, but only the Netherlands has succeeded in breaking the vicious circle of early exit. They argue that these different trajectories are due to differences in the way in which France and the Netherlands have used new types of institutional arrangements. While France has drawn on traditional, standardised and pull-orientated measures, the Netherlands has used new flexible welfare programmes based on the paradigm of 'flexicurity', a paradigm also discussed in Chapter Two. However, the transition from early exit to late exit is not easily interpretable from a citizenship perspective. If early exit has been compensated by generous benefits, early exit and early retirement may actually have developed into a citizen right and an escape route from devastating working conditions. In the case of reductions in benefits in combination with the instalment of new work obligations, late exit may be interpreted as a loss of citizen rights – and vice versa.

We then approach the fourth major theme of this book, moving from a state-centred to a society-centred perspective on changing welfare states and citizenship. The purpose of this change of perspective is to point to some of the pitfalls, potential dangers, and problems in relation to mainstream discussions of citizenship and marginalisation.

In Chapter Eleven, Birgit Pfau-Effinger criticises a state-centred, normative and essentialist approach to social citizenship by making a series of observations using the question of gender equality as her point of departure. She maintains that there is no single desirable or 'correct' form of gender relations. For instance, promoting part-time work could benefit women in one context and disfavour women in another. What is 'good' or 'bad' in terms of gender equality is dependent on the societal context. She states that citizenship delineates a relationship between the state and the individual, but individuals do not react automatically or in a predetermined way to the symbolic and economic signals of the welfare state, since social practices are highly influenced by the cultural basis and the cultural ideals to which individuals refer. Her third observation is that cultural orientations may deviate from the steering aims of the welfare state; that the relationship between the welfare state and cultural ideals may be marked by contradictions and asynchronies. Actually, such cultural contradictions constitute social change. For instance, Birgit Pfau-Effinger demonstrates convincingly how the emergence of the feminist movement in Germany was fuelled by cultural and institutional contradictions. In the theoretical framework put forward by Birgit Pfau-Effinger, cultural values, meanings and ideals become indispensable as a prime drive in the analysis of the causes, contents and effects of citizenship.

Finally, in Chapter Twelve, Asmund Born and Per H. Jensen discuss some major problems associated with the way in which the concepts of marginalisation and exclusion have been used in mainstream debates on citizenship. Most often, the concepts are used detached from any basic assumptions about society. This tends to undermine critical reflections because the concepts are loaded with more or less arbitrary content according to the political affinities of the researcher. This, in turn, favours instrumental thinking, triggering cascades of suggestions for new or alternative remedies of social integration. The challenge is to reconstruct the concepts and their relationships to society in order to restore critical reflections on the functioning of highly differentiated societies. In this perspective, it is argued that the concepts of inclusion/exclusion shall not be seen as representatives of objective phenomena. Rather, they are to be seen as a way to organise the gaze, that is, they are to be observed as epistemic tools, through which a societal self-observation is possible and organised.

The contributions summarised here do not add up to a single, common conclusion. Rather, they point to a field of research where old and new issues, and different scientific disciplines may meet, since the concept of citizenship provides a sufficiently broad framework for this. At the same time, such a framework gives a common direction to a large number of discussions, reminding us of what is the ultimate goal of policies (and of employment), and that this is not only a discussion about efficiency and social justice but also, ultimately, a discussion about the conditions of democracy.

Reference

Pierson, P. (1994) *Dismantling the welfare state*, Cambridge: Cambridge University Press.

Index